Algebra 2

**LARSON
BOSWELL
KANOLD
STIFF**

Applications • Equations • Graphs

Notetaking Guide

The Notetaking Guide contains a lesson-by-lesson framework that allows students to take notes on and review the main concepts of each lesson in the textbook. Each Notetaking Guide lesson features worked-out examples and Checkpoint exercises. Each example has a number of write-on lines for students to complete, either in class as the example is discussed or at home as part of a review of the lesson. Upon completion, each chapter of the Notetaking Guide can be used by students to help review for the test on that particular chapter.

McDougal Littell
A DIVISION OF HOUGHTON MIFFLIN COMPANY
Evanston, Illinois • Boston • Dallas

ISBN-13: 978-0-618-47681-7   ISBN-10: 0-618-47681-4

5 6 7 8 9–CSM–09 08 07 06

Contents

Algebra 2 Notetaking Guide

Contents

Contents

Contents

1.1 Real Numbers and Number Operations

• Use the real number line.
• Use properties of real numbers.

Your Notes

VOCABULARY

Origin of a real number line

Graph of a real number

Coordinate

Opposite

Reciprocal

SUBSETS OF THE REAL NUMBERS

Whole Numbers 0, 1, 2, 3, ...

Integers ... , −3, −2, −1, 0, 1, 2, 3, ...

Rational Numbers Numbers such as $\frac{3}{4}$, $\frac{1}{3}$, and $-\frac{3}{5}$ that can be written as the ratio of two integers. When written as decimals, rational numbers _____. For example, $\frac{3}{4} = $ _____ and $\frac{1}{3} = $ _____.

Irrational Numbers Real numbers that are not rational, such as $\sqrt{3}$ and π. When written as decimals, irrational numbers _____.

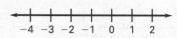 **Graphing and Ordering Real Numbers**

Use a number line to graph and order the real numbers 1 and −3.

Solution

Begin by graphing both numbers.

```
←─┼──┼──┼──┼──┼──┼──┼─→
  −4 −3 −2 −1  0  1  2
```

Because −3 is to the _____ of 1, it follows that −3 is _____ _____ 1, which can be written as −3 __ 1. It can also be written as 1 __ −3, which is read as "1 is _____ −3."

Example 2 *Ordering Temperatures*

Some of the coldest temperatures recorded in Georgia during the winter of 2002–2003 are listed below.

$$6°F, \quad -2°F, \quad 3°F, \quad 0°F, \quad 7°F$$

a. Order the temperatures from least to greatest.

b. How many of the temperatures were at or below 0°F?

Solution

a. From least to greatest, the temperatures are _____ _____ .

b. _____, were at or below 0°F.

✔ *Checkpoint* **Complete the following exercise.**

1. Graph the real numbers $\sqrt{7}$, −2, $-\dfrac{7}{3}$, $\dfrac{5}{2}$, and 0.75. Then write the numbers from least to greatest.

```
←─┼──┼──┼──┼──┼──┼──┼─→
  −3 −2 −1  0  1  2  3
```

PROPERTIES OF ADDITION AND MULTIPLICATION

Let a, b, and c be real numbers.

Property	Addition	Multiplication
Closure	$a + b$ is a _____ number.	ab is a _____ number.
Commutative	$a + b = $ _____	$ab = $ _____
Associative	$(a + b) + c = $ _____	$(ab)c = $ _____
Identity	$a + 0 = $ __, $0 + a = $ __	$a \cdot 1 = $ __, $1 \cdot a = $ __
Inverse	$a + ($____$) = 0$	$a \cdot $ _____ $= 1, a \neq $ __
Distributive	$a(b + c) = $ _____	

Example 3 *Operations with Real Numbers*

a. The difference of 4 and -5 is:

_____ $= $ _____ $= $ __ .   Add the opposite of -5, and simplify.

b. The quotient of 12 and $\dfrac{1}{2}$ is:

$= $ _____ $= $ __ .   Multiply by the reciprocal of $\dfrac{1}{2}$, and simplify.

____

✔ *Checkpoint* Identify the property shown.

2. $5(3) = 3(5)$	**3.** $5(3 + 2) = 5 \cdot 3 + 5 \cdot 2$

Complete the following exercise.

4. Find the difference of -6 and -12.

1.2 Algebraic Expressions and Models

Goals • Evaluate algebraic expressions.
• Simplify algebraic expressions.

Your Notes

VOCABULARY

Numerical expression

Base of a power

Exponent

Power

Variable

Algebraic expression

Mathematical model

Terms of an expression

Coefficient

Like terms

Constant term

Equivalent algebraic expressions

Identity

Example 1 *Evaluating Powers*

a. $(-2)^4 = $ _____ $= $ ___

b. $-2^4 = $ _____ $= $ ____

ORDER OF OPERATIONS

1. First, do operations that occur within _____.

2. Next, evaluate _____.

3. Then, do multiplications and divisions from _____.

4. Finally, do additions and subtractions from _____.

Example 2 *Using Order of Operations*

$$3 + 4(8 - 6)^2 = 3 + 4(\_\_)^2 \qquad \text{Add within parentheses.}$$
$$= 3 + 4(\_\_) \qquad \text{Evaluate power.}$$
$$= 3 + \_\_\_ \qquad \text{Multiply.}$$
$$= \_\_\_ \qquad \text{Add.}$$

Example 3 *Evaluating an Algebraic Expression*

Evaluate $2x^2 - 6x - 3$ when $x = 3$.

$$2x^2 - 6x - 3 = 2(\_\_)^2 - 6(\_\_) - 3 \qquad \text{Substitute for } x.$$
$$= 2(\_\_) - 6(\_\_) - 3 \qquad \text{Evaluate power.}$$
$$= \_\_\_ - \_\_\_ - 3 \qquad \text{Multiply.}$$
$$= \_\_\_ \qquad \text{Add.}$$

✔ *Checkpoint* **Complete the following exercises.**

1. Evaluate $7 + 8(-2 + 4)^2$.   2. Evaluate $-4x^2 + 2x + 9$ when $x = 2$.

Example 4 *Writing and Evaluating a Real-Life Model*

You have $40 and are buying books that cost $12 each. Write an expression that shows how much money you have left after buying *n* books. Evaluate the expression when *n* = 1 and *n* = 3.

Solution

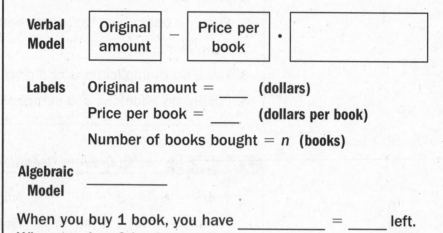

Verbal Model

| Original amount | − | Price per book | · | |

Labels   Original amount = ____ (dollars)

Price per book = ____ (dollars per book)

Number of books bought = *n* (books)

Algebraic Model   _____

When you buy 1 book, you have _____ = ____ left.
When you buy 3 books, you have _____ = ____ left.

Example 5 *Simplifying by Combining Like Terms*

$4(x + 2) - 2(x + 2)$
= _____   Distributive property
= _____   Group like terms.
= _____   Combine like terms.

✓ *Checkpoint* Complete the following exercises.

3. You have a $10 phone card. Each minute on the phone costs 12 cents. Write an expression that shows how much money is left on the card after *x* minutes on the phone. Evaluate the expression for *x* = 20 and *x* = 60.

_____

4. Simplify the expression $-9j - j + 7j^2$.

Homework

1.3 Solving Linear Equations

Goals • Solve linear equations.
• Use linear equations to solve real-life problems.

Your Notes

VOCABULARY

Equation

Linear equation

Solution of an equation in one variable

Equivalent equations

TRANSFORMATIONS THAT PRODUCE EQUIVALENT EQUATIONS

Addition Property of Equality *Add* the same number to both sides: If $a = b$, then $\_\_ + c = \_\_ + c$.

Subtraction Property of Equality *Subtract* the same number from both sides: If $a = b$, then $\_\_ - c = \_\_ - c$.

Multiplication Property of Equality *Multiply* both sides by the same nonzero number: If $a = b$ and $c \neq 0$, then $\_\_ c = \_\_ c$.

Division Property of Equality *Divide* both sides by the same nonzero number: If $a = b$ and $c \neq 0$, then $\_\_ \div c = \_\_ \div c$.

Example 1   *Solving an Equation with a Variable on One Side*

$$5x - 14 = 21 \qquad \text{Original equation}$$
$$5x = \_\_\_ \qquad \text{Add } \_\_\_ \text{ to each side.}$$
$$x = \_\_ \qquad \text{Divide each side by } \_\_.$$

Example 2   *Solving an Equation with a Variable on Both Sides*

$$2x + 6 = 21 - x \qquad \text{Original equation}$$

$$\underline{} + 6 = 21 \qquad \text{Add } \underline{} \text{ to each side.}$$

$$\underline{} = \underline{} \qquad \text{Subtract } \underline{} \text{ from each side.}$$

$$x = \underline{} \qquad \text{Divide each side by } \underline{}.$$

✔ *Checkpoint* Solve the equation.

1. $9x + 6 = -21$ **2.** $-3x + 5 = 31 - 7x$

Example 3   *Using the Distributive Property*

$$-3(x + 8) = 2(x + 3) + 10x \qquad \text{Original equation}$$

$$\underline{} = \underline{} + 10x \qquad \text{Distributive property}$$

$$\underline{} = \underline{} \qquad \text{Combine like terms.}$$

$$\underline{} = \underline{} \qquad \text{Add } \underline{} \text{ to each side.}$$

$$\underline{} = \underline{} \qquad \text{Subtract } \underline{} \text{ from each side.}$$

$$\underline{} = x \qquad \text{Divide each side by } \underline{}.$$

Example 4   *Solving an Equation with Fractions*

$$\frac{2}{3}x - \frac{1}{2} = \frac{7}{6} + \frac{1}{2}x \qquad \text{Original equation}$$

$$\underline{}\left(\frac{2}{3}x - \frac{1}{2}\right) = \underline{}\left(\frac{7}{6} + \frac{1}{2}x\right) \qquad \text{Multiply each side by the LCD, } \underline{}.$$

$$\underline{} = \underline{} \qquad \text{Distributive property}$$

$$\underline{} = \underline{} \qquad \text{Subtract } \underline{} \text{ from each side.}$$

$$x = \underline{} \qquad \text{Add } \underline{} \text{ to each side.}$$

✔ *Checkpoint* **Solve the equation.**

3. $3(2x - 8) = 2x - 2(x + 3)$ **4.** $\frac{5}{4}x + 3 = x - \frac{1}{4}$

Example 5   *Writing and Using a Linear Equation*

A waitress has a base salary of $3 per hour and makes approximately $15 per hour in tips. How many hours must she work to make $135?

Solution

Verbal Model

Total income	=	Base salary	·		+

Tips per hour	·	

Labels   Total income = _____   (dollars)

Base salary = ___   (dollars per hour)

Tip rate = ____   (dollars per hour)

Hours worked = ___   (hours)

Algebraic Model

_____ = _____   Write linear equation.

_____ = ____   Combine like terms.

_____ = x   Divide each side by ___.

The waitress must work ____ hours to earn $135.

✔ *Checkpoint* **Complete the following exercise.**

Homework

5. A bellhop has a base salary of $7 per hour and makes $8 per hour in tips. How many hours must he work to make $120?

1.4 Rewriting Equations and Formulas

Goals • Rewrite equations with more than one variable.
• Rewrite common formulas.

Your Notes

Example 1 *Rewriting an Equation with Two Variables*

Solve $9y + 4x = 7$ for y.

Solution

$9y + 4x = 7$	Write original equation.
$9y =$ _____	Subtract ____ from each side.
$y = $ _____ − _____	Divide each side by __.

Example 2 *Calculating the Value of a Variable*

Given the equation $xy + 3x = 2$, find the value of y when $x = 2$ and $x = -2$.

Solution

$xy + 3x = 2$	Write original equation.
$xy = $ _____	Subtract ____ from each side.
$y = $ _____	Divide each side by __.

When $x = 2$:   When $x = -2$:

$y = $ _____ $=$ ____ $y = $ _____ $=$ ____

✔ **Checkpoint** Solve the equation for y. Then find the value of y for the given value of x.

1. $2y - 2x = 6,\ x = 4$ **2.** $3xy + x = 5,\ x = 2$

Example 3 *Writing an Equation with Variables*

You are selling boxes of cookies for a fundraiser. The boxes come in large and small. Write an equation with more than one variable that represents the amount of money raised.

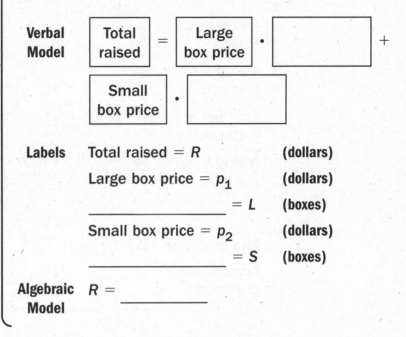

| Verbal Model | Total raised | = | Large box price | · | | + |

| | Small box price | · | | |

Labels   Total raised = R (dollars)

Large box price = p_1 (dollars)

_____ = L (boxes)

Small box price = p_2 (dollars)

_____ = S (boxes)

Algebraic Model $R =$ _____

✔ *Checkpoint* **Complete the following exercise.**

---

3. Assume that the situation in Example 3 also includes size medium boxes of cookies. Write an equation with more than one variable representing the amount of money raised.

COMMON FORMULAS

	Formula	**Variables**
Simple Interest	$I =$ ____	$I =$ interest, $P =$ principal, $r =$ rate, $t =$ time
Temperature	$F = \dfrac{}{}C + 32$	$F =$ degrees Fahrenheit, $C =$ degrees Celsius

continued

Common Formulas Continued

	Formula	Variables
Distance	$d =$ ___	$d =$ distance, $r =$ rate, $t =$ time
Area of a Triangle	$A =$ ____	$A =$ area, $b =$ base, $h =$ height
Area of a Rectangle	$A =$ ___	$A =$ area, $l =$ length, $w =$ width
Perimeter of a Rectangle	$P =$ _____	$P =$ perimeter, $l =$ length, $w =$ width
Area of a Trapezoid	$A = \dfrac{(b_1 + b_2)h}{}$	$A =$ area, $b_1 =$ one base, $b_2 =$ other base, $h =$ height
Area of a Circle	$A =$ ___	$A =$ area, $r =$ radius
Circumference of a Circle	$C =$ ___	$C =$ circumference, $r =$ radius

Example 4 *Rewriting a Common Formula*

Solve $F = \dfrac{9}{5}C + 32$ for C.

$F = \dfrac{9}{5}C + 32$ Write original equation.

_____ $= \dfrac{C}{}$ Subtract ___ from each side.

_____ $= C$ Multiply each side by ___ .

✔ *Checkpoint* Solve the formula for the indicated variable.

4. Solve $I = Prt$ for t.

5. Solve $A = \dfrac{1}{2}(b_1 + b_2)h$ for h.

Problem Solving Using Algebraic Models

Goals • Use a general problem solving plan.
• Use other problem solving strategies.

Your Notes

VOCABULARY

Verbal model

Algebraic model

Example 1 *Writing and Using a Simple Model*

Corporate Average Fuel Economy (CAFE) standards require auto manufacturers to produce cars so that the average fuel efficiency between all of its car models is at least 27.5 miles per gallon. Your new car travels about 385 miles on 11 gallons of gas. Is your car above or below the CAFE standard?

Solution

Verbal Model $\boxed{\text{Fuel efficiency}} = \boxed{\text{Total miles}} \div \boxed{}$

Labels Fuel efficiency = x (miles per gallon)

Total miles = ____   (miles)

Amount of gasoline = ___   (gallons)

Algebraic Model $x = $ _____

$x = $ ___

Your car's fuel efficiency is ____ miles per gallon, which is _____ the CAFE standard.

Example 2 *Writing and Using a Model*

You used all of a $50 gift certificate watching movies at the local theater and you want to know how much you have spent watching evening showings. Afternoon showings are $4 and evening showings are $6. You have seen a total of 10 movies.

Solution

Verbal Model

Evening showings

| Total cost | = | Movie cost | · | | | + |

Afternoon showings

| Movie cost | · | |

Labels

Total cost = ___   (dollars)

Movie cost (evening) = ___   (dollars)

Number of movies (evening) = x (movies)

Movie cost (afternoon) = ___   (dollars)

Number of movies (afternoon) = _____ (movies)

Algebraic Model

___ = _____

___ = _____

___ = ___

___ = x

You watched ___ evening showings.

The cost was ___(6) = $___ .

✔ *Checkpoint* **Complete the following exercise.**

1. Driving to a concert, you average 24 miles per hour in the city and 65 miles per hour on the highway. If the 142 mile trip takes 2.5 hours, how much of the time were you driving on the highway?

Example 3 *Drawing a Diagram*

A car and a truck are 245 miles apart traveling towards each other until they meet. The car averages 65 miles per hour and the truck averages 55 miles per hour. The truck started one hour after the car. After how long do the two automobiles meet? How many miles will each automobile have traveled?

Solution Begin by drawing and labeling a diagram.

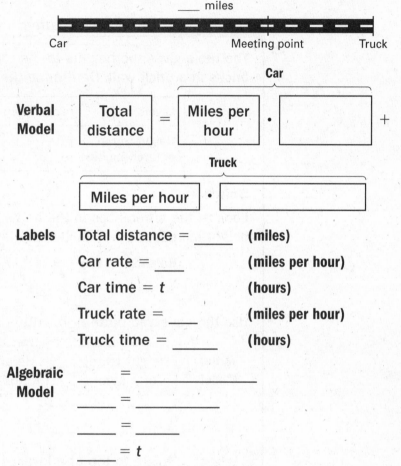

Labels   Total distance = _____   (miles)

Car rate = _____   (miles per hour)

Car time = t (hours)

Truck rate = _____   (miles per hour)

Truck time = _____   (hours)

Algebraic   _____ = _____
Model
_____ = _____

_____ = _____

_____ = t

The automobiles meet after _____ hours. The number of miles each will have traveled is as shown.

Car: $\dfrac{65 \text{ miles}}{\text{hour}}$ • _____ ~~hours~~ = _____ miles

Truck: $\dfrac{55 \text{ miles}}{\text{hour}}$ • (_____) ~~hours~~ = _____ miles

✔ *Checkpoint* **Complete the following exercise.**

> **2.** Assume the truck in Example 3 left 30 minutes after the car. After how long do the two automobiles meet?

Example 4 *Looking for a Pattern*

The table gives the heights to the top of the first few layers of bricks in a brick wall. Determine the height of 18 layers.

Layers	Foundation	1	2	3	4
Height to top of layer (inches)	6	9	12	15	18

Solution

Look at the differences in the heights given in the table. The height increases by ___ inches per layer.

Heights: 6   9   12   15   18
+__ +__ +__ +__

Use the observed pattern to write a model for the height.

Verbal Model | Height to top of a layer | = | Height of foundation | + | Height per layer | .

Labels   Height to top of a layer = h (inches)

Height of foundation = ___   (inches)

Height per layer = ___   (inches per layer)

Layer number = n (layers)

Algebraic Model $h =$ _____   Write algebraic model.

$h =$ _____   Substitute for n.

$h =$ ___   Simplify.

The height to the top of 18 layers is ___ inches, or ___ feet.

✓ *Checkpoint* **Complete the following exercise.**

3. The table gives the heights to the top of the first few layers of bricks in a brick wall. Determine the height of 20 layers.

Layers	Foundation	1	2	3	4
Height to top of layer (inches)	2	7	12	17	22

Homework

1.6 Solving Linear Inequalities

Goals • Solve simple inequalities.
• Solve compound inequalities.

Your Notes

VOCABULARY

Linear inequality in one variable

Solution of an inequality in one variable

Graph of an inequality

Compound inequality

TRANSFORMATIONS PRODUCING EQUIVALENT INEQUALITIES

• *Add* the same number to both sides.

• *Subtract* the same number from both sides.

• *Multiply* both sides by the same _____ number.

• *Divide* both sides by the same _____ number.

• *Multiply* both sides by the same _____ number and _____ the inequality.

• *Divide* both sides by the same _____ number and _____ the inequality.

Example 1 *Solving an Inequality with a Variable on One Side*

$5x + 7 > -3$ Original inequality

$5x > $ _____   Subtract ___ from each side.

$x > $ ___   Divide each side by ___.

The solutions are all real numbers greater than ____.

Example 2 *Solving an Inequality with a Variable on Both Sides*

Solve $2x - 2 \le 3x + 1$.

$2x - 2 \le 3x + 1$ Write original inequality.

$\underline{\hspace{2cm}} \le \underline{\hspace{1cm}}$ Subtract _____ from each side.

$\underline{\hspace{1.5cm}} \le \underline{\hspace{1cm}}$ Add ___ to each side.

$x \, \underline{\hspace{2cm}}$ Divide each side by _____, _____ the inequality.

The solutions are all real numbers $\underline{\hspace{4cm}}$

$\underline{\hspace{1.5cm}}$.

Example 3 *Using a Simple Inequality*

A basketball player's average point total *A* in the last

5 games is $\dfrac{x + 123}{5}$ where *x* is her score in the fifth game.

Describe the scores *x* that will give her an average of at least 30 points.

Solution

$A \ge \underline{\hspace{1.5cm}}$ The average is to be at least _____ points per game.

$\underline{\hspace{2cm}} \ge \underline{\hspace{1cm}}$ Substitute for *A*.

$\underline{\hspace{2cm}} \ge \underline{\hspace{1.5cm}}$ Multiply each side by ___.

$x \ge \underline{\hspace{1.5cm}}$ Subtract _____ from each side.

The scores are greater than or equal to ___.

✔ **Checkpoint** Complete the following exercises.

1. Solve $-2x + 5 > -1$.   **2.** Solve $9 - 6x \le 9 + 2x$.

3. A plant's height *h* (in feet) can be modeled by
$h = 0.3x + 1$, where *x* is the age of the plant in years.
Describe possible ages of the plant if it is over 4 feet tall.

Example 4   *Solving an "And" Compound Inequality*

Solve $-9 < 2x - 3 < 7$. Then graph the solution.

Solution

To solve, isolate the variable between the two inequality signs.

$$-9 < 2x - 3 < 7 \qquad \text{Write original inequality.}$$

$$\underline{\quad} < 2x < \underline{\quad} \qquad \text{Add } \underline{\quad} \text{ to each expression.}$$

$$\underline{\quad} < x < \underline{\quad} \qquad \text{Divide each expression by } \underline{\quad}.$$

Because x is between ____ and __, the solutions are all real numbers _____. Check several of these in the original inequality. Graph the solution below.

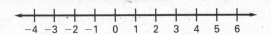

Example 5   *Solving an "Or" Compound Inequality*

Solve $4x - 2 \leq 2$ or $2x - 3 \geq 3$.

Solution

A solution of this compound inequality is a solution of either of its simple parts, so you should solve each part separately.

Solution of first inequality

$$4x - 2 \leq 2 \qquad \text{Write inequality.}$$

$$4x \leq \underline{\quad} \qquad \text{Add } \underline{\quad} \text{ to each side.}$$

$$x \leq \underline{\quad} \qquad \text{Divide each side by } \underline{\quad}.$$

Solution of second inequality

$$2x - 3 \geq 3 \qquad \text{Write inequality.}$$

$$2x \geq \underline{\quad} \qquad \text{Add } \underline{\quad} \text{ to each side.}$$

$$x \geq \underline{\quad} \qquad \text{Divide each side by } \underline{\quad}.$$

The solutions are all real numbers _____. Check several of these numbers to see that they satisfy one of the simple parts of the original inequality. Graph the solution below.

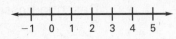

✔ *Checkpoint* Solve the inequality.

4. $3 < 4x + 7 \le 7$	5. $2x + 4 < -6$ or $3x \ge 21$

Example 6 *Using an "And" Compound Inequality*

Under ideal conditions, water will remain a liquid when the temperature F (in degrees Fahrenheit) satisfies the inequality $32 < F < 212$. Write the inequality in degrees Celsius.

Solution

Let C represent the temperature in degrees Celsius and use the formula $F = \dfrac{9}{5}C + 32$.

$32 < F < 212$ Write original inequality.

$32 < \underline{\hspace{2cm}} < 212$ Substitute for F.

$\underline{\hspace{3cm}}$ Subtract ____ from each expression.

$\underline{\hspace{3cm}}$ Multiply each expression by ____ , the reciprocal of $\dfrac{9}{5}$.

Under ideal conditions, water will remain a liquid as long as the temperature stays between ___°C and ____°C.

✔ *Checkpoint* Complete the following exercise.

6. You want to keep at least $10 in your wallet at all times, but no more than $50. Write an inequality describing the situation.

1.7 **Solving Absolute Value Equations and Inequalities**

Goals • Solve absolute value equations and inequalities.
• Use absolute values in real-life problems.

Your Notes

VOCABULARY

Absolute value of a real number

SOLVING AN ABSOLUTE VALUE EQUATION

The absolute value equation $|ax + b| = c$, where $c > 0$, is equivalent to the compound statement $ax + b = $ ___ or $ax + b = $ ___ .

Example 1 *Solving an Absolute Value Equation*

$|4x + 2| = 6$		**Original equation**
$4x + 2 = $ ___ or $4x + 2 = $ ___		**Expression can be** ___ **or** ___ .
$4x = $ ___ or $4x = $ ___		**Subtract** ___ **from each side.**
$x = $ ___ or $x = $ ___		**Divide each side by** ___ .

TRANSFORMATIONS OF ABSOLUTE VALUE INEQUALITIES

• The inequality $|ax + b| < c$, where $c > 0$, means that $ax + b$ is _____ $-c$ and c. This is equivalent to ___ $< ax + b <$ ___ .

• The inequality $|ax + b| > c$, where $c > 0$, means that $ax + b$ is _____ $-c$ and c. This is equivalent to $ax + b <$ ___ or $ax + b >$ ___ .

In the first transformation, $<$ can be replaced by ___ . In the second transformation, $>$ can be replaced by ___ .

Your Notes

Example 2   *Solving an Inequality of the form* $|ax + b| < c$

Solve $|2x - 3| < 3$.

Solution

$\quad\quad |2x - 3| < 3$ Write original inequality.

$\quad \underline{\quad} < 2x - 3 < \underline{\quad}$ Write equivalent compound inequality.

$\quad\quad \underline{\quad\quad\quad\quad}$ Add __ to each expression.

$\quad\quad \underline{\quad\quad\quad}$ Divide each expression by __.

The solutions are all real numbers $\underline{\quad\quad\quad\quad\quad\quad\quad}$

$\underline{\quad\quad}$. Check several solutions in the original inequality.
Graph the solution below.

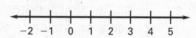

Example 3   *Solving an Inequality of the form* $|ax + b| \geq c$

Solve $|2x + 7| \geq 3$.

Solution

This absolute value inequality is equivalent to $2x + 7$ $\underline{\quad\quad}$
or $2x + 7$ $\underline{\quad\quad}$.

Solve first inequality   **Solve second inequality**

$2x + 7$ $\underline{\quad\quad}$ Write inequality. $2x + 7$ $\underline{\quad\quad}$

$\quad\quad 2x$ $\underline{\quad\quad}$ Subtract __ $2x$ $\underline{\quad\quad}$
                from each side.

$\quad\quad\quad x$ $\underline{\quad\quad}$ Divide each side x $\underline{\quad\quad}$
                by __.

The solutions are all real numbers $\underline{\quad\quad\quad\quad\quad\quad\quad}$

$\underline{\quad\quad\quad\quad\quad\quad\quad\quad\quad\quad\quad}$. Check several solutions in

the original inequality. Graph the solution below.

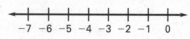

✔ *Checkpoint* **Solve the equation or inequality.**

1. $|5x - 2| = 3$ **2.** $|3x + 4| < 2$ **3.** $|2x - 3| \geq 5$

Example 4   *Write a Model for Tolerance*

A dog food manufacturer has a tolerance of 0.25 pound per bag of dog food advertised as weighing 5 pounds. Write and solve an absolute value inequality that describes the acceptable weights for "5 pound" bags.

Verbal Model | Actual weight | $-$ | Ideal weight | $\leq$ | ⬚ |

Labels   Actual weight $= x$ **(pounds)**

Ideal weight $= $ ___   **(pounds)**

Tolerance $= $ _____   **(pounds)**

Algebraic Model $|x - 5| \leq$ _____   Write algebraic model.

_____ $\leq x - 5 \leq$ _____   Write equivalent compound inequality.

_____ $\leq x \leq$ _____   Add ___ to each expression.

The weights can range between _____ pounds and _____ pounds, inclusive.

✔ *Checkpoint* **Complete the following exercise.**

4. A toy manufacturer has a tolerance of 0.1 inch on a ball that is supposed to have a diameter of 1 inch. Write and solve an inequality describing the acceptable diameters for a ball.

2.1 Functions and Their Graphs

Goals • Represent relations and functions.
• Graph and evaluate linear functions.

Your Notes

VOCABULARY

Relation

Domain of a relation

Range of a relation

Function

Ordered pair

Coordinate plane

Equation in two variables

Solution of an equation in two variables

Independent variable

Dependent variable

Graph of an equation in two variables

Linear function

Function notation

Example 1   *Identifying Functions*

Identify the domain and range. Is the relation a function?

a.   b.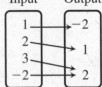

a. The domain consists of _____, and the range consists of _____. The relation _____ a function because _____.

b. The domain consists of _____, and the range consists of _____. The relation _____ a function because _____.

Example 2   *Graphing Relations*

Graph the relations given in Example 1.

a. Write the relation as a set of ordered pairs: (____, __), (____, __), (__, __), (__, ____). Plot the points.

b. Write the relation as a set of ordered pairs: (__, ____), (__, __), (__, __), (____, __). Plot the points.

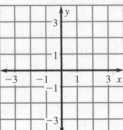   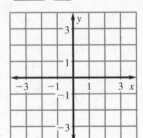

✔ *Checkpoint* **Complete the following exercise.**

1. Identify the domain and range and tell whether the relation is a function. Write the relation as a set of ordered pairs.

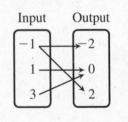

VERTICAL LINE TEST FOR FUNCTIONS

A relation is a function if and only if no vertical line
_____ the graph of the relation at more than one
point.

Example 3 *Using the Vertical Line Test in Real Life*

The graph shows the scores *s* and
time spent studying *t* for several
students who took a test. Are the
scores a function of the time spent
studying? Explain.

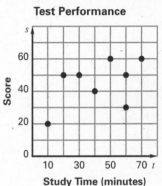

Test Performance

Solution

The scores are _____ of
the time spent studying because
there is a vertical line that
intersects the graph at more than
one point. A vertical line passes through both (___, ___) and
(___, ___).

GRAPHING EQUATIONS IN TWO VARIABLES

To graph an equation in two variables, follow these steps.

Step 1 Construct a table of _____.

Step 2 Graph enough solutions to recognize a _____.

Step 3 Connect the points with a _____ or a _____.

Example 4 *Graphing a Function*

Graph the function $y = x - 1$.

1. Make a table of values.

Choose *x*.	−3	−1	0	1	3
Evaluate *y*.					

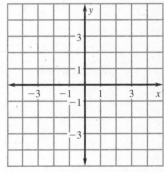

2. Plot the points. Notice the five
   points lie on a _____.

3. Draw a _____ through the points.

✔ *Checkpoint* **Complete the following exercises.**

2. Use the graph to determine if the plotted points represent a function.

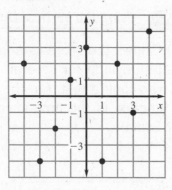

3. Graph the function $y = 2x + 1$.

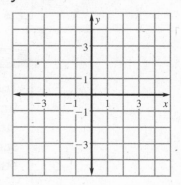

Example 5 **Evaluating Functions**

Evaluate the function when $x = 2$.

a. $f(x) = -3x + 4$

b. $f(x) = x^2 - 4x - 1$

Solution

a. $f(x) = -3x + 4$ Write function.

    $f(\underline{}) = -3(\underline{}) + 4$ Substitute for x.

    $= \underline{}$ Simplify.

b. $f(x) = x^2 - 4x - 1$ Write function.

    $f(\underline{}) = \underline{}^2 - 4(\underline{}) - 1$ Substitute for x.

    $= \underline{}$ Simplify.

✔ *Checkpoint* **Evaluate the function for $x = -1$.**

Homework

4. $f(x) = 3x^2 + 2$

5. $f(x) = -x + 9$

2.2 Slope and Rate of Change

Goals • Find slopes of lines.
• Use slope to solve real-life problems.

Your Notes

VOCABULARY

Slope

Parallel lines

Perpendicular lines

THE SLOPE OF A LINE

The slope of the nonvertical line passing through the points (x_1, y_1) and (x_2, y_2) is:

$$m = \frac{y_2 - y_1}{x_2 - x_1} = \frac{\text{rise}}{\text{run}}$$

Example 1   Finding the Slope of a Line

Find the slope of the line passing through $(-2, 0)$ and $(1, 2)$.

Solution

Let $(x_1, y_1) = (-2, 0)$ and $(x_2, y_2) = (1, 2)$.

$$m = \frac{y_2 - y_1}{x_2 - x_1}$$
⟵ **Rise: Difference of y-values**
⟵ **Run: Difference of x-values**

$$= \frac{\boxed{} - \boxed{}}{\boxed{} - (\boxed{})}$$
Substitute values.

$$= \frac{\boxed{}}{\boxed{} + \boxed{}} = \underline{}$$
Simplify.

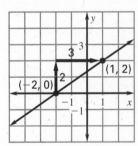

CLASSIFICATION OF LINES BY SLOPE

• A line with a _____ slope *rises* from left to right.
  (*m* ___ 0)

• A line with a _____ slope *falls* from left to right.
  (*m* ___ 0)

• A line with a slope of _____ is *horizontal*.
  (*m* _____)

• A line with an _____ slope is *vertical*.
  (*m* _____)

Positive Slope   **Negative Slope**   **Zero Slope**   **Undefined Slope**

Example 2   *Classifying Lines Using Slope*

Without graphing, tell whether the line through the given points *rises*, *falls*, *is horizontal*, or *is vertical*.

a. $(-4, 3), (4, 3)$ **b.** $(-2, 2), (3, 0)$

Solution

a. $m = \dfrac{\boxed{} - \boxed{}}{\boxed{} - (\boxed{})} = $ _____   Because *m* ___ 0, the line is _____.

b. $m = \dfrac{\boxed{} - \boxed{}}{\boxed{} - (\boxed{})} = $ _____   Because *m* ___ 0, the line _____.

Example 3   *Comparing Steepness of Lines*

Tell which line is steeper.   Line 1: through $(-1, 0)$ and $(0, 5)$
Line 2: through $(2, 4)$ and $(3, 7)$

Solution

The slope of line 1 is $m_1 = \dfrac{\square - \square}{\square - (\square)} = \underline{}$ and the

slope of line 2 is $m_2 = \dfrac{\square - \square}{\square - \square} = \underline{}$.

Because the lines have positive slopes and $\underline{} > \underline{}$,
line $\underline{}$ is steeper than line $\underline{}$.

✓ *Checkpoint* **Complete the following exercises.**

1. Find the slope of the line passing through $(2, -4)$ and $(-5, 1)$.

_____

2. Without graphing, tell whether the line through $(0, 3)$ and $(5, -5)$ *rises, falls, is horizontal,* or *is vertical.*

_____

3. Which line is steeper?
Line 1: through $(-5, 1)$ and $(0, 3)$
Line 2: through $(0, 7)$ and $(3, 9)$

SLOPES OF PARALLEL AND PERPENDICULAR LINES

Consider two different nonvertical lines l_1 and l_2 with slopes m_1 and m_2.

Parallel Lines The lines are parallel if and only if they have the _____ slope.

m_1 ___ m_2

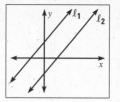

Perpendicular Lines The lines are perpendicular if and only if their slopes are _____ of each other.

$m_1 = $ _____ or $m_1 m_2 = $ ___

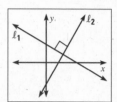

Example 4 **Classify Parallel and Perpendicular Lines**

Tell whether the lines are *parallel*, *perpendicular*, or *neither*.

a. Line 1: through (1, 1) and (0, 4)
   Line 2: through (−2, 3) and (0, −3)

b. Line 1: through (−1, −1) and (2, 3)
   Line 2: through (4, −3) and (−3, 2)

Solution

a. The slopes of the two lines are:

$$m_1 = \frac{}{} = \frac{}{} = \underline{}$$

$$m_2 = \frac{}{} = \frac{}{} = \underline{}$$

Because m_1 ___ m_2, and the lines are _____, you can conclude that the lines are _____.

b. The slopes of the two lines are:

$$m_1 = \frac{}{} = \frac{}{}$$

$$m_2 = \frac{}{} = \frac{}{}$$

Because m_1 and m_2 _____ equal and _____ negative reciprocals of each other, the lines are _____ _____.

Example 5   *Geometrical Use of Slope*

The roof of a house rises 5 feet over a horizontal distance of 15 feet.

a. Find the slope of the roof.

b. If the roof was rebuilt with a slope of $\dfrac{2}{5}$ and still has a horizontal distance of 15 feet, what is the rise of the roof?

Solution

a. $m = \dfrac{\text{rise}}{\text{run}} = \dfrac{}{} = \dfrac{}{}$

The slope of the roof is $\dfrac{}{}$.

b. Let y represent the rise of the roof.

$\dfrac{\text{rise}}{\text{run}} = \dfrac{}{}$ Write a proportion.

$\dfrac{}{} = \dfrac{}{}$ The rise is y and the run is ___.

$\dfrac{}{} = $ Cross multiply.

$y = $ Solve for y.

The rise of the roof is ___ feet.

✓ **Checkpoint** **Complete the following exercises.**

4. Which line is parallel to the line through $(-4, 2)$ and $(2, 1)$?

Line 1: through $(-1, 0)$ and $(0, 6)$
Line 2: through $(7, 1)$ and $(1, 2)$

Homework

5. Find the slope of a road that rises 20 feet over a horizontal distance of 200 feet. Then find the rise over a 250 foot section of road with the same slope.

2.3 Quick Graphs of Linear Equations

Goals • Use the slope-intercept form of a linear equation.
• Use the standard form of a linear equation.

Your Notes

VOCABULARY

y-intercept

_____

Slope-intercept form

_____

Standard form of a linear equation

_____

x-intercept

GRAPHING EQUATIONS IN SLOPE-INTERCEPT FORM

The slope-intercept form of an equation gives you a quick
way to graph the equation.

Step 1 Write the equation in slope-intercept form by solving
for __.

Step 2 Find the __-intercept and use it to plot the point
where the line crosses the __-axis.

Step 3 Find the _____ and use it to plot a second point on
the line.

Step 4 Draw a _____ through the two points.

Your Notes

Example 1 *Graphing with the Slope-Intercept Form*

Graph $y + 1 = \dfrac{2}{3}x$.

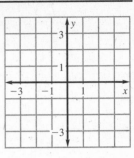

1. Write the equation in slope-intercept form: $y = $ _____ .

2. The y-intercept is ____ , so plot the point (__ , ____).

3. The slope is ____ , so plot a second point on the line by moving __ units to the right and __ units up. This point is (__ , __).

4. Draw a line through the two points.

Example 2 *Using the Slope-Intercept Form*

Your monthly car payments on a new car are made according to the equation $p = 15{,}000 - 250t$ where p is the amount you owe and t is the number of months.

a. What is the original amount you owe?

b. What is the monthly payment?

c. Graph the model.

Solution

a. First rewrite the equation as $p = $ _____ so that it is in slope-intercept form. Then you can see that the p-intercept is _____ . So, the original amount you owe (when $t = 0$) is $ _____ .

b. From the slope-intercept form you can see that the slope is $m = $ _____ . This means that the amount you owe is changing at a rate of _____ per month. Your monthly payment is _____ .

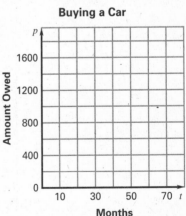

Buying a Car

c. Graph the model. Notice that the line stops when it reaches the t-axis (at $t = $ ____) so the car is paid for at that point.

GRAPHING EQUATIONS IN STANDARD FORM

Step 1 Write the equation in standard form.

Step 2 Find the x-intercept by letting ___ = 0 and solving for ___. Use the x-intercept to plot the point where the line crosses the x-axis.

Step 3 Find the y-intercept by letting ___ = 0 and solving for ___. Use the y-intercept to plot the point where the line crosses the y-axis.

Step 4 Draw a line through the two points.

Example 3   *Drawing Quick Graphs*

Graph $2y - 3x = 6$.

Method 1 **Use Standard Form**

1. $-3x + 2y = 6$ **Standard form**

2. $-3x + 2(\underline{\ \ }) = 6$ **Let $y = \underline{\ \ }$.**

    $x = \underline{\ \ \ }$ **Solve for x.**

    Plot the x-intercept at (___, 0).

3. $-3(\underline{\ \ }) + 2y = 6$ **Let $x = \underline{\ \ }$.**

    $y = \underline{\ \ }$ **Solve for y.**

    Plot the y-intercept at (0, ___).

4. Draw a line through the two points.

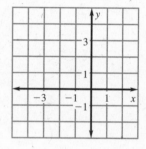

Method 2 **Use Slope-Intercept Form**

1. $2y - 3x = 6$

    $2y = 6 + \underline{\ \ \ }$

    $y = \dfrac{\underline{\ \ \ \ \ \ \ \ }}{}$ **Slope-intercept form**

2. The y-intercept is ___, so plot (0, ___).

3. The slope is $\underline{\ \ \ }$, so plot a second point by moving ___ units right and ___ units up. This point is (___, ___).

4. Draw a line through the two points.

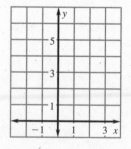

HORIZONTAL AND VERTICAL LINES

Horizontal Line The graph of $y = c$ is a horizontal line
through (__, __).

Vertical Line The graph of $x = c$ is a vertical line through
(__, __).

Example 4 *Graphing Horizontal and Vertical Lines*

Graph (a) $x = 3$ and (b) $y = -2$.

a. The graph of $x = 3$ is a _____
line that passes through the point
(__, 0). Notice that every point on the
line has an *x*-coordinate of __.

b. The graph of $y = -2$ is a _____
line that passes through the point
(0, ___). Notice that every point on
the line has a *y*-coordinate of ___.

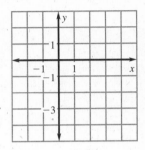

✔ *Checkpoint* **Complete the following exercises.**

1. The number of gallons of gas left
in your gas tank is given by
$g = 12 - 4t$, with *t* in hours. Find
the hourly gas use. Determine in
how many hours the tank will be
empty. Graph the model.

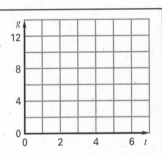

Graph the equation.

2. $2y + 4x = 4$ **3.** $y = 2$

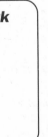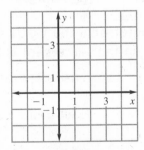   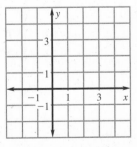

2.4 Writing Equations of Lines

Goals
• Write linear equations.
• Write direct variation equations.

Your Notes

VOCABULARY

Direct variation

Constant of variation

WRITING AN EQUATION OF A LINE

Slope-Intercept Form Given the slope m and the y-intercept b, use this equation: $y = $ _____

Point-Slope Form Given the slope m and a point (x_1, y_1), use this equation: $y - y_1 = $ _____

Two Points Given two points (x_1, y_1) and (x_2, y_2), use the

formula $m = $ to find the slope m. Then use the
_____

point-slope form with this slope and either of the given points to write an equation of the line.

Example 1   *Writing an Equation Given m and b*

Write an equation of the line shown.

From the graph you can see that the

slope is $m = $. You can also see
____

that the line intersects the y-axis at the

point (0, __), so the y-intercept is $b = $ __.

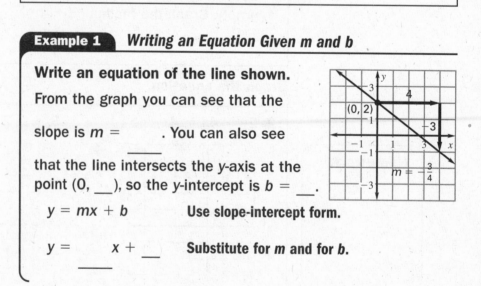

$y = mx + b$ Use slope-intercept form.

$y = $ $x + $ __   Substitute for m and for b.
____

Example 2 *Writing an Equation Given the Slope and a Point*

Write an equation of the line that passes through (1, 2) and has a slope of 2.

Because you know the slope and a point on the line, you should use the point-slope form to write an equation of the line. Let $(x_1, y_1) = (\underline{\ }, \underline{\ })$ and $m = \underline{\ }$.

$y - y_1 = m(x - x_1)$ Use point slope form.

$y - \underline{\ } = \underline{\ }(x - \underline{\ })$ Substitute for m, x_1, and y_1.

Once you have used the point-slope form to find an equation, you can simplify the result to the slope-intercept form.

$y - \underline{\ } = \underline{\ }(x - \underline{\ })$ Write point-slope form.

$y - \underline{\ } = \underline{\ }x - \underline{\ }$ Distributive property

$y = \underline{\ }x$ Write in slope-intercept form.

Example 3 *Write Equations of Perpendicular and Parallel Lines*

Write an equation of the line that passes through (2, 0) and is (a) perpendicular and (b) parallel to the line $y = 2x - 1$.

Solution

a. The given line has a slope of $m_1 = \underline{\ }$. So, a line perpendicular to this line has a slope of

$m_2 = -\dfrac{1}{m_1} = \dfrac{}{\underline{\ \ \ \ }}$. Because you know the slope and a

point on the line, use the point-slope form with $(x_1, y_1) = (\underline{\ }, \underline{\ })$ to find an equation of the line.

$y - y_1 = m_2(x - x_1)$ Use point-slope form.

$y - \underline{\ } = \dfrac{}{\underline{\ \ \ \ }}(x - \underline{\ })$ Substitute for m_2, x_1, and y_1.

$y = \dfrac{}{\underline{\ \ \ \ }}$ Distributive property

b. For a parallel line use $m_2 = m_1 = \underline{\ }$ and $(x_1, y_1) = (\underline{\ }, \underline{\ })$.

$y - y_1 = m_2(x - x_1)$ Use point-slope form.

$y - \underline{\ } = \underline{\ }(x - \underline{\ })$ Substitute for m_2, x_1, and y_1.

$y = \underline{\ \ \ \ }$ Distributive property

✅ *Checkpoint* **Complete the following exercises.**

1. Write an equation of the line shown.

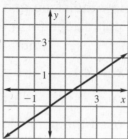

2. Write an equation of the line that passes through $(-2, 1)$ and is
(a) perpendicular and
(b) parallel to $y = x - 3$.

Example 4   *Writing an Equation Given Two Points*

Write an equation of the line that passes through $(-1, 3)$ and $(3, -2)$.

Solution

The line passes through $(x_1, y_1) = (-1, 3)$ and $(x_2, y_2) = (3, -2)$, so its slope is $m = \dfrac{y_2 - y_1}{x_2 - x_1} = \underline{\hspace{2cm}} = \underline{\hspace{1cm}}.$

Because you know the slope and a point on the line, use the point-slope form to find an equation of the line.

$y - y_1 = m(x - x_1)$ **Use point-slope form.**

$\underline{\hspace{1.5cm}} = \underline{\hspace{2.5cm}}$ **Substitute for m, x_1, and y_1.**

$\underline{\hspace{1.5cm}} = \underline{\hspace{2.5cm}}$ **Distributive property**

$y = \underline{\hspace{2.5cm}}$ **Write in slope-intercept form.**

Example 5 *Writing and Using a Direct Variation Equation*

The variables x and y vary directly, and $y = 6$ when $x = 1.5$.

a. Write and graph an equation relating x and y.

b. Find y when $x = 3$.

Solution

a. Use the given values of x and y to find the constant of variation.

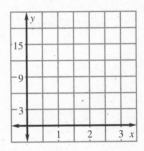

$y = kx$	Write direct variation equation.
$\_\_ = k(\underline{\hspace{1cm}})$	Substitute for y and for x.
$\_\_ = k$	Solve for k.

b. When $x = 3$, the value of y is $y = \underline{\hspace{1.5cm}} = \underline{\hspace{1cm}}$.

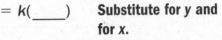

✓ *Checkpoint* **Complete the following exercises.**

3. Write an equation of the line that passes through $(3, -1)$ and $(1, 3)$.

4. The variables x and y vary directly, and $y = 2$ when $x = 3$. Write and graph an equation relating x and y. Find y when $x = 5$.

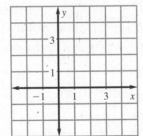

Homework

2.5 Correlation and Best-Fitting Lines

Goals • Use scatter plots and correlation.
• Approximate best-fitting lines.

Your Notes

VOCABULARY

Scatter plot

Positive correlation

Negative correlation

Relatively no correlation

APPROXIMATING A BEST-FITTING LINE: GRAPHICAL APPROACH

Step 1 Carefully draw a _____ of the data.

Step 2 Sketch the _____ that appears to follow most closely the pattern given by the points. There should be as many points above the line as below it.

Step 3 Choose _____ on the line and estimate the coordinates of each point. These two points do not have to be original data points.

Step 4 Find an _____ of the line that passes through the two points from Step 3. This equation models the data.

Example 1 **Fitting a Line to Data**

The data pairs give the speed of a car during a 30-second interval, with t in seconds and y in miles per hour. Approximate the best-fitting line for the data. (0, 0), (5, 15), (10, 23), (15, 38), (20, 45), (25, 60), (30, 65)

Solution

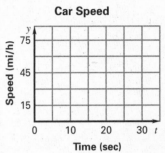

Car Speed

1. Begin by drawing a _____ _____ of the data.

2. Next, sketch the line that appears to best fit the data.

3. Then, choose two points on the line. From the scatter plot shown, you might choose (0, __) and (20, ___).

4. Finally, find an equation of the line. The line that passes through the two points has a slope of:

$$m = \frac{\quad\quad}{\rule{2cm}{0.4pt}} = \underline{\quad}.$$

Use the point-slope form to write the equation.

$y - y_1 = m(t - t_1)$ Use point-slope form.

$y - \underline{\ } = \underline{\quad\quad}$ Substitute for m, t_1, and y_1.

$y = \underline{\quad}$ Simplify.

✔ **Checkpoint** **Complete the following exercise.**

1. Describe the correlation shown by the scatter plot. Then approximate the best-fitting line for the data.

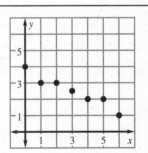

Example 2 _Using a Fitted Line_

The table shows the amount of imported oil _y_ (in millions of barrels per day) to the United States in each year _t_.

t	1991	1992	1993	1994	1995	1996
y	7.6	7.9	8.6	9.0	8.8	9.5
t	1997	1998	1999	2000	2001	2002
y	10.2	10.7	10.9	11.5	11.9	11.4

a. Approximate the best-fitting line for the data.

b. Use the fitted line to estimate the number of barrels per day that will be imported in 2005.

Solution

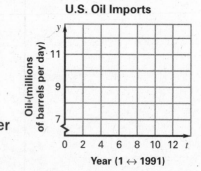

U.S. Oil Imports

a. _Draw_ a scatter plot of the data. Let $t = 1$ represent _____.

Sketch the line that appears to best fit the data.

Choose two points on the scatter plot shown, you might choose (2, ____) and (6, ____).

Find an equation of the line that passes through the two

points and has a slope of $m = \dfrac{}{} = $ ____.

Approximate the best-fitting line as follows:

$$y - y_1 = m(t - t_1) \qquad \text{Use point-slope form.}$$
$$y - \underline{} = \underline{} \qquad \text{Substitute for } m, t_1, \text{ and } y_1.$$
$$y = \underline{} \qquad \text{Simplify.}$$

b. To estimate the number of barrels imported per day in 2005, use the model from part (a) and use ____ for _t_.

$$y = \underline{} \qquad \text{Write linear model.}$$
$$y = \underline{} \qquad \text{Substitute for } t.$$
$$y = \underline{} \qquad \text{Simplify.}$$

An estimated ____ million barrels of oil per day will be imported in 2005.

2.6 Linear Inequalities in Two Variables

Goals • Graph linear inequalities.
• Use linear inequalities to solve real-life problems.

Your Notes

VOCABULARY

Linear inequality in two variables

Solution of an inequality in two variables

Half-planes

Example 1 *Checking Solutions of Inequalities*

Check whether the ordered pairs (a) (5, 1) and (b) (0, 0) are solutions of $x - 4y < 1$.

Ordered Pair	Substitute	Conclusion
a. (5, 1)	__ − 4(__) = _____	(5, 1) _____ a solution.
b. (0, 0)	__ − 4(__) = _____	(0, 0) _____ a solution.

GRAPHING A LINEAR INEQUALITY

The graph of a linear inequality in two variables is a half-plane. To graph a linear inequality, follow these steps:

Step 1 Graph the boundary line of the inequality. Use a _____ line for < or > and a _____ line for ≤ or ≥.

Step 2 Test a point _____ the boundary to see if it is a solution of the inequality. Shade the appropriate half-plane.

Example 2 _Graphing Linear Inequalities in One Variable_

Graph $x > -2$ in a coordinate plane.

Solution

Graph the boundary line $x = -2$. Use a _____ line because $x > -2$.

Test the point (0, 0). Because (0, 0) _____ a solution of the inequality, shade the half-plane to the _____ the line.

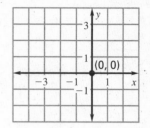

Example 3 _Graphing Linear Inequalities in Two Variables_

Graph (a) $y < x$ and (b) $2y + 2x \leq 4$.

Solution

a. **Graph** the boundary line $y = x$. Use a _____ line because $y < x$.

Test the point (1, 0). Because (1, 0) _____ a solution of the inequality, shade the half-plane _____ the line.

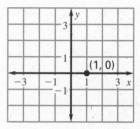

b. **Graph** the boundary line $2y + 2x = 4$. Use a _____ line because $2y + 2x \leq 4$.

Test the point (0, 0). Because (0, 0) _____ a solution of the inequality, shade the half-plane _____ the line.

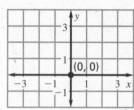

✔ **Checkpoint** Complete the following exercises.

1. Is (0, 0) a solution of $-y + x < -2$?

2. Graph $-y + x < -2$.

Example 4   *Writing and Using a Linear Inequality*

You have $40 and want to buy peanuts and refreshments for your friends at a baseball game. Peanuts are $3 per bag and refreshments are $4 each.

a. Write a linear inequality in two variables to represent the number of refreshments and bags of peanuts you can buy.

b. Graph the inequality and discuss three possible solutions.

Solution

a.   Verbal Model | Peanut price | · | Amount of peanuts | + | Refreshment price | ·

| Number of refreshments | $\leq$ | |

     Labels   Peanut price = ___   **(dollars)**

                 Amount of peanuts = x   **(bags)**

                 Refreshment price = ___   **(dollars)**

                 Number of refreshments = y   **(refreshments)**

                 Spending money = ___   **(dollars)**

     Algebraic Model   _____

b. *Graph* the boundary line _____ . Use a _____ line because _____ .

Test the point (0, 0). Because (0, 0) ___ a solution of the inequality, shade the half-plane _____ the line.

Possible solutions are points within the shaded region.

Buying for Friends

One solution is to buy no bags of peanuts and ___ refreshments. The total cost will be $___ .

You could buy 5 bags of peanuts and ___ refreshments. The total cost will be $___ .

You could buy 8 bags of peanuts and ___ refreshments. The total cost will be $___ .

Homework

2.7 Piecewise Functions

Goals • Represent piecewise functions.
• Use piecewise functions to model real-life quantities.

Your Notes

VOCABULARY

Piecewise function _____

_____

Step function

Example 1 *Evaluating a Piecewise Function*

Evaluate $f(x)$ when (a) $x = -3$ and (b) $x = -1$.

$$f(x) = \begin{cases} x - 4, & \text{if } x < -1 \\ 3x - 1, & \text{if } x \geq -1 \end{cases}$$

a. $f(x) = x - 4$ Because -3 ___ -1, use
                                             _____ equation.

     $f(\underline{\quad}) = \underline{\qquad} = \underline{\quad}$ Substitute for x.

b. $f(x) = 3x - 1$ Because -1 ___ -1, use
                                             _____ equation.

     $f(\underline{\quad}) = \underline{\qquad} = \underline{\quad}$ Substitute for x.

Example 2 *Graphing a Piecewise Function*

Graph this function: $f(x) = \begin{cases} -x + 1, & \text{if } x < 0 \\ 2x + 1, & \text{if } x \geq 0 \end{cases}$

Solution

To the left of $x = 0$, the graph is given by $y = \underline{\qquad}$.

To the right of and including $x = 0$, the graph is given by $y = \underline{\qquad}$.

The graph is composed of two rays with common initial point (___, ___).

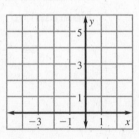

Example 3 *Graphing a Step Function*

Graph this function: $f(x) = \begin{cases} -1, & \text{if } -3 \leq x < -1 \\ 1, & \text{if } -1 \leq x < 1 \\ 3, & \text{if } 1 \leq x < 3 \end{cases}$

Solution

The graph is composed of _____ line segments. The first line segment is given by the equation $y =$ ____ and represents the graph when x is greater than or equal to ____ and less than ____.

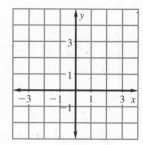

The _____ dot at $(-1, 1)$ indicates that $f(-1)$ ___ 1.

The _____ dot at $(1, 1)$ indicates that $f(1)$ ___ 1.

Example 4 *Writing a Piecewise Function*

Write equations for the piecewise function whose graph is shown.

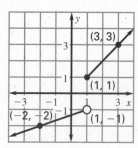

Solution

To the _____ of $x = 1$, the graph is part of the line passing through $(-2, -2)$ and $(1, -1)$. An equation of this line is

$y =$ _____ .

To the _____ of and including $x = 1$, the graph is part of the line passing through $(1, 1)$ and $(3, 3)$. An equation of this line is given by $y =$ ___. The equations for the piecewise function are:

$f(x) = \begin{cases} \underline{\hspace{1.5cm}}, & \text{if } x \underline{\hspace{0.8cm}} \\ \underline{\hspace{0.5cm}}, & \text{if } x \underline{\hspace{0.8cm}} \end{cases}$

Example 5   *Using a Step Function*

Parking costs $1 per hour or a $4 maximum for 6 hours. Write and graph a piecewise function for the costs.

Solution

For times up to one hour, the charge is $__. For each additional hour, the charge is an additional $__ until you reach $__. Let t be the number of hours you park.

Parking Cost

$$f(t) = \begin{cases} \_\_, & \text{if } 0 \_\_ t \_\_ 1 \\ \_\_, & \text{if } 1 \_\_ t \_\_ 2 \\ \_\_, & \text{if } 2 \_\_ t \_\_ 3 \\ \_\_, & \text{if } 3 \_\_ t \_\_ 6 \end{cases}$$

✔ *Checkpoint* **Complete the following exercises.**

1. Graph $f(x)$ and evaluate for $x = 0$, $x = 2$, and $x = 3$.

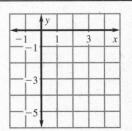

$$f(x) = \begin{cases} x - 2, & \text{if } x \leq 2 \\ -x - 2, & \text{if } x > 2 \end{cases}$$

2. Write an equation for the graph shown.

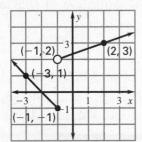

$(-1, 2)$ $(2, 3)$
$(-3, 1)$
$(-1, -1)$

3. Shipping costs $3 on purchases up to $10, $5 on purchases up to $50, and $8 on purchases over $50 up to $100. Write a piecewise function for this situation.

2.8 Absolute Value Functions

Goals • Represent absolute value functions.
 • Use absolute value functions to model real-life situations.

Your Notes

VOCABULARY

Vertex of an absolute value graph

GRAPHING ABSOLUTE VALUE FUNCTIONS

The graph of $y = a|x - h| + k$ has the following characteristics.

• The graph has vertex (__, __) and is symmetric in the line $x =$ __.

• The graph is V-shaped. It opens _____ if $a > 0$ and opens _____ if $a < 0$.

• The graph is _____ than the graph of $y = |x|$ if $|a| < 1$.

• The graph is _____ than the graph of $y = |x|$ if $|a| > 1$.

Example 1 *Graphing an Absolute Value Function*

Graph $y = 2|x + 1| - 2$.

Solution

To graph $y = 2|x + 1| - 2$, plot the vertex at (____, ____). Then plot another point on the graph, such as (0, __). Use symmetry to plot a third point, (____, __). Connect these three points with a V-shaped graph. Note that $a =$ __ > 0 and $|a| > 1$, so the graph opens _____ and is _____ than the graph of $y = |x|$.

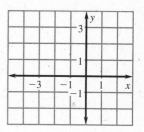

Example 2   *Writing an Absolute Value Function*

Write an equation of the graph shown.

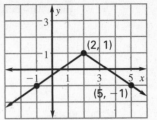

Solution

The vertex of the graph is (__ , __),
so the equation has the form
$y = a|x - \_\_| + \_\_$.

To find the value of *a*, substitute the
coordinates of the point (__ , ____) into the equation and
solve.

$y = a|x - \_\_| + \_\_$ Write equation.

$\_\_\_ = a|\underline{\hspace{1cm}}| + \_\_$ Substitute for *y* and for *x*.

$\dfrac{}{\_\_\_} = \underline{\hspace{1cm}}$ Simplify.

$\dfrac{}{\_\_\_} = \_\_\_$ Subtract __ from each side.

$\dfrac{}{\_\_\_\_} = a$ Divide each side by __ .

An equation of the graph is $y = \underline{\hspace{3cm}}$.

Example 3   *Interpreting an Absolute Value Function*

The roof of a building can be modeled by the function
$y = -\dfrac{4}{3}|x - 9| + 12$, where *x* and *y* are measured in feet
and the *x*-axis represents the base of the roof.

a. Graph the function.

b. Interpret the domain and range of the function.

Solution

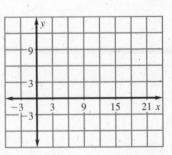

a. The vertex is (__ , ____) and the
graph opens _____ . It is
_____ than the graph of
$y = |x|$.

b. The domain is _____ , so
the roof is ___ feet wide. The
range is _____ , so the top
of the roof is ___ feet above its
base.

Your Notes

Checkpoint **Complete the following exercises.**

1. Graph $y = \dfrac{2}{3}|x + 1| - 1$.   2. Write an equation of the graph shown.

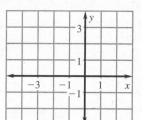

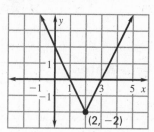

| Example 4 | *Interpreting an Absolute Value Graph* |

While playing miniature golf, you hit the ball off of a wall to try to make it in the hole. The ball is located at (1, 2) and the hole is at (6, 2). The point where the ball hits the wall is (3, 0).

a. Write an equation for the path of the ball.

b. Do you make your putt?

Solution

a. The vertex of the path of the ball is (__, __), so the equation has the form $y =$ _____. Substitute the coordinates of the point (__, __) into the equation and solve for *a*.

　　__ $=$ _____　　**Substitute for *x* and for *y*.**

　　__ $=$ __　　　　　**Solve for *a*.**

An equation for the path of the ball is $y =$ _____.

b. You will make your shot if (__, __) lies on the path of the ball.

　　__ $\overset{?}{=}$ _____　　**Substitute for *x* and for *y*.**

　　__ __ _____　　**Simplify.**

The point (__, __) _____ the equation, so you _____ make your shot.

Homework

3.1 Solving Linear Systems by Graphing

Goals • Graph and solve systems of linear equations.
• Use linear systems to solve real-life problems.

Your Notes

VOCABULARY

System of two linear equations

Solution of a system of linear equations

Example 1   *Checking Solutions of a Linear System*

Check whether (a) $(-1, -4)$ and (b) $(1, 2)$ are solutions of the following system.

$$3x - y = 1 \qquad \text{Equation 1}$$
$$x + y = 3 \qquad \text{Equation 2}$$

Solution

a. $3(\_\_\_) - (\_\_\_) = \_\_$ Equation 1 _____.

$(\_\_\_) + (\_\_\_) = \_\_\_$ Equation 2 _____.

b. $3(\_\_) - (\_\_) = \_\_$ Equation 1 _____.

$(\_\_) + (\_\_) = \_\_$ Equation 2 _____.

Because $(1, 2)$ _____ a solution of each equation and $(-1, -4)$ _____, $(1, 2)$ _____ a solution of the system and $(-1, -4)$ _____.

Example 2 *Solving a System Graphically*

Solve the system.

$$-2x + y = 5 \quad \text{Equation 1}$$
$$x + 3y = 8 \quad \text{Equation 2}$$

Solution

Begin by graphing both equations. From the graph, the lines appear to intersect at (___, ___). You can check this algebraically as follows.

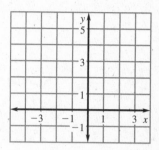

$$-2(\underline{\quad}) + \underline{\quad} = \underline{\quad}$$
$$\underline{\quad} + 3(\underline{\quad}) = \underline{\quad}$$

The solution is (___, ___).

Example 3 *Systems with Many or No Solutions*

Tell how many solutions the linear system has.

a. $x - 3y = -1$
   $x - 3y = 1$

b. $-x - 3y = -1$
   $3x + 9y = 3$

Solution

a. Graph the linear system.

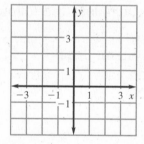

The graphs of the equations are two _____ lines. Because the two lines have _____, the system has _____ _____.

b. Graph the linear system.

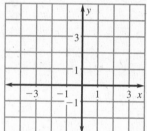

The graphs of the equations are the _____. So, each point on the line is a solution and the system has _____ _____.

NUMBER OF SOLUTIONS OF A LINEAR SYSTEM

The relationship between the graph of a linear system and the system's number of solutions is described below.

Graphical Interpretation	Algebraic Interpretation
The graph of the system is a pair of lines that intersect in one point.	The system has _____ _____.
The graph of the system is a single line.	The system has _____ _____.
The graph of the system is a pair of parallel lines so that there is no point of intersection.	The system has _____ _____.

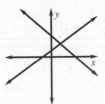

Exactly one solution

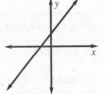

Infinitely many solutions

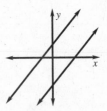

No solution

✓ *Checkpoint* Complete the following exercises.

1. Solve the system. Check your solution.
$$x + 7y = 29$$
$$-9x + y = -5$$

2. Tell how many solutions the linear system has.
$$\frac{2}{3}x + y = 2$$
$$4x + 6y = 12$$

Example 4   *Writing and Using a Linear System*

You are putting a fence around a rectangular yard and you want the length to be twice the width. You will use 120 feet of fencing. What are the dimensions of the fence?

Solution

Verbal Model

| Length | = 2([_____])

2(| Length |) + 2(| Width |) = [_____]

Labels   **Equation 1**   Length = l (feet)

                      Width = w (feet)

           Equation 2   Length = l (feet)

                      Width = w (feet)

                      Perimeter = ____   (feet)

Algebraic Model l = ____   **Equation 1**

          $2l + 2w$ = ____   **Equation 2**

Graph the linear system. The lines appear to intersect at the point (____, ____). Check this algebraically.

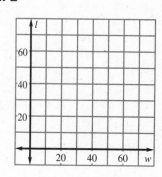

   2(____) = ____

   2(____) + 2(____) = ____

The solution is (____, ____), which means that the fence has a length of ____ feet and a width of ____ feet.

✔ *Checkpoint* **Complete the following exercise.**

3. You decide instead to use 105 feet of fencing in Example 4 and you want the length to be 4 times the width. Write a linear system for this situation.

Solving Linear Systems Algebraically

Goals • Use algebraic methods to solve linear systems.
• Use linear systems to model real-life situations.

Your Notes

THE SUBSTITUTION METHOD

Step 1 Solve one of the equations for one of its variables.

Step 2 Substitute the expression from _____ into the other equation and solve for the other variable.

Step 3 Substitute the value from _____ into the revised equation from Step 1 and solve.

Example 1 *The Substitution Method*

Solve the linear system using the substitution method.

$$x - 2y = 4 \qquad \textbf{Equation 1}$$
$$2x - 3y = 1 \qquad \textbf{Equation 2}$$

Solution

1. Solve Equation 1 for x.

   $x - 2y = 4$ **Write Equation 1.**

   $x = $ _____   **Revised Equation 1**

2. Substitute this expression into Equation 2 and solve for y.

   $2x - 3y = 1$ **Write Equation 2.**

   $2(\underline{}) - 3y = 1$ **Substitute for x.**

   $y = $ ____   **Solve for y.**

3. Substitute the value of y into revised Equation 1 and solve for x.

   $x = $ _____   **Write revised Equation 1.**

   $x = $ _____   **Substitute for y.**

   $x = $ ____   **Simplify.**

The solution is (____ , ____). Check the solution by substituting back into the original equations.

THE LINEAR COMBINATION METHOD

Step 1 Multiply one or both of the equations by a
_____ to obtain coefficients that differ only in
_____ for one of the variables.

Step 2 Add the revised equations from _____ . Combining
like terms will _____ one of the variables.
Solve for the remaining variable.

Step 3 Substitute the value obtained in _____ into either
of the original equations and solve for the other
variable.

Example 2 *The Linear Combination Method*

Solve the linear system using $2x - 3y = 1$ **Equation 1**
the linear combination method. $-4x + 2y = 6$ **Equation 2**

1. Multiply the first equation by ___ so that the *x*-coefficients
   differ only in sign.

   $2x - 3y = 1$ × ___ ⟶ [   ]   **Equation 1**

   $-4x + 2y = 6$ ⟶ $-4x + 2y = 6$ **Equation 2**

2. Add the revised equations [   ]
   and solve for *y*.
              $y =$ ___

3. Substitute the value of *y* into one of the original
   equations. Solve for *x*.

$2x - 3y = 1$	**Write Equation 1.**
$2x - 3(\_\_\_) = 1$	**Substitute for *y*.**
$2x + \_\_ = 1$	**Simplify.**
$x =$ _____	**Solve for *x*.**

The solution is _____ .

Check You can check the solution
algebraically using the method shown
in Example 1. You can also use a
graphing calculator to check the
solution.

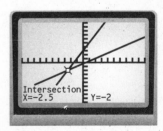

Intersection
X=−2.5   Y=−2

✔ *Checkpoint* Complete the following exercises.

1. Solve the linear system using the substitution method.

$x - y = 3$
$-3x + 4y = 2$

2. Solve the linear system using the linear combination method.

$5x + 6y = -2$
$2x + 3y = 1$

Example 3 | *The Linear Combination Method*

Solve the linear system using the linear combination method.

$2x + 5y = 6$ **Equation 1**
$-3x - 2y = 2$ **Equation 2**

Solution

Multiply the first equation by ___ and the second equation by ___ so that the coefficients of x differ only in sign.

$2x + 5y = 6$ × ___ ➡ [   ]

$-3x - 2y = 2$ × ___ ➡ [   ]

[   ]

Add the revised equations and solve for y.

$y = $ ___

Substitute the value of y into one of the original equations. Solve for x.

$2x + 5y = 6$ Write Equation 1.

$2x + 5(\_\_) = 6$ Substitute for y.

$x = $ ___   Solve for x.

The solution is (___ , ___). Check the solution algebraically or graphically.

Example 4   *Linear Systems with Many or No Solutions*

Solve the linear system.

a. $4x - 2y = 5$ **b.** $-3x + 6y = 9$
    $2x - y = 3$ $4x - 8y = -12$

Solution

a. Because the coefficient of y in the second equation is
   ____, use substitution. Solve the second equation for y.

      $2x - y = 3$

      _____ $= y$

Substitute the expression for y into the first equation.

          $4x - 2y = 5$ **Write first equation.**

    $4x - 2(_____) = 5$ **Substitute for y.**

       $\_\_ = \_\_$ **Simplify.**

Because the statement _____ is _____, there

_____.

b. Because no coefficient is _____, use the linear
combination method. Multiply the first equation by __ and
the second equation by __.

    $-3x + 6y = 9$ $\times \_\_$ ⟹   [_____]

    $4x - 8y = -12$ $\times \_\_$ ⟹   [_____]

                                   [_____]

Add the revised equations.

Because the equation _____ is _____, there

_____.

✔ **Checkpoint** Solve the linear system.

3. $2x + 7y = -4$ **4.** $3x - 5y = 10$
    $-6x - 21y = 12$ $7x - 11y = 20$

3.3 Graphing and Solving Systems of Linear Inequalities

Goals • Graph a system of linear inequalities.
• Use systems of linear inequalities to solve real-life problems.

VOCABULARY

System of linear inequalities in two variables

Solution of a system of linear inequalities

Graph of a system of linear inequalities

GRAPHING A SYSTEM OF LINEAR INEQUALITIES

To graph a system of linear inequalities, do the following for each inequality in the system:

• Graph the line that corresponds to the inequality. Use a _____ line for an inequality with < or > and a _____ line for an inequality with ≤ or ≥.

• Lightly shade the half-plane that is the graph of the inequality. Colored pencils may help you distinguish the different half-planes.

The graph of the system is the region common to all of the half-planes. If you used colored pencils, it is the region that has been shaded with _____ color.

Example 1 *Graphing a System of Two Inequalities*

Graph the system. $y \geq x - 1$ **Inequality 1**
                          $y < -2x + 1$ **Inequality 2**

Begin by graphing each linear inequality. Use different shades for each half-plane.

The graph of the system is the intersection of the two shaded regions.

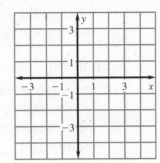

Shade the half-plane on and _____ $y = x - 1$.

Shade the half-plane to the _____ of $y = -2x + 1$.

Example 2 *Graphing a System of Three Inequalities*

Graph the system. $x \geq 0$ **Inequality 1**
                          $y \geq 0$ **Inequality 2**
                          $2y + 3x < 7$ **Inequality 3**

The graph of the system is a _____ region.

The inequality $x \geq 0$ implies that the region is on and to the _____ of the y-axis.

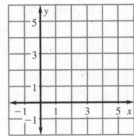

The inequality $2y + 3x < 7$ implies that the region is _____ the line $2y + 3x = 7$.

The inequality $y \geq 0$ implies that the region is on and _____ the x-axis.

✔ **Checkpoint** **Complete the following exercise.**

1. Graph the system.

   $x \geq 1$
   $y \geq 2$
   $y \leq 5 - x$

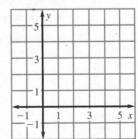

Example 3 *Writing and Using a System of Inequalities*

You are selling $5 adult tickets and $3 youth tickets for a school play. You want to sell at least $600 worth of tickets.

a. Write and graph a system of linear inequalities that describes the information given above.

b. You sell 80 adult tickets and 100 youth tickets. Did you reach your sales goal?

Solution

a. Let y represent the number of youth tickets sold. Let x represent the number of adult tickets sold. From the given information, you can write the following system of inequalities.

$x \geq$ ___   **Must sell at least ___ adult tickets.**

$y \geq$ ___   **Must sell at least ___ youth tickets.**

_____   **Total sales must be at least $ ___.**

Graph the system of inequalities.

b. From the graph you can see that (80, 100) ___ in the solution region, so selling 80 adult tickets and 100 youth tickets ___ reach your sales goal.

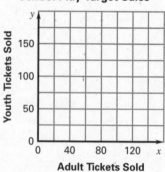

School Play Target Sales

✔ *Checkpoint* **Complete the following exercise.**

2. Assume that in Example 3, the auditorium can only hold up to 200 people. Write and graph a system of linear inequalities with this addition.

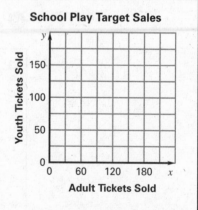

School Play Target Sales

Homework

3.4 Linear Programming

Goals • Solve linear programming problems.
• Use linear programming to solve real-life problems.

Your Notes

VOCABULARY

Optimization

Linear programming

Objective function

Constraints

Feasible region

OPTIMAL SOLUTION OF A LINEAR PROGRAMMING PROBLEM

If an objective function has a maximum or a minimum value, then it must occur at a _____ of the feasible region. Moreover, the objective function will have both a maximum and a minimum value if the feasible region is

_____.

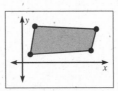

Bounded region

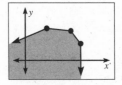

Unbounded region

Example 1 *Solving a Linear Programming Problem*

Find the minimum value and the maximum value of

$C = 2y + 3x$ **Objective function**

subject to the following constraints.

$x \leq 2$
$y \geq -1$ **Constraints**
$y - x \leq 3$

Solution

The feasible region determined by the constraints is shown. The three vertices are $(-4, -1)$, $(2, -1)$, and $(2, 5)$. To find the minimum and maximum values of C, evaluate $C = 2y + 3x$ at each of the three vertices.

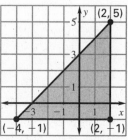

At $(-4, -1)$: $C =$ _____

At $(2, -1)$: $C =$ _____

At $(2, 5)$: $C =$ _____

The minimum value of C is _____. It occurs when $x =$ ____ and $y =$ ____. The maximum value of C is ____. It occurs when $x =$ __ and $y =$ __.

✔ *Checkpoint* **Complete the following exercise.**

1. Find the minimum value and maximum value of $C = x - 2y$ subject to the following constraints.

$x \geq 1$
$y \geq x + 1$
$y \leq 7 - x$

Example 2   *A Region that is Unbounded*

Find the minimum value and the maximum value of

$C = y + 2x$ **Objective function**

subject to the following constraints.

$x \geq 0$
$y \geq 0$ **Constraints**
$2y + 3x \geq 8$
$3y + x \geq 5$

Solution

The feasible region determined by the constraints is shown. The three vertices are $(0, 4)$, $(2, 1)$, and $(5, 0)$. Evaluate $C = y + 2x$ at each of the vertices.

At $(0, 4)$: $C =$ _____

At $(2, 1)$: $C =$ _____

At $(5, 0)$: $C =$ _____

If you evaluate other points in the feasible region, you will see that as the points get farther from the origin, the value of the objective function _____ without bound. So, the objective function has no _____ value. The value of the objective function is always at least ___, so the _____ value is ___.

✔ *Checkpoint* Complete the following exercise.

2. Find the minimum value and the maximum value of $C = 3x + y$ subject to the following constraints.

$x \leq 4$
$x \geq 0$
$y + 2x \geq 9$
$3y - x \geq 6$

Example 3 **Finding Maximum Profit**

You are making fruit baskets with oranges, bananas, and apples. The table gives the amount of fruit required for the two arrangements. Each day you have 240 oranges, 270 bananas, and 320 apples. Arrangement A earns a profit of $10 per basket and Arrangement B earns $8 per basket. How many of each fruit basket should you make per day to maximize your profit?

Fruit	Arrangement A	Arrangement B
Oranges	4	6
Bananas	6	6
Apples	8	6

Solution

Write an objective function. Let a and b represent the number of each type of fruit basket made. Because you want to maximize the profit P, the objective function is: $P =$ _____ .

Write the constraints in terms of a and b.

___a + ___$b \le$ ____   Oranges: up to _____

___a + ___$b \le$ ____   Bananas: up to _____

___a + ___$b \le$ ____   Apples: up to _____

$a \ge$ ___   Amount cannot be _____ .

$b \ge$ ___   Amount cannot be _____ .

Calculate the profit at each vertex of the feasible region.

At (0, 40): $P =$ _____

At (15, 30): $P =$ _____

At (25, 20): $P =$ _____

At (40, 0): $P =$ _____

Maximum profit is obtained by making ___ Arrangement A baskets and ___ Arrangement B baskets.

Homework

3.5 Graphing Linear Equations in Three Variables

Goals • Graph linear equations in three variables and evaluate linear functions of two variables.
• Use functions of two variables to model real-life situations.

Your Notes

VOCABULARY

Three-dimensional coordinate system

z-axis

Ordered triple

Octants

Linear equation in three variables

Function of two variables

Example 1 *Plotting Points in Three Dimensions*

Plot $(-4, -1, 3)$ in a three-dimensional coordinate system.

To plot $(-4, -1, 3)$, find the point $(\_\_\_\_, \_\_\_\_)$ in the xy-plane. The point $(-4, -1, 3)$ lies 3 units _____.

Example 2 | *Graphing a Linear Equation in Three Variables*

Sketch the graph of $2x - 2y + 3z = 6$.

Find points at which the graph intersects the axes. Let $x = 0$ and $y = 0$, and solve for z to get $z =$ __. This tells you that the z-intercept is __, so plot (__, __, __). In a similar way, you can find that the x-intercept is __ and the y-intercept is ___. After plotting the intercepts, connect the points with lines to form the triangular region of the plane.

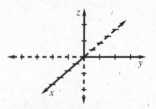

Example 3 | *Evaluating a Function of Two Variables*

Write the linear equation $2x - 2y + 3z = 6$ as a function of x and y. Then evaluate the function when $x = 1$ and $y = 1$. Interpret the result geometrically.

$2x - 2y + 3z = 6$ Write original equation.

$3z =$ _____   Isolate z-term.

$z =$ _____   Solve for z.

$f(x, y) =$ _____   Replace z with $f(x, y)$.

$f(1, 1) =$ _____ $=$ __. This tells you that the graph of f contains the point (__, __, __).

✔ *Checkpoint* **Complete the following exercise.**

1. Graph $3x + 4y - 4z = 12$. Then write the equation as a function of x and y and evaluate $f(0, 2)$.

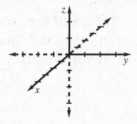

Your Notes

Example 4 **Modeling a Real-Life Situation**

You are painting the inside of your house and plan to use two colors of paint: white and blue. White costs $12 per gallon and blue costs $15 per gallon. You also buy supplies totaling $40.

a. Write a model for the total amount you spend as a function of the number of gallons of white and blue paint you use.

b. Evaluate the model for 3 gallons of white paint and 2 gallons of blue paint.

Solution

a. Verbal Model

| Total cost | = | White paint cost | · | | + |

| Blue paint cost | · | | + | Supplies |

Labels   Total Cost = C   (dollars)

White paint cost = ____   (dollars per gallon)

White paint amount = w   (gallons)

Blue paint cost = ____   (dollars per gallon)

Blue paint amount = b   (gallons)

Supplies = ____   (dollars)

Algebraic Model   C = _____

b. Substitute w = __ and b = __ into the function to find the total cost.

C = _____   Write original function.

= _____   Substitute for w and b.

= ____   Simplify.

The total cost is $____.

Homework

Solving Systems of Linear Equations in Three Variables

Goals • Solve systems of linear equations in three variables.
• Use linear systems in three variables to model real-life situations.

Your Notes

VOCABULARY

System of three linear equations
_____

Solution of a system of three linear equations
_____

THE LINEAR COMBINATION METHOD (3-VARIABLE SYSTEMS)

Step 1 Use the linear combination method to rewrite the linear system in three variables as a linear system in _____ variables.

Step 2 Solve the new linear system for both of its variables.

Step 3 Substitute the values found in _____ into one of the original equations and solve for the remaining variable.

Note: If you obtain a _____ equation, such as $0 = 1$, in any of the steps, then the system has _____. If you obtain an _____, such as $0 = 0$, then the system has _____.

Example 1   *Using the Linear Combination Method*

Solve the system.
$$4x + 2y - z = 1 \qquad \text{Equation 1}$$
$$x - 3y + 2z = 14 \qquad \text{Equation 2}$$
$$-x + y + z = -1 \qquad \text{Equation 3}$$

1. Eliminate a variable in two of the original equations.

$$4x + 2y - z = 1$$

Add ___ times the third
equation to the first.

$$\boxed{}$$

New Equation 1

$$x - 3y + 2z = 14$$
$$-x + y + z = -1$$

Add the second and
third equations.

$$\boxed{}$$

New Equation 2

2. Solve the new system of linear equations.

$$\boxed{}$$

Add ____ times new Equation 2
to new Equation 1.

$$\boxed{}$$

$$y = \underline{} \qquad \text{Solve for } y.$$

$$z = \underline{} \qquad \text{Substitute } y \text{ in new Equation 1 or 2.}$$

3. Substitute y and z into an original equation. Solve for x.

$$-x + y + z = -1 \qquad \text{Equation 3}$$

Substitute for y and for z.

$$x = \underline{} \qquad \text{Solve for } x.$$

The solution is the ordered triple (__, ____, __). Check this
solution in each of the original equations.

✔ *Checkpoint* **Complete the following exercise.**

1. Solve the system

$$x + 3y - 4z = -3$$
$$-2x + 2y + z = 0$$
$$3x - 2y + 2z = 8$$

Example 2 **Solving a System with Many Solutions**

Solve the system. $x + 2y + 2z = 4$ **Equation 1**
                          $2x - 2y + 4z = 8$ **Equation 2**
                          $2x + 2y + 4z = 8$ **Equation 3**

Rewrite the linear system in three variables as a linear system in two variables.

$x + 2y + 2z = 4$ Add the first equation
$\underline{2x - 2y + 4z = 8}$ to the second.

[   ]   New Equation 1

$2x - 2y + 4z = 8$ Add the second equation
$\underline{2x + 2y + 4z = 8}$ to the third.

[   ]   New Equation 2

The result is a system of linear equations in two variables.

_____   New Equation 1

_____   New Equation 2

Solve the new system by adding ____ times the first equation to __ times the second equation. This produces the _____ _____. So, the system has _____.

Describe the solution. Rewrite new Equation 1 to get $x =$ _____. Substituting this into original equation 1 produces $y =$ __. So, any ordered triple of the form (_____, __, __) is a solution of the system. For instance, (__, __, 2), (__, __, 1), and (__, __, 0) are all solutions.

✔ **Checkpoint** Solve the system.

2. $x + y - 2z = 3$ **3.** $x + 2y - 4z = 7$
    $2x + 2y - 4z = 1$ $-x - y + 2z = -4$
    $-x - 3y + z = 5$ $x + 4y - 8z = 13$

Homework

4.1 Matrix Operations

Goals • Add and subtract matrices, multiply a matrix by a scalar, and solve matrix equations.
• Use matrices in real-life situations.

Your Notes

VOCABULARY

Matrix

Dimensions of a matrix

Entries of a matrix

Equal matrices

Scalar

Scalar multiplication

Example 1 *Comparing Matrices*

a. The following matrices are _____ because corresponding entries are _____ .

$$\begin{bmatrix} 0.25 & 2 \\ 1 & -\dfrac{3}{5} \end{bmatrix} - \begin{bmatrix} \dfrac{1}{4} & 2 \\ 1 & -0.6 \end{bmatrix}$$

b. The following matrices are _____ because corresponding entries in the first row are _____ .

$$\begin{bmatrix} -1 & 3 \\ 1 & -2 \end{bmatrix} - \begin{bmatrix} 1 & -3 \\ 1 & -2 \end{bmatrix}$$

Example 2   *Adding and Subtracting Matrices*

Perform the indicated operation, if possible.

a. $\begin{bmatrix} 2 \\ 1 \end{bmatrix} + \begin{bmatrix} 2 & 0 & 7 \\ 1 & -1 & 0 \end{bmatrix}$

b. $\begin{bmatrix} 3 & -2 \\ 0 & -2 \end{bmatrix} - \begin{bmatrix} -1 & 2 \\ 5 & 3 \end{bmatrix}$

Solution

a. Because the dimensions of $\begin{bmatrix} 2 \\ 1 \end{bmatrix}$ are _____, and the

dimensions of $\begin{bmatrix} 2 & 0 & 7 \\ 1 & -1 & 0 \end{bmatrix}$ are _____, you _____ add

the matrices.

b. The dimensions are _____. So, subtract the matrices.

$$\begin{bmatrix} 3 & -2 \\ 0 & -2 \end{bmatrix} - \begin{bmatrix} -1 & 2 \\ 5 & 3 \end{bmatrix} = \begin{bmatrix} \underline{} & \underline{} \\ \underline{} & \underline{} \end{bmatrix}$$

$$= \begin{bmatrix} \underline{} & \underline{} \\ \underline{} & \underline{} \end{bmatrix}$$

Example 3   *Multiplying a Matrix by a Scalar*

Perform the indicated operation(s), if possible.

a. $2\begin{bmatrix} 3 & 2 \\ -1 & 3 \end{bmatrix}$

b. $3\begin{bmatrix} 1 & 2 \\ -2 & 3 \end{bmatrix} - \begin{bmatrix} 2 & 6 \\ -6 & 8 \end{bmatrix}$

Solution

a. $2\begin{bmatrix} 3 & 2 \\ -1 & 3 \end{bmatrix} = \begin{bmatrix} \underline{} & \underline{} \\ \underline{} & \underline{} \end{bmatrix} = \begin{bmatrix} \underline{} & \underline{} \\ \underline{} & \underline{} \end{bmatrix}$

b. $3\begin{bmatrix} 1 & 2 \\ -2 & 3 \end{bmatrix} - \begin{bmatrix} 2 & 6 \\ -6 & 8 \end{bmatrix} = \begin{bmatrix} \underline{} & \underline{} \\ \underline{} & \underline{} \end{bmatrix} - \begin{bmatrix} 2 & 6 \\ -6 & 8 \end{bmatrix}$

$$= \begin{bmatrix} \underline{} & \underline{} \\ \underline{} & \underline{} \end{bmatrix} - \begin{bmatrix} 2 & 6 \\ -6 & 8 \end{bmatrix}$$

$$= \underline{}$$

✓ *Checkpoint* **Complete the following exercises.**

1. Tell whether the matrices are *equal* or *not equal*.

$$\begin{bmatrix} 2 & -6 & \dfrac{-3}{8} & 8 \end{bmatrix} \text{ and } \begin{bmatrix} 2 & -\dfrac{24}{4} & -0.375 & 8 \end{bmatrix}$$

2. Perform the indicated operations.

$$2\begin{bmatrix} -1 & 5 \\ 3 & -2 \end{bmatrix} - \begin{bmatrix} -3 & 2 \\ -4 & 0 \end{bmatrix} + \begin{bmatrix} 0 & 1 \\ 2 & 1 \end{bmatrix}$$

Example 4   *Solving a Matrix Equation*

Solve the matrix equation for *x* and *y*:

$$2\left(\begin{bmatrix} -2 & 3 \\ x & 5 \end{bmatrix} + \begin{bmatrix} y & 7 \\ -4 & 10 \end{bmatrix}\right) = \begin{bmatrix} -10 & 20 \\ 10 & 30 \end{bmatrix}$$

Solution

Simplify the left side of the equation.

$$2\left(\begin{bmatrix} -2 & 3 \\ x & 5 \end{bmatrix} + \begin{bmatrix} y & 7 \\ -4 & 10 \end{bmatrix}\right) = \begin{bmatrix} -10 & 20 \\ 10 & 30 \end{bmatrix}$$

$$2\begin{bmatrix} \underline{\quad\quad} & \underline{\quad} \\ \underline{\quad\quad} & \underline{\quad} \end{bmatrix} = \begin{bmatrix} -10 & 20 \\ 10 & 30 \end{bmatrix}$$

$$\begin{bmatrix} \underline{\quad\quad} & \underline{\quad} \\ \underline{\quad\quad} & \underline{\quad} \end{bmatrix} = \begin{bmatrix} -10 & 20 \\ 10 & 30 \end{bmatrix}$$

Equate corresponding entries and solve the two resulting equations.

$$\underline{\quad\quad\quad} = -10 \qquad\qquad \underline{\quad\quad\quad} = 10$$

$$y = \underline{\quad} \qquad\qquad\qquad x = \underline{\quad}$$

✔ *Checkpoint* **Complete the following exercise.**

3. Solve the matrix equation for *x* and *y*:

$$-\left(\begin{bmatrix} 3 & x \\ -5 & 0 \end{bmatrix} + \begin{bmatrix} y & 2 \\ -1 & 3 \end{bmatrix}\right) = \begin{bmatrix} 0 & -2 \\ 6 & -3 \end{bmatrix}$$

PROPERTIES OF MATRIX OPERATIONS

Let *A*, *B*, and *C* be matrices with the same dimensions and let *c* be a scalar.

Associative Property of Addition $(A + B) + C =$ _____

Commutative Property of Addition $A + B =$ _____

Distributive Property of Addition $c(A + B) =$ _____

Distributive Property of Subtraction $c(A - B) =$ _____

Example 5 *Using Matrices to Organize Data*

Use matrices to organize the following information.

The population estimate for Gallatin County for July 1, 2001 was 36,315 males and 33,532 females. For Glacier County, the estimate was 6452 males and 6633 females.

The population estimate for Gallatin County for July 1, 2002 was 36,998 males and 34,208 females. For Glacier County, the estimate was 6434 males and 6672 females.

Solution

Homework

Organize the data in a _____ matrix.

	July 1, 2001		July 1, 2002	
	Male	Female	Male	Female
Gallatin County	_____	_____	_____	_____
Glacier County	_____	_____	_____	_____

4.2 Multiplying Matrices

Goals • Multiply two matrices.
• Use matrix multiplication in real-life situations.

Your Notes

Example 1   *Describing Matrix Products*

State whether the product AB is defined. If so, give the dimensions of AB.

a. A: 3×4, B: 2×4 **b.** A: 3×4, B: 4×3

Solution

a. Because the number of _____ in A (four) _____ _____ the number of _____ in B (two), the product AB _____ defined.

b. Because A is a 3×4 matrix and B is a 4×3 matrix, the product AB ___ defined and is a _____ matrix.

Example 2   *Finding the Product of Two Matrices*

Find AB if $A = \begin{bmatrix} 2 & 1 \\ -3 & 4 \\ 5 & -2 \end{bmatrix}$ and $B = \begin{bmatrix} 3 & -2 \\ -1 & 5 \end{bmatrix}$.

Solution

$$AB = \begin{bmatrix} 2 & 1 \\ -3 & 4 \\ 5 & -2 \end{bmatrix} \begin{bmatrix} 3 & -2 \\ -1 & 5 \end{bmatrix}$$

$$= \begin{bmatrix} 2(\underline{}) + 1(\underline{}) & 2(\underline{}) + 1(\underline{}) \\ -3(\underline{}) + 4(\underline{}) & -3(\underline{}) + 4(\underline{}) \\ 5(\underline{}) - 2(\underline{}) & 5(\underline{}) - 2(\underline{}) \end{bmatrix}$$

$$= \underline{}$$

✔ *Checkpoint* **Complete the following exercise.**

1. Given *A* and *B*, give the dimensions of *AB*. Then find *AB*.

$$A = \begin{bmatrix} 1 & 0 \\ 2 & -3 \end{bmatrix}, B = \begin{bmatrix} 2 & -1 \\ 3 & 0 \end{bmatrix}$$

Example 3 *Finding the Product of Two Matrices*

If $A = \begin{bmatrix} -2 & 4 \\ 0 & 3 \end{bmatrix}$ and $B = \begin{bmatrix} 2 & 1 \\ 4 & -3 \end{bmatrix}$, find *AB* and *BA*.

$$AB = \begin{bmatrix} -2 & 4 \\ 0 & 3 \end{bmatrix}\begin{bmatrix} 2 & 1 \\ 4 & -3 \end{bmatrix} = \underline{\hspace{2cm}}$$

$$BA = \begin{bmatrix} 2 & 1 \\ 4 & -3 \end{bmatrix}\begin{bmatrix} -2 & 4 \\ 0 & 3 \end{bmatrix} = \underline{\hspace{2cm}}$$

Example 4 *Using Matrix Operations*

If $A = \begin{bmatrix} 3 & 1 \\ -2 & -1 \end{bmatrix}, B = \begin{bmatrix} 2 & 1 \\ 0 & -3 \end{bmatrix}$, and $C = \begin{bmatrix} 4 & 2 \\ -3 & 2 \end{bmatrix}$,

simplify each expression.

a. (A + B)C   **b.** AC + BC

Solution

a. $(A + B)C = \left(\begin{bmatrix} 3 & 1 \\ -2 & -1 \end{bmatrix} + \begin{bmatrix} 2 & 1 \\ 0 & -3 \end{bmatrix}\right)\begin{bmatrix} 4 & 2 \\ -3 & 2 \end{bmatrix}$

$$= \underline{\hspace{2cm}}\begin{bmatrix} 4 & 2 \\ -3 & 2 \end{bmatrix} = \underline{\hspace{2cm}}$$

b. $AC + BC = \begin{bmatrix} 3 & 1 \\ -2 & -1 \end{bmatrix}\begin{bmatrix} 4 & 2 \\ -3 & 2 \end{bmatrix} + \begin{bmatrix} 2 & 1 \\ 0 & -3 \end{bmatrix}\begin{bmatrix} 4 & 2 \\ -3 & 2 \end{bmatrix}$

$$= \underline{\hspace{2cm}} + \underline{\hspace{2cm}} = \underline{\hspace{2cm}}$$

PROPERTIES OF MATRIX MULTIPLICATION

Let *A*, *B*, and *C* be matrices and let *c* be a scalar.

Associative Property of Matrix Multiplication $A(BC) = $ _____

Left Distributive Property $A(B + C) = $ _____

Right Distributive Property $(A + B)C = $ _____

Associative Property of Scalar Multiplication $c(AB) = (cA)$__ $ = $ __(cB)

Example 5   *Using Matrices to Calculate the Total Cost*

Tim wants 4 notebooks, 5 pens, and 10 pencils for the new school year. Leslye wants 5 notebooks, 8 pens, and 8 pencils. Each notebook is $4, each pen is $2, and each pencil is $1. Use matrix multiplication to find the total cost for each person.

Solution

Write the supplies and the costs in matrix form. Set up the matrices so that the _____ of the supplies matrix match the _____ of the cost matrix.

Supplies
Notebooks Pens Pencils   Cost
Dollars

Tim
Leslye _____   Notebooks
Pens
Pencils ____

The total cost for each person can be obtained by multiplying the _____ matrix by the _____ matrix.

$$\begin{bmatrix} 4 & 5 & 10 \\ 5 & 8 & 8 \end{bmatrix} \begin{bmatrix} 4 \\ 2 \\ 1 \end{bmatrix} = \underline{\hspace{3cm}} = \underline{\hspace{1cm}}$$

The labels for the matrix are as follows.

Total Cost
Dollars
Tim
Leslye _____

The total cost of supplies is $____ for Tim and $____ for Leslye.

Homework

4.3 Determinants and Cramer's Rule

Goals • Evaluate determinants.
• Use Cramer's Rule.

Your Notes

VOCABULARY

Determinant

Cramer's rule

Coefficient matrix

THE DETERMINANT OF A MATRIX

Determinant of a 2 × 2 matrix

$$\det \begin{bmatrix} a & b \\ c & d \end{bmatrix} = \begin{vmatrix} a & b \\ c & d \end{vmatrix} = \underline{\quad} - \underline{\quad}$$

Determinant of a 3 × 3 matrix

$$\det \begin{bmatrix} a & b & c \\ d & e & f \\ g & h & i \end{bmatrix} =$$

$$\begin{vmatrix} a & b & c \\ d & e & f \\ g & h & i \end{vmatrix} \begin{matrix} a & b \\ d & e \\ g & h \end{matrix} = (aei + bfg + cdh) - (gec + hfa + idb)$$

Example 1   *Evaluating Determinants*

Evaluate the determinant of (a) $\begin{bmatrix} 5 & -3 \\ 2 & 4 \end{bmatrix}$ and

(b) $\begin{bmatrix} -2 & 0 & 1 \\ 4 & -1 & 0 \\ 0 & 2 & 1 \end{bmatrix}$.

a. $\begin{vmatrix} 5 & -3 \\ 2 & 4 \end{vmatrix} = 5(\underline{\ \ \ }) - 2(\underline{\ \ \ \ }) = \underline{\ \ \ \ \ \ \ } = \underline{\ \ }$

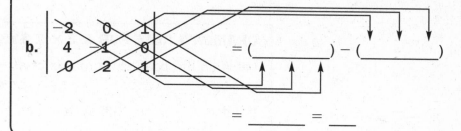

b. $\begin{vmatrix} -2 & 0 & 1 \\ 4 & -1 & 0 \\ 0 & 2 & 1 \end{vmatrix} = (\underline{\ \ \ \ \ \ \ }) - (\underline{\ \ \ \ \ \ \ })$

$= \underline{\ \ \ \ \ \ } = \underline{\ \ \ }$

AREA OF A TRIANGLE

The area of a triangle with vertices (x_1, y_1), (x_2, y_2), and (x_3, y_3) is

$$\text{Area} = \pm \frac{\ \ \ }{\ \ \ } \begin{vmatrix} x_1 & y_1 & 1 \\ x_2 & y_2 & 1 \\ x_3 & y_3 & 1 \end{vmatrix}$$

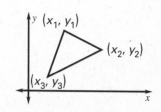

where the symbol $\pm$ indicates that the appropriate sign should be chosen to yield a _____ value.

Example 2   *The Area of a Triangle*

The area of the triangle shown is:

$$\text{Area} = \pm \frac{1}{2} \begin{vmatrix} & & 1 \\ & & 1 \\ \underline{\ \ } & & 1 \end{vmatrix}$$

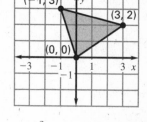

$= \pm \dfrac{1}{2} \Big[\underline{\hspace{5cm}} \Big] = \underline{\ \ \ \ }$

Your Notes

✔ *Checkpoint* **Complete the following exercises.**

1. Evaluate the determinant

of $\begin{bmatrix} -5 & 2 \\ 4 & -3 \end{bmatrix}$.

2. Find the area of a triangle with vertices $(3, 0)$, $(-2, 2)$, and $(-2, -2)$.

CRAMER'S RULE FOR A 2 × 2 SYSTEM

Let A be the coefficient matrix of $ax + by = e$
$ cx + dy = f$

If det $A \neq$ ___, then the system has _____ solution.

$$x = \frac{\begin{vmatrix} e & b \\ f & d \end{vmatrix}}{\det A} \quad \text{and} \quad y = \frac{\begin{vmatrix} a & e \\ c & f \end{vmatrix}}{\det A}$$

Example 3 *Using Cramer's Rule for a 2 × 2 System*

Use Cramer's rule to solve this system: $2x - 3y = 2$
$ -3x + 6y = 0$

Evaluate the determinant of the _____ matrix.

$\begin{vmatrix} \\ \end{vmatrix} = \underline{} = \underline{}$

Apply Cramer's rule because the determinant is not ___.

$x = \dfrac{\boxed{}}{\boxed{}} = \dfrac{}{} = \underline{}$

$y = \dfrac{\boxed{}}{\boxed{}} = \dfrac{}{} = \underline{}$

The solution is (___ , ___).

84   **Algebra 2 Notetaking Guide** • Chapter 4

CRAMER'S RULE FOR A 3 × 3 SYSTEM

Let A be the coefficient matrix of this linear system:

$$ax + by + cz = j$$
$$dx + ey + fz = k$$
$$gx + hy + iz = l$$

If det $A \neq$ ___, then the system has _____ solution.

$$x = \frac{\begin{vmatrix} j & b & c \\ k & e & f \\ l & h & i \end{vmatrix}}{\det A}, \quad y = \frac{\begin{vmatrix} a & j & c \\ d & k & f \\ g & l & i \end{vmatrix}}{\det A}, \quad z = \frac{\begin{vmatrix} a & b & j \\ d & e & k \\ g & h & l \end{vmatrix}}{\det A}$$

Example 4   *Using Cramer's Rule for a 3 × 3 System*

Use Cramer's rule to solve this system:

$$x - 4y + 2z = 2$$
$$-x + 6y - z = 1$$
$$2x - 5y + z = 4$$

Solution

Evaluate the determinant of the _____ matrix.

$$\begin{vmatrix} \\ \\ \end{vmatrix} = \underline{\hspace{4cm}}$$

Apply Cramer's rule because the determinant is not ___.

$$x = \underline{\hspace{3cm}} = \underline{\hspace{2cm}} = \underline{\hspace{1cm}}$$

$$y = \underline{\hspace{3cm}} = \underline{\hspace{2cm}} = \underline{\hspace{1cm}}$$

$$z = \underline{\hspace{3cm}} = \underline{\hspace{2cm}} = \underline{\hspace{1cm}}$$

The solution is (___, ___, ___).

Homework

4.4 Identity and Inverse Matrices

Goals • Find and use inverse matrices.
• Use inverse matrices in real-life situations.

Your Notes

VOCABULARY

Identity matrix

Inverse matrices

THE INVERSE OF A 2 × 2 MATRIX

The inverse of the matrix $A = \begin{bmatrix} a & b \\ c & d \end{bmatrix}$ is

$$A^{-1} = \frac{1}{\boxed{}} \begin{bmatrix} d & -b \\ -c & a \end{bmatrix} = \frac{1}{\boxed{}} \begin{bmatrix} d & -b \\ -c & a \end{bmatrix}$$

provided _____ $\neq 0$.

Example 1 *Finding the Inverse of a 2 × 2 Matrix*

Find the inverse of $A = \begin{bmatrix} 2 & 1 \\ -5 & -1 \end{bmatrix}$.

Solution

$$A^{-1} = \frac{1}{\boxed{}} \begin{bmatrix} \boxed{} \end{bmatrix} = \frac{1}{\boxed{}} \underline{}$$

$$= \underline{}$$

Check the inverse by showing that $AA^{-1} = I = A^{-1}A$.

Example 2   *Solving a Matrix Equation*

Solve the matrix equation $AX = B$ for the 2×2 matrix X.

$$\overset{A}{\begin{bmatrix} 5 & 1 \\ -4 & -1 \end{bmatrix}} X = \overset{B}{\begin{bmatrix} 11 & 13 \\ -9 & -10 \end{bmatrix}}$$

Solution

Begin by finding the inverse of A.

$$A^{-1} = \underline{\hspace{1cm}}\underline{\hspace{1.5cm}} = \underline{\hspace{1.5cm}}$$

To solve the equation for X, multiply both sides of the equation by _____ on the left.

$$\underline{\hspace{2cm}}\begin{bmatrix} 5 & 1 \\ -4 & -1 \end{bmatrix} X$$

$$= \underline{\hspace{1.5cm}}\begin{bmatrix} 11 & 13 \\ -9 & -10 \end{bmatrix} \qquad A^{-1}AX = A^{-1}B$$

$$X = \underline{\hspace{3cm}} \qquad IX = A^{-1}B$$

$$X = \underline{\hspace{2cm}} \qquad X = A^{-1}B$$

✔ *Checkpoint* **Complete the following exercise.**

1. Solve the matrix equation $AX = B$ for the 2×2 matrix X.

$$\begin{bmatrix} 3 & -2 \\ -7 & 5 \end{bmatrix} X = \begin{bmatrix} 1 & 1 \\ -2 & -2 \end{bmatrix}$$

Example 3　　*Converting a Message*

Use the list where a blank space is 0, A = 1, B = 2, C = 3, and so on, to convert the message HI JOE to row matrices.

　H　I　_　J　O　E

　[_____][_____][_____]

Example 4　　*Encoding a Message*

Use A = $\begin{bmatrix} 1 & 3 \\ -3 & 2 \end{bmatrix}$ to encode the message HI JOE.

Solution

The coded matrices are obtained by multiplying each _____ row matrix by the matrix A on the _____.

Uncoded Row Matrix	Encoding Matrix A	Coded Row Matrix
_____	$\begin{bmatrix} 1 & 3 \\ -3 & 2 \end{bmatrix}$ =	_____
_____	$\begin{bmatrix} 1 & 3 \\ -3 & 2 \end{bmatrix}$ =	_____
_____	$\begin{bmatrix} 1 & 3 \\ -3 & 2 \end{bmatrix}$ =	_____

The coded message is _____.

✔ *Checkpoint* **Complete the following exercises.**

2. Use the list in Example 3 to convert GOOD DAY to row matrices.

3. Use A = $\begin{bmatrix} 2 & -1 \\ 4 & 3 \end{bmatrix}$ to encode GOOD DAY.

Example 5 *Decoding a Message*

Use the inverse of $A = \begin{bmatrix} 1 & 1 \\ -3 & -2 \end{bmatrix}$ to decode this message:

−38, −23, 3, 7, −73, −48, 5, 5, −35, −23

Solution

First find A^{-1}: $A^{-1} =$ _____ _____ = _____

Partition the message into groups of two to form coded row matrices. Multiply each coded row matrix by _____ on the right to obtain the _____ row matrices.

Coded Row Matrix	Decoding Matrix A^{-1}	Uncoded Row Matrix
[−38 −23]	_____ =	_____
[3 7]	_____ =	_____
[−73 −48]	_____ =	_____
[5 5]	_____ =	_____
[−35 −23]	_____ =	_____

Read the message as

_____

✔ **Checkpoint** Complete the following exercise.

4. Use the inverse of $A = \begin{bmatrix} 5 & -3 \\ -2 & 1 \end{bmatrix}$ and the list in Example 3 to decode 20, −13, 17, −11, −40, 20, 30, −19, −8, 4, 61, −38.

4.5 Solving Systems Using Inverse Matrices

Goals • Solve systems using inverse matrices.
• Use systems to solve real-life problems.

Your Notes

VOCABULARY

Matrix of variables

Matrix of constants

Example 1 *Writing a Matrix Equation*

Write the system of linear equations as a matrix equation.

$4x - 3y = 10$ **Equation 1**

$-3x + 2y = 7$ **Equation 2**

Solution   A   X   B

$$\begin{bmatrix} \end{bmatrix}\begin{bmatrix} x \\ y \end{bmatrix} = \begin{bmatrix} \end{bmatrix}$$

Example 2 *Solving a Linear System*

Use matrices to solve the linear system in Example 1.

Begin by writing the linear system in matrix form, as in Example 1. Then find the inverse of matrix A.

$A^{-1} = \underline{\hspace{3cm}} = \underline{\hspace{3cm}}$

$\overline{\hspace{2cm}} \ \overline{\hspace{2cm}} \ \overline{\hspace{2cm}}$

Finally, multiply the matrix of constants by _____.

$X = A^{-1}B = \underline{\hspace{3cm}} = \underline{\hspace{3cm}} = \begin{bmatrix} x \\ y \end{bmatrix}$

$\overline{\hspace{3cm}} \ \overline{\hspace{1.5cm}} \ \overline{\hspace{2cm}}$

The solution of the system is (_____, _____).

✓ *Checkpoint* **Complete the following exercise.**

1. Write and solve the system of linear equations using matrices.

$$3x - 2y = 1$$
$$-4x + 3y = 1$$

Example 3 *Using a Graphing Calculator*

Use a matrix equation and a graphing calculator to solve the linear system.

$$2x - y + z = -3 \quad \textbf{Equation 1}$$
$$-x + 2y - 2z = 3 \quad \textbf{Equation 2}$$
$$-3x + 2y + 2z = 1 \quad \textbf{Equation 3}$$

Solution

The matrix equation that represents the system is

$$\underline{\hspace{3cm}} \ \underline{\hspace{1.5cm}} = \underline{\hspace{1.5cm}} .$$

Enter the coefficient matrix A and the matrix of constants B into a graphing calculator. Then find the solution $X = A^{-1}B$.

The solution is (___ , ___ , ___).

Example 4   *Writing and Using a Linear System*

You and two friends each spend $26 buying avocados, loaves of bread, and packages of chicken. You buy 4, 3, and 1 of each, respectively. One friend buys 2, 2, and 2 of each, while the other buys 2, 6, and 1 of each. How much does each item cost?

Solution

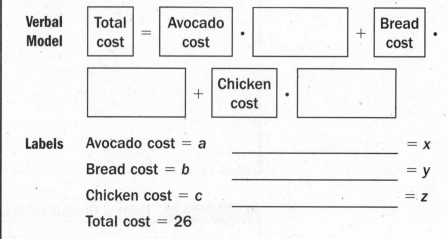

Verbal Model

| Total cost | = | Avocado cost | · | | | + | Bread cost | · |

| | | + | Chicken cost | · | |

Labels   Avocado cost = a _____ = x

Bread cost = b _____ = y

Chicken cost = c _____ = z

Total cost = 26

Algebraic Model   _____

Write the system of equations using the information about purchasing amounts and total cost.

_____   **Equation 1**

_____   **Equation 2**

_____   **Equation 3**

In matrix form, the system is   =   .

_____   ____   _____

Enter the coefficient matrix A and the matrix of constants B into a graphing calculator. Then find the solution $X = A^{-1}B$.

```
[A]⁻¹[B]
          [[3 ]
           [2 ]
           [8 ]]
■
```

Avocados cost $__ each, loaves of bread are $__ each, and packages of chicken are $__ each.

Homework

5.1 Graphing Quadratic Functions

Goals • Graph quadratic functions.
• Use quadratic functions to solve real-life problems.

Your Notes

VOCABULARY

Quadratic function

Parabola

Vertex of a parabola

Axis of symmetry of a parabola

Standard form

THE GRAPH OF A QUADRATIC FUNCTION

The graph of $y = ax^2 + bx + c$ is a parabola with these characteristics:

• The parabola opens up if a ___ 0 and opens down if a ___ 0. The parabola is wider than the graph of $y = x^2$ if $|a|$ ___ 1 and narrower than the graph of $y = x^2$ if $|a|$ ___ 1.

• The x-coordinate of the vertex is _____ .

• The axis of symmetry is the vertical line $x = $ _____ .

Example 1   *Graphing a Quadratic Function*

Graph $y = -x^2 + 2x - 2$.

Solution

Note that the coefficients for this function are $a = $ ____ , $b = $ __ , and $c = $ ____ . Because a __ 0, the parabola opens _____ .

Find and plot the vertex. The x- and y-coordinates are:

$$x = -\frac{b}{2a} = \underline{\hspace{3em}} = \underline{\hspace{1em}}$$

$$y = \underline{\hspace{8em}}$$

So, the vertex is (__ , ____).

Draw the axis of symmetry $x = $ __ .

Plot two points on one side of the axis of symmetry, such as (2, ____) and (3, ____). Use symmetry to plot two more points, such as (0, ____) and (−1, ___).

Draw a parabola through the plotted points.

VERTEX AND INTERCEPT FORMS OF QUADRATIC FUNCTIONS

Form of Quadratic Function	Characteristics of Graph
Vertex form: $\quad y = a(x - h)^2 + k$	The vertex is (__ , __). Axis of symmetry is $x = $ __ .
Intercept form: $\quad y = a(x - p)(x - q)$	The x-intercepts are __ and __ . Axis of symmetry is halfway between (__ , __) and (__ , __).

For both forms, the graph opens up if a __ 0 and down if a __ 0.

Example 2 *Graphing a Quadratic Function in Vertex Form*

Graph $y = 2(x - 3)^2 - 2$.

Solution

The function is in vertex form where $a = \underline{\hphantom{0}}$, $h = \underline{\hphantom{0}}$, and $k = \underline{\hphantom{00}}$. Because $a \underline{\hphantom{0}} 0$, the parabola opens _____. To graph the function, first plot the vertex $(h, k) = (\underline{\hphantom{0}}, \underline{\hphantom{00}})$. Draw the axis of symmetry $x = \underline{\hphantom{0}}$ and plot two points on one side of it, such as $(2, \underline{\hphantom{0}})$ and $(1, \underline{\hphantom{0}})$. Use symmetry to complete the graph.

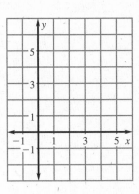

✔ **Checkpoint** **Graph the quadratic function.**

1. $y = \dfrac{1}{2}x^2 - x - 1$

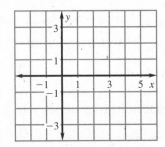

2. $y = -(x + 1)^2 + 3$

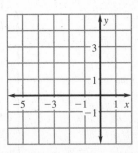

Example 3 *Graphing a Quadratic Function in Intercept Form*

Graph $y = (x - 3)(x - 1)$.

Solution

The quadratic function is in intercept form $y = a(x - p)(x - q)$ where $a = \underline{\hphantom{0}}$, $p = \underline{\hphantom{0}}$, and $q = \underline{\hphantom{0}}$. The x-intercepts occur at $(\underline{\hphantom{0}}, \underline{\hphantom{0}})$ and $(\underline{\hphantom{0}}, \underline{\hphantom{0}})$. The axis of symmetry lies halfway between these points, at $x = \underline{\hphantom{0}}$. So, the x-coordinate of the vertex is $x = \underline{\hphantom{0}}$ and the y-coordinate of the vertex is $y = \underline{\hspace{2cm}}$.

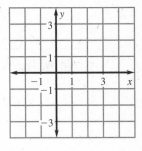

Example 4   *Writing Quadratic Functions in Standard Form*

Write $y = 2(x - 2)(x + 3)$ in standard form.

Solution

$y = 2(x - 2)(x + 3)$ Write original function.

$= 2(\underline{\hspace{3cm}})$ Multiply using FOIL.

$= 2(\underline{\hspace{2cm}})$ Combine like terms.

$= \underline{\hspace{3cm}}$ Use distributive property.

Example 5   *Using a Quadratic Model in Standard Form*

The path of a ball after you kicked it can be modeled by $y = -0.1x^2 + 4x$, where x is the horizontal distance in feet and y is the height in feet of the ball. What was the height of the ball at its highest point? How many feet had the ball traveled horizontally at this height?

Solution

Because $a = \underline{\hspace{1cm}}$, the graph of the quadratic function opens $\underline{\hspace{1.5cm}}$ and has a maximum value. The maximum value occurs at $x = \dfrac{\underline{\hspace{1cm}}}{\underline{\hspace{1.5cm}}} = \underline{\hspace{0.8cm}}$.

The corresponding value of y is
$y = \underline{\hspace{3.5cm}} = \underline{\hspace{0.8cm}}$.

The maximum height of the ball was $\underline{\hspace{0.8cm}}$ feet. At this height the ball had traveled $\underline{\hspace{0.8cm}}$ feet horizontally.

✔ *Checkpoint* **Complete the following exercises.**

3. Write $y = 2(x - 3)^2 + 4$ in standard form.

Homework

4. In Example 5, assume the path can be modeled by $y = -0.2x^2 + 4x + 1$. What is the height of the ball at its highest point?

5.2 Solving Quadratic Equations by Factoring

Goals • Factor quadratic expressions and solve quadratic equations by factoring.
• Find zeros of quadratic functions.

Your Notes

VOCABULARY

Binomial

Trinomial

Factoring

Monomial

Quadratic equation in one variable

Zero of a function

Example 1   *Factoring a Trinomial of the Form $x^2 + bx + c$*

Factor $x^2 - 9x + 14$.

Solution

You want $x^2 - 9x + 14 = (x + m)(x + n)$ where $mn =$ ____
and $m + n =$ ____ .

Factors of 14 (m, n)	1, ____	−1, ____	2, ____	−2, ____
Sum of factors ($m + n$)	____	____	____	____

The table shows that $m =$ ____ and $n =$ ____ . So,
$x^2 - 9x + 14 = ($ ____ $)($ ____ $)$.

Example 2 *Factoring a Trinomial of the Form $ax^2 + bx + c$*

Factor $2x^2 + 13x + 6$.

Solution

You want $2x^2 + 13x + 6 = (kx + m)(lx + n)$ where k and l are factors of __ and m and n are (_____) factors of __. Check possible factorizations by multiplying.

$(2x + 3)(x + 2) =$ _____

$(2x + 2)(x + 3) =$ _____

$(2x + 6)(x + 1) =$ _____

$(2x + 1)(x + 6) =$ _____

The correct factorization is
$2x^2 + 13x + 6 =$ _____ .

SPECIAL FACTORING PATTERNS

Difference of Two Squares   **Example**

$a^2 - b^2 = (a + b)(a - b)$ $x^2 - 9 = ($_____$)($_____$)$

Perfect Square Trinomial   **Example**

$a^2 + 2ab + b^2 = (a + b)^2$ $x^2 + 12x + 36 = ($_____$)^2$

$a^2 - 2ab + b^2 = (a - b)^2$ $x^2 - 8x + 16 = ($_____$)^2$

Example 3 *Factoring with Special Patterns*

Factor the quadratic expression.

a. $9x^2 - 16 = ($___$)^2 -$ ___^{2} Difference of two

$= ($_____$)($_____$)$ squares

b. $16y^2 + 40y + 25$ Perfect square trinomial

$= ($___$)^2 + 2($____$)($___$) +$ ___^{2}

$= ($_____$)^2$

c. $64x^2 - 32x + 4$ Perfect square trinomial

$= ($___$)^2 - 2($___$)($___$) +$ ___^{2}

$= ($_____$)^2$

Example 4   *Factoring Monomials First*

Factor the quadratic expression.

a. $12x^2 - 3 = 3$ _____ $= 3$ _____

b. $3u^2 - 9u + 6 = 3$ _____ $= 3$ _____

c. $7v^2 - 42v = 7v$ _____

d. $2x^2 + 8x + 2 = 2$ _____

✔ *Checkpoint* **Factor the expression.**

1. $6c^2 - 48c - 54$ **2.** $81x^2 - 1$

_____

3. $49h^2 + 42h + 9$ **4.** $16x^2 - 4$

ZERO PRODUCT PROPERTY

Let A and B be real numbers or algebraic expressions. If $AB = 0$, then $A =$ ___ or $B =$ ___.

Example 5   *Solving Quadratic Equations*

Solve $4x^2 + 13x + 11 = -3x - 5$.

Solution

$4x^2 + 13x + 11 = -3x - 5$ Write original equation.

_____ $= 0$ Write in standard form.

_____ $= 0$ Divide each side by ___.

_____ $= 0$ Factor.

_____ $= 0$ Use zero product property.

$x =$ ____   Solve for x.

The solution is ___. Check this in the original equation.

✅ **Checkpoint** Solve the quadratic equation.

5. $x^2 + 15x + 26 = 0$　　　　6. $2x^2 + x + 3 =$
　　　　　　　　　　　　　　　　　　　$-5x + 19 + x^2$

Example 6   *Finding the Zeros of a Quadratic Function*

Find the zeros of $y = x^2 + 4x + 3$.

Use factoring to write the function in intercept form.

$y = x^2 + 4x + 3$

$= \underline{\hspace{3cm}}$

The zeros of the function are _____ and _____.

Check Graph $y = x^2 + 4x + 3$. The graph passes through (____, 0) and (____, 0), so the zeros are _____ and _____.

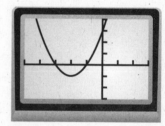

✅ **Checkpoint** Complete the following exercise.

7. Find the zeros of $y = 3x^2 - x - 2$.

Homework

5.3 Solving Quadratic Equations by Finding Square Roots

Goals • Solve quadratic equations.
• Use quadratic equations to solve real-life problems.

Your Notes

VOCABULARY

Square root

Radical sign

Radicand

Radical

Rationalizing the denominator

PROPERTIES OF SQUARE ROOTS ($a > 0$, $b > 0$)

Product Property: $\sqrt{ab} =$ _____ • _____

Quotient Property: $\sqrt{\dfrac{a}{b}} = \dfrac{\boxed{}}{\boxed{}}$

Example 1   *Using Properties of Square Roots*

Simplify the expression.

a. $\sqrt{27}$ = _____ · _____ = _____

b. $\sqrt{5} \cdot \sqrt{15}$ = _____ = _____ · _____ = _____

c. $\sqrt{\dfrac{5}{36}}$ = $\dfrac{\boxed{}}{\boxed{}}$ = _____

d. $\sqrt{\dfrac{13}{3}}$ = $\dfrac{\boxed{}}{\boxed{}}$ · $\dfrac{\boxed{}}{\boxed{}}$ = _____

✔ *Checkpoint* **Simplify the expression.**

1. $\sqrt{5} \cdot \sqrt{8}$ 2. $\sqrt{\dfrac{3}{5}}$

Example 2   *Solving a Quadratic Equation*

Solve $\dfrac{1}{2}(x - 2)^2 = 8$.

Solution

$\dfrac{1}{2}(x - 2)^2 = 8$ Write original equation.

_____ = ___   Multiply each side by ___.

_____ = _____   Take square roots of each side.

x = _____   Add ___ to each side.

The solutions are _____.

Check Check the solutions either by substituting them into
the original equation or by graphing $y =$
_____
and observing the x-intercepts.

Example 3 *Modeling a Falling Object's Height*

An acorn falls out of a tree from a height of 40 feet. How many seconds does the acorn take to reach the ground?

Solution

The initial height is $h_0 =$ ____ feet, so the height as a function of time is $h = -16t^2 + 40$. Find the value of t for which $h = 0$ to determine how long it takes the acorn to reach the ground.

Method 1: Make a table of values.

The table shows that $h = 0$ has a value of t between $t =$ __ and $t =$ __. It takes between _____ _____ for the acorn to reach the ground.

t	0	1	2
h			

Method 2: Solve a quadratic equation.

$h = -16t^2 + 40$ Write height function.

__ $= -16t^2 + 40$ Substitute ___ for h.

_____   Subtract ____ from each side.

_____   Divide each side by ____ .

_____   Take positive square root.

_____   Use a calculator.

The acorn takes about _____ to reach the ground.

✔ *Checkpoint* **Complete the following exercises.**

3. Solve $5x^2 - 30 = 70$.   4. Solve $\frac{1}{3}(x + 7)^2 = 8$.

5. You drop a football from a window 20 feet above the ground. For how much time is the football falling if your friend catches it at a height of 4 feet?

5.4 Complex Numbers

Goals • Perform operations with complex numbers.
• Apply complex numbers to fractal geometry.

Your Notes

VOCABULARY

Imaginary unit *i*

Complex number

Standard form of a complex number

Imaginary number

Pure imaginary number

Complex plane

Complex conjugates

Absolute value of a complex number

THE SQUARE ROOT OF A NEGATIVE NUMBER

Property	Example
1. If r is a positive real number, then $\sqrt{-r} = i\sqrt{r}$.	$\sqrt{-5} = $ _____
2. By Property (1), it follows that $(i\sqrt{r})^2 = -r$.	$(i\sqrt{5})^2 = i^2 \cdot 5 = $ _____

Example 1   *Solving a Quadratic Equation*

Solve $2x^2 + 3 = -15$.

Solution

$2x^2 + 3 = -15$ Write original equation.

_____   Subtract ___ from each side.

_____   Divide each side by ___.

_____   Take square roots of each side.

_____   Write in terms of i.

_____   Simplify the radical.

The solutions are _____.

Example 2   *Plotting Complex Numbers*

Plot the complex numbers in the complex plane.

a. $1 + i$ **b.** $-2 - 2i$ **c.** $3 - 3i$

Solution

a. To plot $1 + i$, start at the origin, move _____, and then _____.

b. To plot $-2 - 2i$, start at the origin, move _____, and then _____.

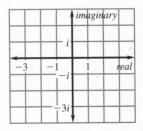

c. To plot $3 - 3i$, start at the origin, move _____, and then _____.

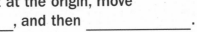

Example 3   *Adding and Subtracting Complex Numbers*

Write the expression $(5 + i) + (1 - 2i)$ as a complex number in standard form.

$(5 + i) + (1 - 2i)$

$= (\underline{}) + (\underline{})i$ **Complex addition**

$= \underline{}$ **Standard form**

✓ *Checkpoint* **Complete the following exercises.**

1. Solve $5x^2 + 2 = -8$.

2. In which quadrant of the complex plane is $1 - 3i$?

_____

3. Write $3 - (7 + 8i) + (5 - 6i)$ as a complex number in standard form.

Example 4   *Multiplying and Dividing Complex Numbers*

Write the expression as a complex number in standard form.

a. $(1 - 4i)(3 + 5i)$ **b.** $\dfrac{6 - 4i}{1 + i}$

Solution

a. $(1 - 4i)(3 + 5i) = $ _____   **Use FOIL.**

$= $ _____   **Simplify and use $i^2 = $ ___.**

$= $ _____   **Standard form**

b. $\dfrac{6 - 4i}{1 + i} = \dfrac{6 - 4i}{1 + i} \cdot \dfrac{}{}$ **Multiply by _____, the conjugate of $1 + i$.**

$= $ _____   **Use FOIL.**

$= $ _____   **Simplify.**

$= $ _____   **Write in standard form.**

✓ *Checkpoint* Write the expression in standard form.

4. $(4 - 5i)(4 + 5i)$

5. $\dfrac{3 + 2i}{2 - i}$

Example 5 *Finding Absolute Values of Complex Numbers*

Find the absolute value of each complex number. Which number is farthest from the origin in the complex plane?

a. $-2 - 3i$ **b.** $2 + i$ **c.** $-1 + 3i$

Solution

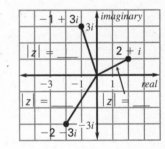

a. $\left| -2 - 3i \right|$

$= \sqrt{\underline{\hspace{3cm}}}$

$= \underline{\hspace{1.5cm}} \approx \underline{\hspace{1cm}}$

b. $\left| 2 + i \right|$

$= \sqrt{\underline{\hspace{3cm}}}$

$= \underline{\hspace{1.5cm}} \approx \underline{\hspace{1cm}}$

c. $\left| -1 + 3i \right|$

$= \sqrt{\underline{\hspace{3cm}}}$

$= \underline{\hspace{1.5cm}} \approx \underline{\hspace{1cm}}$

Because _____ has the greatest absolute value, it is farthest from the origin in the complex plane.

COMPLEX NUMBERS IN THE MANDELBROT SET

To determine whether a complex number c is in the Mandelbrot set, consider the function $f(z) = z^2 + c$ and this infinite list of complex numbers: $z_0 = 0$, $z_1 = f(z_0)$, $z_2 = f(z_1)$, $z_3 = f(z_2)$, ...

• If the absolute values $|z_0|$, $|z_1|$, $|z_2|$, $|z_3|$, ... are all _____ some fixed number N, then c _____ the Mandelbrot set.

• If the absolute values $|z_0|$, $|z_1|$, $|z_2|$, $|z_3|$, ... become _____, then c _____ the Mandelbrot set.

Example 6   *Complex Numbers in the Mandelbrot Set*

Tell whether $c = -i$ belongs to the Mandelbrot set.

Solution

Let $f(z) = z^2 - i$.

$z_0 = 0$ $|z_0| = $ __

$z_1 = f(\underline{}) = $ _____ $|z_1| = $ __

$z_2 = f(\underline{}) = $ _____ $|z_2| \approx $ ____

$z_3 = f(\underline{}) = $ _____ $|z_3| \approx $ __

$z_4 = f(\underline{}) = $ _____ $|z_4| \approx $ ____

The absolute values _____, so all the absolute values are _____. Therefore, $c = -i$ _____ to the Mandelbrot set.

✔ *Checkpoint* **Complete the following exercises.**

6. Find the absolute value of $8 - 6i$.

7. Tell whether $c = 2$ belongs to the Mandelbrot set.

Homework

5.5 Completing the Square

Goals • Solve quadratic equations by completing the square.
• Write quadratic functions in vertex form.

Your Notes

VOCABULARY

Completing the square

Example 1 *Completing the Square*

Find the value of c that makes $x^2 + 12x + c$ a perfect square trinomial, then write the expression as the square of a binomial.

Solution

In the expression $x^2 + 12x + c$, notice that $b = $ ___.
Therefore:

$$c = \left(\frac{b}{2}\right)^2 = \underline{\qquad} = \underline{\quad}$$

Use this value of c to write $x^2 + 12x + c$ as a perfect square trinomial, and then as the square of a binomial.

$x^2 + 12x + c = $ _____ **Perfect square trinomial**

$\qquad\qquad = $ _____ **Square of binomial:**

$$\left(x + \frac{b}{2}\right)^2$$

✔ *Checkpoint* **Complete the following exercise.**

---

1. Find the value of c that makes $x^2 - 5x + c$ a perfect square trinomial. Write the expression as the square of a binomial.

Example 2   *Solving a Quadratic Equation*

Solve the equation by completing the square.

$2x^2 + 8x + 12 = 0$

Solution

$2x^2 + 8x + 12 = 0$ Write original equation.

_____   Divide each side by the coefficient of x^2.

_____   Write the left side in the form $x^2 + bx$.

_____   Complete the square.

_____   Write the left side as a binomial squared.

_____   Take square roots of each side.

_____   Solve for x.

✔ *Checkpoint* **Complete the following exercise.**

2. Solve $x^2 + 4x + 1 = 0$ by completing the square.

Example 3 *Writing a Quadratic Function in Vertex Form*

Write the quadratic function $y = x^2 + 6x + 7$ in vertex form. What is the vertex of the function's graph?

$$y = x^2 + 6x + 7$$ Original equation

$$y + \underline{} = (x^2 + 6x + \underline{}) + 7$$ Complete the square.

$$y + \underline{} = (\underline{})^2 + 7$$ Write as a binomial squared.

$$y = \underline{}$$ Solve for y.

The vertex is at _____ .

✔ *Checkpoint* Complete the following exercises.

3. Write $y = x^2 - 2x - 4$ in vertex form.

Homework

5.6 The Quadratic Formula and the Discriminant

Goals • Solve equations using the quadratic formula.
• Use the quadratic formula in real-life situations.

Your Notes

VOCABULARY

Discriminant of a quadratic equation

THE QUADRATIC FORMULA

Let a, b, and c be real numbers such that $a \neq 0$. The solutions of the quadratic equation $ax^2 + bx + c = 0$ are:

$$x = \frac{\underline{\quad} \pm \sqrt{\underline{\quad} - 4\underline{\quad}}}{2\underline{\quad}}$$

Example 1 *Quadratic Equation with Two Real Solutions*

Solve $3x^2 - 3x - 5 = 0$.

$3x^2 - 3x - 5 = 0$ Original equation

$x = \dfrac{\underline{\quad} \pm \sqrt{\underline{\quad} - 4\underline{\quad}}}{2\underline{\quad}}$ Quadratic formula

$x = \dfrac{\underline{\quad} \pm \sqrt{\underline{\quad} - 4\underline{\quad}}}{2\underline{\quad}}$ $a = \underline{\quad}$, $b = \underline{\quad}$, $c = \underline{\quad}$

$x = \underline{\hspace{2cm}}$ Simplify.

The solutions are

$x = \underline{\hspace{3cm}}$ and $x = \underline{\hspace{3cm}}$.

Your Notes

Example 2 *Quadratic Equation with One Real Solution*

Solve $x^2 + 4x + 11 = 7$.

$x^2 + 4x + 11 = 7$	Write original equation.
$x^2 + 4x + 4 = 0$	$a = \underline{\ }, b = \underline{\ }, c = \underline{\ }$
$x = $ _____	Quadratic formula
$x = $ _____	Simplify.
$x = $ ____	Simplify.

The solution is ____.

Check Substitute ____ for x in the original equation.

$(\underline{\ })^2 + 4(\underline{\ }) + 11 \overset{?}{=} 7$

$\underline{\ } = 7$

Example 3 *Quadratic Equation with Two Imaginary Solutions*

Solve $x^2 - 4x = -8$.

$x^2 - 4x = -8$	Write original equation.
$x^2 - 4x + 8 = 0$	$a = \underline{\ }, b = \underline{\ }, c = \underline{\ }$
$x = $ _____	Quadratic formula
$x = $ _____	Simplify.
$x = $ _____	Write using the imaginary unit i.
$x = $ _____	Simplify.

The solutions are _____.

Check Substitute an imaginary solution into the original equation.

$(\underline{\ })^2 - 4(\underline{\ }) \overset{?}{=} -8$

$\underline{\hspace{2cm}} \overset{?}{=} -8$

$\underline{\ } = -8$

✔ *Checkpoint* Solve the quadratic equation.

1. $x^2 + 3x = 10$ | | **2.** $x^2 + 7 = 8x - 9$

3. $x^2 - 6x + 3 = -7$

NUMBER AND TYPE OF SOLUTIONS OF A QUADRATIC EQUATION

Consider the quadratic equation $ax^2 + bx + c = 0$.

- If $b^2 - 4ac > 0$, then the equation has

  _____.

- If $b^2 - 4ac = 0$, then the equation has

  _____.

- If $b^2 - 4ac < 0$, then the equation has

  _____.

Example 4 *Using the Discriminant*

Find the discriminant of the quadratic equation and give the number and type of solutions of the equation.

a. $x^2 + 2x - 3 = 0$ **b.** $x^2 + 2x + 1 = 0$

c. $x^2 + 2x + 5 = 0$

Solution

Discriminant | Solution(s)

$b^2 - 4ac$ | $x = \dfrac{-b \pm \sqrt{b^2 - 4ac}}{2a}$

a. _____ | _____

b. _____ | _____

c. _____ | _____

Example 5 *Solving a Vertical Motion Problem*

A diver jumps from a height of 40 feet above the water with an initial velocity of 4 feet per second. For how long is the diver in the air?

Solution

Because the diver jumps, use the model
$h = -16t^2 + v_0 t + h_0$ with $v_0 =$ ___ and $h_0 =$ ___. To determine how long the diver is in the air, find the value of t for which $h =$ ___.

$h = -16t^2 + v_0 t + h_0$ Write original equation.

_____ $h =$ ___ , $v_0 =$ ___ , $h_0 =$ ___ .

_____   Quadratic formula: $a =$ _____ , $b =$ ___ , $c =$ ___

_____   Use a calculator.

Reject the solution _____ because the time in the air cannot be _____ . The diver is in the air for about _____ seconds.

✅ *Checkpoint* **Complete the following exercises.**

4. Find the discriminant of $2x^2 + 4x = 2$ and give the number and type of solutions. Then find the solutions.

_____

5. A ball is thrown from a height of 6 feet with an initial vertical velocity of 32 ft/sec. If the ball is caught at a height of 2 feet, for how long is the ball in the air?

Homework

Graphing and Solving Quadratic Inequalities

Goals • Graph quadratic inequalities in two variables.
• Solve quadratic inequalities in one variable.

Your Notes

VOCABULARY

Quadratic inequality in two variables

Quadratic inequality in one variable

GRAPHING A QUADRATIC INEQUALITY IN TWO VARIABLES

To graph one of the four types of quadratic inequalities, follow these steps:

Step 1 Draw the parabola with equation $y = ax^2 + bx + c$. Make the parabola _____ for inequalities with $<$ or $>$ and _____ for inequalities with $\leq$ or $\geq$.

Step 2 Choose a point (x, y) _____ the parabola and check whether the point is a solution of the inequality.

Step 3 If the point in Step 2 is a solution, shade the region _____ the parabola. If it is not a solution, shade the region _____ the parabola.

Your Notes

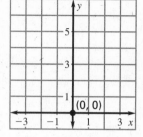

Example 1 *Graphing a Quadratic Inequality*

Graph $y \leq -x^2 + x + 5$.

1. Graph $y = -x^2 + x + 5$. The symbol is $\leq$, so make the parabola _____.

2. Test a point inside the parabola, such as $(0, 0)$. _____

   _____

   So, $(0, 0)$ _____ of the inequality.

3. Shade the region _____ the parabola.

Example 2 *Graph a System of Quadratic Inequalities*

Graph the system of quadratic inequalities.

$y \leq -x^2 - 3x + 1$ **Inequality 1**

$y > x^2 - 3$ **Inequality 2**

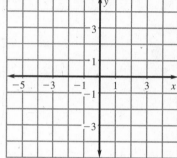

Solution

Graph the inequality $y \leq -x^2 - 3x + 1$. The graph is the region _____ and including the parabola $y =$ _____.

Graph the inequality $y > x^2 - 3$. The graph is the region _____ (but not including) the parabola $y =$ _____.

Identify the region where the two graphs overlap. This region is the graph of the system.

✔ *Checkpoint* **Complete the following exercise.**

1. Graph the system:
   $y < -2x^2 + 2x + 1$
   $y > x^2 - x - 2$

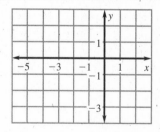

Example 3 *Solving a Quadratic Inequality by Graphing*

Solve $-3x^2 + 4x + 2 \leq 0$.

Solution

The solution consists of the x-values for which the graph of $y = -3x^2 + 4x + 2$ lies _____ the x-axis. Find the graph's x-intercepts by letting $y = 0$ and using _____ to solve for x.

$0 = -3x^2 + 4x + 2$

$x =$

_____

$x =$ _____ = _____

$x \approx$ _____ or $x \approx$ _____

Sketch a parabola that opens _____ with _____ and _____ as x-intercepts. The graph lies _____ the x-axis to the left of (and including) $x =$ _____ and to the right of (and including) $x =$ _____.

The solution is approximately _____.

✔ *Checkpoint* Solve the quadratic inequality.

2. $2x^2 - 3x - 5 \leq 0$

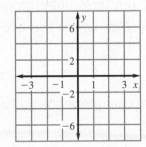

3. $x^2 - 2x - 3 > 0$

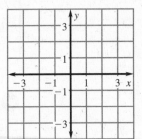

Example 4 *Solving a Quadratic Inequality Algebraically*

Solve $x^2 + 5x \geq 6$.

First write and solve the equation obtained by replacing the inequality symbol with _____.

$x^2 + 5x \geq 6$	Write original inequality.
_____	Write corresponding equation.
_____	Write in standard form.
_____	Factor.
_____	Zero product property

The numbers _____ are called the critical x-values of the inequality $x^2 + 5x \geq 6$. Plot _____ on a number line, using _____ dots. The critical x-values partition the number line into three intervals. Test an x-value in each interval to see if it satisfies the inequality.

Test $x =$ ____ :   Test $x =$ ___ :

_____   _____

Test $x =$ ___ :

_____

The solution is _____ .

✔ **Checkpoint** Solve the quadratic inequality algebraically.

4. $2x^2 + x < 3$

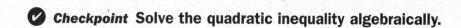

5.8 Modeling with Quadratic Functions

Goals
- Write quadratic functions.
- Use technology to find quadratic models.

Your Notes

VOCABULARY

Best-fitting quadratic model

Example 1   *Write a Quadratic Function in Vertex Form*

Write a quadratic function for the parabola shown.

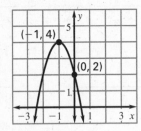

(−1, 4)

(0, 2)

Solution

Because you are given the vertex $(h, k) =$ _____ , use the vertex form of the quadratic function.

$$y = a(x - h)^2 + k$$

$$y = a(\underline{\quad\quad})^2 + \underline{\quad}$$

Use the other given point, _____ , to find a.

$$\underline{\quad} = a(\underline{\quad\quad})^2 + \underline{\quad}$$ **Substitute for x and for y.**

_____   **Simplify coefficient of a.**

_____   **Subtract ___ from each side.**

A quadratic function for the parabola is

_____ .

Example 2   *Write a Quadratic Function in Intercept Form*

Write a quadratic function for the parabola shown.

Solution

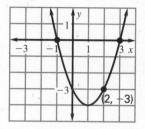

Because you are given the *x*-intercepts
p = ____ and *q* = __, use the intercept
form of the quadratic function.

$y = a(x - p)(x - q)$

$y = a(\underline{\hspace{1cm}})(\underline{\hspace{1cm}})$

Use the other given point, _____, to find *a*.

____ = $a(\underline{\hspace{1cm}})(\underline{\hspace{1cm}})$	**Substitute for *x* and for *y*.**
____ = ____ *a*	**Simplify coefficient of *a*.**
___ = *a*	**Divide each side by ____.**

A quadratic function for the parabola is _____.

✔ *Checkpoint* **Complete the following exercise.**

1. Write an equation in vertex form and in intercept form
   for the parabola with vertex $(1, -4)$ going through
   $(-1, 0)$ and $(3, 0)$.

Example 3   *Finding a Quadratic Model for a Data Set*

The table shows the path taken by a paper airplane where *x* measures horizontal distance (meters) and *y* measures height (meters). Find a quadratic model in standard form for the data.

Horizontal distance, x	0	1	2	3	4	5	6	7	8
Height, y	0.7	1.75	2.4	2.7	2.8	2.3	1.6	1.2	0.4

Plot the data pairs.

Draw the parabola that best fits the data.

Estimate coordinates of three points on the parabola: (0, 1), (4, 3), and (7, 1).

Substitute the coordinates of the points into the model $y = ax^2 + bx + c$ to obtain a system of three linear equations.

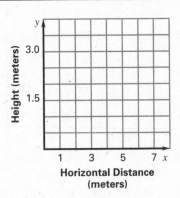

_____

_____

_____

Solve the linear system: $a =$ ____ , $b =$ ___ , and $c =$ __ .

A quadratic model for the data is _____ .

✔ **Checkpoint** **Complete the following exercise.**

2. The table shows the path taken by an object where *t* measures time (seconds) and *y* measures height (feet). Find a quadratic model in standard form for the data using the first, sixth, and eighth points.

Time, t	0	1	2	3	4	5	6	7
Height, y	5	14	19	26	25	18	14	4

Example 4   *Use Quadratic Regression to Find a Model*

Use a graphing calculator to find the best-fitting quadratic model for the data in Example 3.

Solution

a. Enter the data in two _____ of a graphing calculator.

Make a _____ of the data.

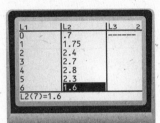

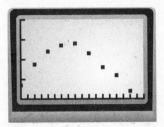

Use the quadratic regression feature to find the best-fitting quadratic model for the data.

Check how well the model fits the data by graphing the _____ and the _____ in the same viewing window.

QuadReg

$y = ax^2 + bx + c$

$a = $ _____

$b = $ _____

$c = $ _____

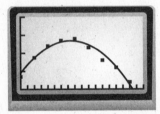

The best-fitting quadratic model is _____.

✓ *Checkpoint* **Complete the following exercise.**

3. Use a graphing calculator to find the best-fitting quadratic model for the data in Checkpoint 2.

Homework

6.1 Using Properties of Exponents

Goals • Use properties of exponents to evaluate and simplify expressions involving powers.
• Use exponents and scientific notation to solve real-life problems.

Your Notes

VOCABULARY

Scientific notation

PROPERTIES OF EXPONENTS

Let a and b be real numbers and let m and n be integers.

Product of powers property $a^m \cdot a^n = a\underline{\quad\quad}$

Power of a power property $(a^m)^n = a\underline{\quad}$

Power of a product property $(ab)^m = a\underline{\quad}b\underline{\quad}$

Negative exponent property $a^{-m} = \underline{\quad\quad}, a \neq 0$

Zero exponent property $a^0 = \underline{\ \ }, a \neq 0$

Quotient of powers property $\dfrac{a^m}{a^n} = a\underline{\quad\quad}, a \neq 0$

Power of a quotient property $\left(\dfrac{a}{b}\right)^m = \underline{\quad\quad}, b \neq 0$

Example 1   *Evaluating Numerical Expressions*

a. $\dfrac{7^6}{7^3} = 7\underline{\quad\quad} = 7\underline{\quad} = \underline{\quad\quad}$

b. $3^{-2} = \underline{\quad\quad} = \underline{\quad\quad}$

c. $(3^2)^2 = 3\underline{\quad\quad} = 3\underline{\quad} = \underline{\quad\quad}$

Example 2   *Simplifying Algebraic Expressions*

a. $\left(\dfrac{x^{-3}}{y^2}\right)^4 =$ _____   **Power of a quotient property**

$=$ _____   **Power of a power property**

$=$ _____   **Negative exponent property**

b. $(-3a)^3 a^9 a^{-7} =$ _____ $a^9 a^{-7}$ **Power of a product property**

$=$ _____   **Product of powers property**

$=$ _____   **Simplify exponent.**

c. $\dfrac{(c^4 d)^2}{c^9 d^2} = \dfrac{\boxed{}}{c^9 d^2}$ **Power of a product property**

$= \dfrac{\boxed{}}{c^9 d^2}$ **Power of a power property**

$=$ _____   **Quotient of powers property**

$=$ _____   **Simplify exponents.**

$=$ ___   **Zero exponent property**

$=$ ___   **Negative exponent property**

✔ *Checkpoint* **Complete the following exercises.**

1. Evaluate $(2^{-2})^3 (2^5)$.   **2.** Simplify $\dfrac{(jk^2)^2}{(j^{-1}k)^3}$.

Example 3   *Comparing Real-Life Volumes*

The radius of a basketball is about 5.7 times greater than the radius of a golf ball. How many times as great as the golf ball's volume is the basketball's volume?

Solution

Let *r* represent the radius of the golf ball.

$$\dfrac{\text{Basketball's volume}}{\text{Golf ball's volume}} = \dfrac{\frac{4}{3}\pi\left(\boxed{}\right)^3}{\frac{4}{3}\pi r^3}$$
     The volume of a sphere is $\frac{4}{3}\pi r^3$.

$$= \dfrac{\frac{4}{3}\pi\,\boxed{}}{\frac{4}{3}\pi r^3}$$
     Power of a product property

$$= \underline{}$$
     Quotient of powers property

$$= \underline{}$$
     Zero exponent property

$$\approx \underline{}$$
     Approximate power.

The basketball's volume is about _____ times as great as the golf ball's volume.

Example 4   *Using Scientific Notation in Real Life*

Greenland covers about 2.2×10^6 square kilometers and has approximately 5.6×10^4 people. About how many square kilometers are there per person?

Solution

$$\dfrac{\text{Land area}}{\text{Population}} = \underline{}$$
     Divide land area by population.

$$= \underline{}$$
     Quotient of powers property

$$\approx \underline{}$$
     Use a calculator.

$$= \underline{}$$
     Write in standard notation.

There are about _____ square kilometers per person.

Homework

6.2 Evaluating and Graphing Polynomial Functions

Goals
- Evaluate polynomial functions.
- Graph polynomial functions.

Your Notes

VOCABULARY

Polynomial function

Leading coefficient

Constant term

Degree

Standard form of a polynomial function

End behavior

Example 1 *Identifying Polynomial Functions*

Decide whether the function is a polynomial function. If it is, write the function in standard form and state its degree, type, and leading coefficient.

a. $f(x) = 2x^{1.2} + 2x^3 - 4x^2$ **b.** $f(x) = 0.32x - x^3 + 71$

a. The function _____ a polynomial function because _____ does not have a _____.

b. The function _____ a polynomial function. Its standard form is _____. It has degree __, so it is a _____ function. The leading coefficient is ___.

✓ *Checkpoint* **Complete the following exercise.**

1. State the degree, type, and leading coefficient of
$f(x) = -x^4 + 2x^3 - 4x^2 - x + 5$.

Example 2 *Using Synthetic Substitution*

Use synthetic substitution to evaluate
$f(x) = 2x^4 - 4x^3 + x^2 + 1$ when $x = 2$.

Write the value of x and the coefficients of $f(x)$ as shown. Bring down the leading coefficient. Multiply by ___ and write the result in the next column. _____ the numbers in that column and write the sum below the line. Continue to multiply and add.

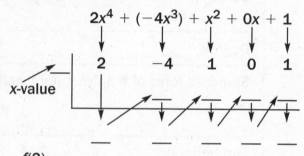

$2x^4 + (-4x^3) + x^2 + 0x + 1$ **Polynomial in standard form**

    2   -4   1   0   1   **Coefficients**

x-value

$f(2) =$ ___

END BEHAVIOR FOR POLYNOMIAL FUNCTIONS

The graph of $f(x) = a_n x^n + a_{n-1} x^{n-1} + \ldots + a_1 x + a_0$ has this end behavior:

- For $a_n > 0$ and n even, $f(x) \rightarrow$ ___ as $x \rightarrow -\infty$ and $f(x) \rightarrow$ ___ as $x \rightarrow +\infty$.

- For $a_n > 0$ and n odd, $f(x) \rightarrow$ ___ as $x \rightarrow -\infty$ and $f(x) \rightarrow$ ___ as $x \rightarrow +\infty$.

- For $a_n < 0$ and n even, $f(x) \rightarrow$ ___ as $x \rightarrow -\infty$ and $f(x) \rightarrow$ ___ as $x \rightarrow +\infty$.

- For $a_n < 0$ and n odd, $f(x) \rightarrow$ ___ as $x \rightarrow -\infty$ and $f(x) \rightarrow$ ___ as $x \rightarrow +\infty$.

Example 3 **Graphing Polynomial Functions**

Graph (a) $f(x) = -x^3 + 2x^2 + x + 1$ and
(b) $f(x) = x^4 - 4x^2 + x + 1$.

Solution

a. Make a table of values and plot
the corresponding points. Connect
the points with a smooth curve and
check the end behavior.

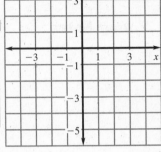

x	−3	−2	−1	0	1	2	3
f(x)							

The degree is _____ and the
leading coefficient is _____,
so $f(x) \rightarrow$ _____ as $x \rightarrow -\infty$ and $f(x) \rightarrow$ _____ as $x \rightarrow +\infty$.

b. Make a table of values and
plot the corresponding points.
Connect the points with a smooth
curve and check the end behavior.

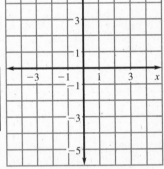

x	−3	−2	−1	0	1	2	3
f(x)							

The degree is _____ and the
leading coefficient is _____,
so $f(x) \rightarrow$ _____ as $x \rightarrow -\infty$ and $f(x) \rightarrow$ _____ as $x \rightarrow +\infty$.

✔ **Checkpoint** Complete the following exercises using the
function $f(x) = -x^4 + x^3 + 4x^2 - 4x - 3$.

2. Evaluate $f(x)$ for $x = 4$
using synthetic
substitution.

3. Graph $f(x)$.

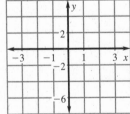

Homework

6.3 Adding, Subtracting, and Multiplying Polynomials

Goals • Add, subtract, and multiply polynomials.
• Use polynomial operations in real-life problems.

Your Notes

Example 1 *Adding Polynomials Vertically and Horizontally*

a.　$2x^3 - 3x^2 + 7x - 5$
　　$+ \ 3x^3 + 2x^2 - 3x$

　　[ ]

b. $(x^3 + 6x + 4) + (-6x^3 + 2x^2 - 9x - 2)$

　　$=$ _____

　　$=$ _____

Example 2 *Subtracting Polynomials Vertically and Horizontally*

a.　$7x^3 + 4x^2 - x - 4$　　　　$7x^3 + 4x^2 - \ x - 4$

　　$- \ (5x^3 - \ x^2 + x - 6)$

b. $(3x^4 + 9x^3 + 2) - (2x^4 + 6x^3 + 2x - 4)$

　　$= 3x^4 + 9x^3 + 2$ _____

　　$=$ _____

Example 3 *Multiplying Polynomials Vertically*

　　　　$x^2 - x + 3$
　　$\times \qquad x + 2$

　　[ ]　　　Multiply $x^2 - x + 3$ by 2.

　　[ ]　　　Multiply $x^2 - x + 3$ by x.

　　[ ]　　　Combine like terms.

Example 4 *Multiplying Polynomials Horizontally*

Multiply the polynomials.

$(x - 2)(3x^2 - x + 5)$

$= (x - 2)\underline{\quad\quad} - (x - 2)\underline{\quad} + (x - 2)\underline{\quad}$

$= \underline{\hspace{4cm}}$

$= \underline{\hspace{3cm}}$

Example 5 *Multiplying Three Binomials*

Multiply the polynomials.

$(x + 2)(x - 1)(x - 3) = (\underline{\hspace{2cm}})(x - 3)$

$= (\underline{\hspace{2cm}})(x) - (\underline{\hspace{2cm}})(3)$

$= \underline{\hspace{4cm}}$

$= \underline{\hspace{3cm}}$

SPECIAL PRODUCT PATTERNS

Sum and Difference

$(a + b)(a - b) = a^2 - b^2$

Square of a Binomial

$(a + b)^2 = a^2 + 2ab + b^2$

$(a - b)^2 = a^2 - 2ab + b^2$

Example

$(x + 3)(x - 3) = \underline{\hspace{2cm}}$

$(y + 4)^2 = \underline{\hspace{2cm}}$

$(3t^2 - 2)^2$

$= \underline{\hspace{2cm}}$

Cube of a Binomial

$(a + b)^3$

$= a^3 + 3a^2b + 3ab^2 + b^3$

$(a - b)^3$

$= a^3 - 3a^2b + 3ab^2 - b^3$

$(x + 1)^3$

$= \underline{\hspace{2cm}}$

$(p - 2)^3$

$= \underline{\hspace{2cm}}$

Example 6   *Using Special Product Patterns*

Multiply the polynomials.

a. $(3z + 4)(3z - 4) = (\underline{})^2 - \underline{}^2$

$$= \underline{}$$

b. $(4x^2 + 3y)^2$

$$= (\underline{})^2 + 2(\underline{})(\underline{}) + (\underline{})^2$$

$$= \underline{}$$

c. $(cd - 4)^3$

$$= (\underline{})^3 - 3(\underline{})^2(\underline{}) + 3(\underline{})(\underline{})^2 - \underline{}^3$$

$$= \underline{}$$

✔ *Checkpoint* **Complete the following exercises.**

1. Add $(-3x^2 + 3x - 7) + (x^2 - 9x + 5)$.

_____

2. Subtract $(6x^3 + x^2 + 1) - (2x^3 - 6x + 3)$.

_____

3. Multiply $(x - 3)(x + 1)(x + 7)$.

Homework

_____

4. Multiply $(2w - 3)^2$.

6.4 Factoring and Solving Polynomial Equations

Goals • Factor polynomial expressions.
• Use factoring to solve polynomial equations.

Your Notes

VOCABULARY

Factor by grouping

Quadratic form

SPECIAL FACTORING PATTERNS

Sum of Two Cubes

$a^3 + b^3 = (a + b)(a^2 - ab + b^2)$

Example

$x^3 + 8 = (x + 2)(\underline{\hspace{2.5cm}})$

Difference of Two Cubes

$a^3 - b^3 = (a - b)(a^2 + ab + b^2)$

Example

$8x^3 - 1 = (2x - 1)(\underline{\hspace{2.5cm}})$

Example 1 *Factoring the Sum or Difference of Cubes*

Factor each polynomial.

a. $x^3 - 64 = x^3 - \underline{\hspace{0.5cm}}^3$

$\qquad\qquad = (x - \underline{\hspace{0.5cm}})(\underline{\hspace{2.5cm}})$

b. $54y^4 + 16y = 2y(\underline{\hspace{2cm}})$

$\qquad\qquad = 2y\left[(\underline{\hspace{0.5cm}})^3 + \underline{\hspace{0.5cm}}^3\right]$

$\qquad\qquad = 2y(\underline{\hspace{1.5cm}})(\underline{\hspace{2cm}})$

Example 2   *Factoring by Grouping*

Factor the polynomial $x^3 - 3x^2 - 4x + 12$.

Solution

$x^3 - 3x^2 - 4x + 12$

$= x^2(\underline{\hspace{1cm}}) - 4(\underline{\hspace{1cm}})$ Factor by grouping.

$= \underline{\hspace{3cm}}$

$= \underline{\hspace{4cm}}$ Difference of squares

Example 3   *Factoring Polynomials in Quadratic Form*

Factor (a) $16x^4 - 1$ and (b) $2x^6 - 10x^4 + 12x^2$.

Solution

a. $16x^4 - 1 = (\underline{\hspace{1cm}})^2 - \underline{\hspace{0.5cm}}^2$

$= \underline{\hspace{3cm}}$

$= \underline{\hspace{4cm}}$

b. $2x^6 - 10x^4 + 12x^2 = 2x^2(\underline{\hspace{3cm}})$

$= \underline{\hspace{3cm}}$

Example 4   *Solving a Polynomial Equation*

Solve $x^4 + 4 = 5x^2$.

Solution

$x^4 + 4 = 5x^2$ Write original equation.

$\underline{\hspace{3cm}} = 0$ Rewrite in standard form.

$\underline{\hspace{3cm}} = 0$ Factor trinomial.

$\underline{\hspace{4cm}} = 0$ Factor difference of squares.

$x = \underline{\hspace{0.5cm}}, x = \underline{\hspace{1cm}}, x = \underline{\hspace{0.5cm}},$ or $x = \underline{\hspace{1cm}}$ Zero product property

The solutions are $\underline{\hspace{3cm}}$. Check these in the original equation.

✓ Checkpoint Factor each polynomial in Exercises 1–3.

1. $x^3 + 216$ 2. $x^3 - x^2 - 2x + 2$

3. $x^4 - 7x^2 + 12$

4. Solve $x^5 - 2x = -x^3$.

Example 5   *Solving a Polynomial Equation in Real Life*

A rectangular swimming pool has a volume of 512 cubic feet. The pool's dimensions are x feet deep by $6x - 8$ feet long by $6x - 16$ feet wide. How deep is the pool?

Verbal Model | Volume | = | | · | Length | · | Width |

Labels   Volume = ____   (cubic feet)

Depth = __   (feet)

Length = _____   (feet)

Width = _____   (feet)

Algebraic Model   512 = _____

0 = _____   Standard form

0 = _____   Factor by grouping.

0 = _____

The only real solution is $x =$ __, so $6x - 8 =$ ___ and $6x - 16 =$ __. The pool is __ feet deep. The dimensions are _____.

Homework

6.5 The Remainder and Factor Theorems

Goals • Divide polynomials and relate the result to the remainder theorem and the factor theorem.
• Use polynomial division in real-life problems.

Your Notes

VOCABULARY

Polynomial long division

Synthetic division

Example 1 *Using Polynomial Long Division*

Divide $4x^4 - x^2 - 18x + 8$ by $x^2 + 2x + 3$.

Write division in the same format you would use when dividing numbers. Include a "0" as the coefficient of x^3.

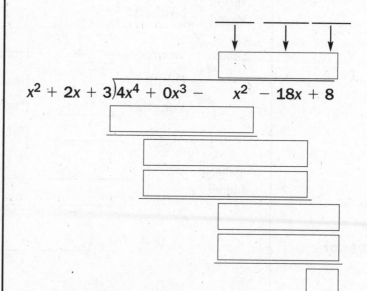

$$x^2 + 2x + 3 \overline{) 4x^4 + 0x^3 - x^2 - 18x + 8}$$

Write the result as follows.

$$\frac{4x^4 - x^2 - 18x + 8}{x^2 + 2x + 3} = \underline{\hspace{3cm}}$$

Your Notes

REMAINDER THEOREM
If a polynomial $f(x)$ is divided by $x - k$, the remainder is $r = $ ____ .

Example 2 *Using Synthetic Division*

Divide $x^3 + x^2 - 5x + 3$ by $x + 2$.

Solution

To find the value of k, rewrite the divisor in the form $x - k$. Because $x + 2 = x - $ ____ , $k = $ ___ .

```
___ | 1   1   -5   3
     |    __  __  __
      __  __  __  __
```

$$\frac{x^3 + x^2 - 5x + 3}{x + 2} = \underline{\hspace{4cm}}$$

FACTOR THEOREM
A polynomial $f(x)$ has a factor $x - k$ if and only if $f(k) = $ __ .

Example 3 *Factoring a Polynomial*

Factor $f(x) = x^3 - 19x - 30$ given that $f(5) = 0$.

Solution

Because $f(5) = 0$, you know that _____ is a factor of $f(x)$. Use synthetic division to find the other factors.

```
___ | 1   0   -19   -30
     |    __   __   __
      __  __   __   __
```

The result gives the coefficients of the quotient.

$$x^3 - 19x - 30 = (\underline{\hspace{1cm}})(\underline{\hspace{2cm}})$$
$$= (\underline{\hspace{1cm}})(\underline{\hspace{1cm}})(\underline{\hspace{1cm}})$$

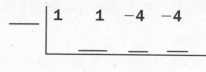 **Finding Zeros of a Polynomial Function**

A zero of $f(x) = x^3 + x^2 - 4x - 4$ is $x = -1$. Find the other zeros.

Solution

Because $f(-1) = 0$, you know that _____ is a factor of $f(x)$. Use synthetic division to find the other factors.

$$\underline{\quad} \,\big|\; \begin{array}{cccc} 1 & 1 & -4 & -4 \end{array}$$

The result gives the coefficients of the quotient.

$f(x) = x^3 + x^2 - 4x - 4$

$\quad = (\underline{\quad})(\underline{\quad})$

$\quad = (\underline{\quad})(\underline{\quad})(\underline{\quad})$

By the factor theorem, the zeros of f are _____.

✔ **Checkpoint** **Complete the following exercises.**

1. Use long division to divide $x^2 + 4x - 1$ by $x + 3$.

2. Use synthetic division to divide $2x^3 - x^2 + 3x + 4$ by $x + 1$.

3. Factor $f(x) = 2x^3 - x^2 - 25x - 12$ given that $f(4) = 0$.

4. A zero of $f(x) = x^4 - 5x^2 + 4$ is 1. Find the other zeros.

Homework

6.6 Finding Rational Zeros

Goals • Find the rational zeros of a polynomial function.
• Use polynomial equations to solve real-life problems.

Your Notes

THE RATIONAL ZERO THEOREM

If $f(x) = a_nx^n + \ldots + a_1x + a_0$ has _____ coefficients, then every rational zero of f has the following form:

$$\frac{p}{q} = \frac{\text{factor of constant term} \;\square}{\text{factor of leading coefficient} \;\square}$$

Example 1 *Using the Rational Zero Theorem*

Find the rational zeros of $f(x) = x^3 + 5x^2 + 2x - 8$.

Solution

List the possible rational zeros. The leading coefficient is ___ and the constant term is ___ . So, the possible rational zeros are:

$$x = \underline{\quad}, \; \underline{\quad}, \; \underline{\quad}, \; \underline{\quad}$$

Test these zeros using synthetic division.

Test $x =$ ___

$$\underline{\quad} \begin{array}{|rrrr} 1 & 5 & 2 & -8 \\ & \underline{\quad} & \underline{\quad} & \underline{\quad} \\ \hline \underline{\quad} & \underline{\quad} & \underline{\quad} & \underline{\quad} \end{array}$$

$\longleftarrow$ ___ is a zero.

Because ___ is a zero of f, write $f(x) =$ _____ .

Factor the trinomial and use the factor theorem.

$$f(x) = \underline{\hspace{6cm}}$$

The zeros of f are _____ .

Example 2   *Using the Rational Zero Theorem*

Find all real zeros of $f(x) = 6x^4 + 7x^3 - 19x^2 - 5x + 6$.

List the possible rational zeros of f:

_____

_____

Choose values to check by using your graphing utility to graph the function. Two reasonable choices are $x = $ ____ and $x = $ ____.

Check the value using synthetic division.

$$-\frac{2}{3} \begin{array}{|ccccc} 6 & 7 & -19 & -5 & 6 \\ & \underline{\quad} & \underline{\quad} & \underline{\quad} & \underline{\quad} \\ \underline{\quad} & \underline{\quad} & \underline{\quad} & \underline{\quad} & \underline{\quad} \end{array}$$

$\longleftarrow$ ____ is a zero.

Factor out a binomial using the result of the synthetic division.

$f(x) = $

_____   **Rewrite as product of factors.**

$= $

_____   **Factor ___ from the second factor.**

$= $

_____   **Multiply the first factor by ___.**

Repeat the steps above for $g(x) = $ _____. Any zero of g will also be a zero of f. The possible rational zeros of g are $x = $ _____. Confirm that the value

$x = $ ____ is a zero by using synthetic division.

$f(x) = $ _____

Find the remaining zeros of f by using the quadratic formula to solve _____.

The real zeros of f are ____ , ____ , _____ , and

_____ .

✓ *Checkpoint* **Complete the following exercise.**

1. Find all real zeros of
   $f(x) = 5x^4 + 6x^3 - 24x^2 - 15x - 2.$

Example 3   *Writing and Using a Polynomial Model*

You are making a wooden rectangular box. You want the volume of the box to be 135 cubic inches. You want the length of each side of the square base to be x inches and the height to be $x + 12$ inches. What are the dimensions?

The volume is $V = Bh$ where $B =$ base area and $h =$ height.

Verbal Model   Volume $=$ [　　　　] $\cdot$ Height

Labels   Volume $=$ ____   (cubic inches)

Area of Base $=$ ___   (square inches)

Height $=$ _____   (inches)

Algebraic Model $135 =$ _____

$135 =$ _____

$0 =$ _____

The possible rational solutions are $x =$ _____ , _____ , _____

, _____ , _____ , _____ , and _____ .

In this case, it makes sense to test only positive x-values.

1 | _____ _____   3 | _____ _____

So, $x =$ __ is a solution. The base should be __ inches by __ inches. The height should be _____ inches.

6.7 Using the Fundamental Theorem of Algebra

Goals • Use the fundamental theorem of algebra.
• Use technology to approximate zeros.

Your Notes

VOCABULARY

Repeated solution

Example 1   *Finding the Number of Solutions or Zeros*

a. The equation $x^3 - 2x^2 + x - 2 = 0$ has _____ solutions:

_____.

b. The function $f(x) = x^4 + 3x^3 - 4x^2$ has _____ zeros:

_____.

Example 2   *Finding the Zeros of a Polynomial Function*

Find all the zeros of $f(x) = x^5 - 2x^4 - 3x^3 + 6x^2 - 4x + 8.$

The possible rational zeros are _____. Using
synthetic division, you can determine that ___ is a repeated
zero and that ____ is also a zero. You can write the function
in factored form as follows:

$f(x) =$ _____.

Complete the factorization.

$f(x) =$ _____

The five zeros are _____.

The graph of f is shown at the right.
Note that only the _____ zeros appear
as x-intercepts. Also note that the graph
only _____ the x-axis at the repeated
zero $x =$ ___, but _____ the x-axis at
the zero $x =$ ____.

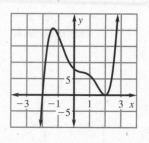

Your Notes

1. State the number of zeros of $f(x) = x^3 - 3x^2 - 5x - 25$ and tell what they are.

2. Find all zeros of $f(x) = x^4 + 7x^2 + 18x + 10$.

Example 3   *Using Zeros to Write Polynomial Functions*

Write a polynomial function f of least degree that has real coefficients, leading coefficient 1, and zeros -1 and $2 + i$.

Solution

Because the coefficients are real and $2 + i$ is a zero, _____ must also be a zero. Use the three zeros and the factor theorem to write $f(x)$ as a product of three factors.

$f(x) = ($_____$)[x - ($_____$)][x - ($_____$)]$ **Factored form**

$= ($_____$)[$_____$][$_____$]$ **Regroup.**

$=$ _____   **Multiply.**

$=$ _____   **Expand, use $i^2 = $ ___.**

$=$ _____   **Simplify.**

$=$ _____   **Multiply.**

$=$ _____   **Combine like terms.**

Check You can check by evaluating $f(x)$ at each of its zeros.

✔ *Checkpoint* **Complete the following exercise.**

3. Write a polynomial function of least degree that has real coefficients, a leading coefficient of 1, and 4, $3i$, and $-3i$ as zeros.

Example 4 **Approximating Real Zeros**

Approximate the real zeros of
$f(x) = x^4 - 5x^3 + 6x^2 - 20x + 8$.

Solution

Use a graphing calculator to approximate the real zeros of the function. Use the *Zero* (or *Root*) feature.

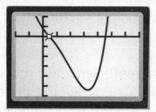 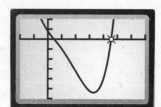

You can see that the real zeros are about _____.

The polynomial function has degree ___, so there must be ____ other zeros. These may be repeats of the real zeros or imaginary. In this case, they are _____ : $x =$ ____.

Homework

✔ *Checkpoint* **Complete the following exercise.**

4. Approximate the real zeros of
$f(x) = x^5 - 6x^4 + 10x^3 - 18x^2 + 21x$.

6.8 Analyzing Graphs of Polynomial Functions

Goals • Analyze the graph of a polynomial function.
• Use polynomial functions in real life.

VOCABULARY

Local maximum

Local minimum

ZEROS, FACTORS, SOLUTIONS, AND INTERCEPTS

Let $f(x) = a_n x^n + a_{n-1} x^{n-1} + \cdots + a_1 x + a_0$ be a polynomial function. The following statements are equivalent.

Zero: ___ is a zero of the polynomial function f.

Factor: _____ is a factor of the polynomial $f(x)$.

Solution: ___ is a solution of the polynomial equation $\overline{f(x)} = 0$.

If k is a real number, then the following is also equivalent.

x-Intercept: ___ is an x-intercept of the graph of the polynomial function f.

Example 1   *Using x-Intercepts to Graph a Polynomial Function*

Graph the function $f(x) = -\dfrac{1}{2}(x + 1)^2(x - 3)$.

Solution

Plot x-intercepts. Because $x + 1$ and $x - 3$ are factors of $f(x)$, ____ and __ are the x-intercepts of the graph of f. Plot the points (___, __) and (__, __).

Plot points between and beyond the x-intercepts.

x	-3	-2	0	1	2	4
y						

Determine the end behavior of the graph. Because $f(x)$ has _____ linear factors of the form $x - k$ and a constant

factor of ____ , it is a _____ function with a _____

leading coefficient. Therefore, $f(x) \to$ ____ as $x \to -\infty$ and $f(x) \to$ ____ as $x \to +\infty$.

Draw the graph so that it passes through the points you plotted and has the appropriate end behavior.

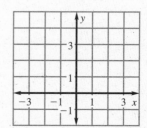

TURNING POINTS OF POLYNOMIAL FUNCTIONS

The graph of every polynomial function of degree n has *at most* _____ turning points. Moreover, if a polynomial function has n distinct real zeros, then its graph has exactly _____ turning points.

Example 2 *Finding Turning Points*

Graph each function. Identify the *x*-intercepts and the points where the local maximums and local minimums occur.

a. $f(x) = -x^3 + 4x^2 - x - 4$

b. $f(x) = -x^4 + 2x^3 + 2x^2 - 3x$

Solution

a. Use a graphing calculator to graph the function.

Notice that the graph has _____ *x*-intercepts and _____ turning points. You can use the graphing calculator's *Zero*, *Maximum*, and *Minimum* features to approximate the coordinates of the points.

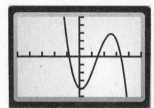

The *x*-intercepts of the graph are _____ _____. The function has a local minimum at (_____, _____) and a local maximum at (_____, _____).

b. Use a graphing calculator to graph the function.

Notice that the graph has _____ *x*-intercepts and _____ turning points. You can use the graphing calculator's *Zero*, *Maximum*, and *Minimum* features to approximate the coordinates of the points.

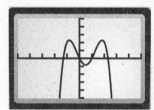

The *x*-intercepts of the graph are _____. The function has local maximums at (_____, _____) and (_____, _____), and it has a local minimum at (____, _____).

✅ *Checkpoint* **Complete the following exercises.**

1. Graph $f(x) = (x - 1)(3x + 1)(2x - 5)$.

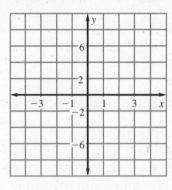

2. Use a graphing calculator to identify the x-intercepts, local maximums, and local minimums of the graph of $f(x) = x^4 - x^3 - 6x^2 + 4x + 2$.

Homework

6.9 Modeling with Polynomial Functions

Goals • Use finite differences.
• Use technology to find polynomial models.

Your Notes

VOCABULARY

Finite differences

Example 1 *Writing a Cubic Function*

Write the cubic function whose
graph is shown at the right.

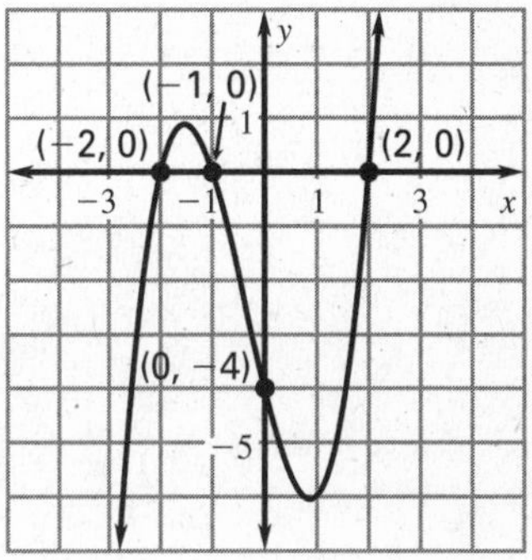

Solution

Use the three given *x*-intercepts
to write

$f(x) = a$_____ .

To find *a*, substitute the coordinates
of the fourth point.

____ $= a$_____ , so $a = $ __.

$f(x) = $ _____

Check Check the graph's end behavior. The degree of *f* is
_____ and *a* __ 0, so $f(x) \rightarrow$ ____ as $x \rightarrow -\infty$ and $f(x) \rightarrow$ ____
as $x \rightarrow +\infty$.

✓ *Checkpoint* **Complete the following exercise.**

1. Write the cubic function of the graph shown.

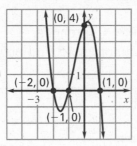

Example 2 *Finding Finite Differences*

An equation for a polynomial function is
$f(n) = n^3 - 2n^2 + 3n + 1$. **Show that this function has constant third-order differences.**

Write the first several function values. Find the first-order differences by subtracting consecutive function values. Then find the second-order differences by subtracting consecutive _____ differences. Finally, find the third-order differences by subtracting consecutive _____ differences.

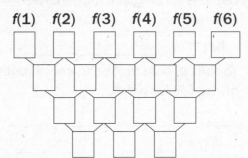

$f(1)$ $f(2)$ $f(3)$ $f(4)$ $f(5)$ $f(6)$ Function values for equally-spaced n-values

First-order differences

Second-order differences

Third-order differences

PROPERTIES OF FINITE DIFFERENCES

1. If a polynomial function $f(x)$ has degree n, then the nth-order differences of function values for equally spaced x-values are _____.

2. Conversely, if the nth-order differences of equally-spaced data are _____, then the data can be represented by a polynomial function of degree n.

Example 3	*Modeling with Finite Differences*

The values of a polynomial function for five consecutive whole numbers are given below. Write a polynomial function for $f(n)$.

$f(1) = 5$, $f(2) = 14$, $f(3) = 27$, $f(4) = 44$, and $f(5) = 65$

Solution

Begin by finding the finite differences.

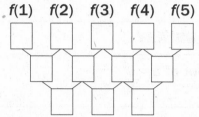

Function values for equally-spaced n-values

First-order differences

Second-order differences

Because the _____ differences are constant, you know that the numbers can be represented by a _____ function which has the form $f(n) =$ _____.

By substituting the first three values into the function, you can obtain a system of three linear equations in _____ variables.

_____ ⟹ _____

_____ ⟹ _____

_____ ⟹ _____

Using a calculator to solve the system gives $a =$ __, $b =$ __, and $c =$ __.

The polynomial function is $f(n) =$ _____.

✔ *Checkpoint* **Complete the following exercise.**

2. Values of a polynomial function for six consecutive whole numbers are given. Write a polynomial function for $f(n)$.
$f(1) = 2$, $f(2) = 8$, $f(3) = 22$, $f(4) = 50$, $f(5) = 98$, and $f(6) = 172$

Homework

7.1 *n*th Roots and Rational Exponents

Goals • Evaluate *n*th roots using radical notation and rational exponent notation.
• Use *n*th roots to solve real-life problems.

Your Notes

VOCABULARY

*n*th root of *a*

Index of a radical

REAL *n*th ROOTS

Let *n* be an integer greater than 1 and let *a* be a real number.

• If *n* is odd, then *a* has one real *n*th root: $\sqrt[n]{a} =$ _____

• If *n* is even and *a* > 0, then *a* has two real *n*th roots:
$\pm\sqrt[n]{a} =$ _____

• If *n* is even and *a* = 0, then *a* has one *n*th root:
$\sqrt[n]{0} = 0^{1/n} =$ ___

• If *n* is even and *a* < 0, then *a* has _____.

Example 1   *Finding nth Roots*

Find the indicated real nth root(s) of a.

a. $n = 3$, $a = 64$ **b.** $n = 4$, $a = 81$

Solution

a. Because $n = 3$ is odd, $a = 64$ has _____.

Because ___^{3} = 64, you can write:

$$\sqrt[3]{64} = \underline{} \quad \text{or} \quad 64^{1/3} = \underline{}$$

b. Because $n = 4$ is even and $a = 81 > 0$, 81 has

_____. Because ___^{4} = 81 and

_____^{4} = 81, you can write:

$$\pm\sqrt[4]{81} = \underline{} \quad \text{or} \quad \pm 81^{1/4} = \underline{}$$

✔ **Checkpoint** Find the indicated nth root(s) of a.

1. $n = 3$, $a = 343$	**2.** $n = 4$, $a = 256$

RATIONAL EXPONENTS

Let $a^{1/n}$ be an nth root of a, and let m be a positive integer.

- $a^{m/n} = (a^{1/n})^m = (\underline{})^m$

- $a^{-m/n} = \dfrac{1}{a^{m/n}} = \dfrac{1}{(a^{1/n})^m} = \dfrac{1}{(\boxed{})^m}, a \neq 0$

Example 2   *Evaluating Expressions with Rational Exponents*

a. $25^{3/2} = $ _____

b. $27^{-2/3} = $ _____

Example 3 **Solving Equations Using nth Roots**

a. $3x^6 = 192$

$x^6 = $ ____

$x = $ _____

$x = $ ____

b. $(x + 3)^5 = 11$

$x + 3 = $ _____

$x = $ _____

$x \approx $ _____

Example 4 **Evaluating a Model with nth Roots**

The population P of a certain animal species after t years can be modeled by $P = C(2.72)^{-t/3}$ where C is the initial population. Find the population after 2 years if the initial population was 1000.

Solution

$P = C(2.72)^{-t/3}$ Write model for population.

$= $ _____   Substitute for C and t.

$\approx $ ____   Use a calculator.

The population of the species is about ____ after 2 years.

✓ **Checkpoint** **Complete the following exercises.**

3. Evaluate $16^{-3/4}$.

4. Solve $(z - 5)^5 = 34$.

5. Solve $y = \dfrac{0.1942x^{-1/3}}{x^3 z^{5/2}}$ for y when $x = 0.3$ and $z = 4$.

7.2 Properties of Rational Exponents

Goals • Use properties of rational exponents.
• Use properties of rational exponents in real life.

VOCABULARY

Simplest form of a radical

_____

Like radicals

PROPERTIES OF RATIONAL EXPONENTS

Let a and b be real numbers and let m and n be rational numbers. The following properties have the same names as those listed in Lesson 6.1, but now apply to rational exponents as illustrated.

Property	Example
1. $a^m \cdot a^n = a^{m+n}$	$3^{1/2} \cdot 3^{3/2}$ $= 3^{(1/2 + 3/2)} = $ _____
2. $(a^m)^n = a^{mn}$	$(4^{3/2})^2 = 4^{(3/2 \cdot 2)} = $ _____
3. $(ab)^m = a^m b^m$	$(9 \cdot 4)^{1/2}$ $= 9^{1/2} \cdot 4^{1/2} = $ _____
4. $a^{-m} = \dfrac{1}{a^m}, a \neq 0$	$25^{-1/2} = \dfrac{1}{25^{1/2}} = $ ___
5. $\dfrac{a^m}{a^n} = a^{m-n}, a \neq 0$	$\dfrac{6^{5/2}}{6^{1/2}} = 6^{(5/2 - 1/2)} = $ _____
6. $\left(\dfrac{a}{b}\right)^m = \dfrac{a^m}{b^m}, b \neq 0$	$\left(\dfrac{8}{27}\right)^{1/3} = \dfrac{8^{1/3}}{27^{1/3}} = $ ___

Example 1 *Using Properties of Rational Exponents*

Use properties of rational exponents to simplify the expression.

a. $7^{2/3} \cdot 7^{1/2} =$ _____

b. $(3^{1/4} \cdot 5^{1/3})^3 =$ _____

  $=$ _____

c. $\dfrac{10^{1/2}}{10^{1/4}} =$ _____

d. $\left(\dfrac{12^{1/6}}{3^{1/6}}\right)^4 =$ _____

Example 2 *Using Properties of Radicals*

Use the properties of radicals to simplify the expression.

a. $\sqrt[5]{16} \cdot \sqrt[5]{2} =$ _____ $=$ _____ $=$ ___   Use the product property.

b. $\dfrac{\sqrt[3]{108}}{\sqrt[3]{4}} =$ _____ $=$ _____ $=$ ___   Use the quotient property.

✔ *Checkpoint* Simplify the expression.

1. $(6^5 \cdot 2^5)^{-1/5}$ **2.** $\dfrac{\sqrt[4]{48}}{\sqrt[4]{3}}$

Example 3 *Writing Radicals in Simplest Form*

Write the expression in simplest form.

$\sqrt[4]{48} =$ _____   Factor out perfect fourth power.

  $=$ ____ · ____   Product property

  $=$ ____   Simplify.

Example 4   *Adding and Subtracting Roots and Radicals*

Perform the indicated operation.

a. $3(5^{3/4}) + 4(5^{3/4}) =$ _____

b. $\sqrt[4]{64} + \sqrt[4]{4} =$ _____ $+$ _____

$\qquad\qquad = $ _____ $\cdot$ _____ $+$ _____

$\qquad\qquad = $ _____

$\qquad\qquad = $ _____

$\qquad\qquad = $ _____

✔ *Checkpoint* **Write the expression in simplest form.**

3. $\sqrt[4]{\dfrac{2}{9}}$

4. $\sqrt[4]{64} - \sqrt[4]{4}$

Example 5   *Simplify Expressions Involving Variables*

Simplify the expression. Assume all variables are positive.

a. $\sqrt[4]{81x^{12}} =$ _____

b. $(8a^9b^3)^{1/3} =$ _____

c. $\sqrt[6]{\dfrac{y^{12}}{x^{24}}} =$

_____

d. $\dfrac{8x^2y^6z^2}{4x^{1/4}y^5} =$ _____

Example 6 *Writing Variable Expressions in Simplest Form*

Write the expression in simplest form. Assume all variables are positive.

$$\sqrt[3]{\dfrac{y^2}{x^5}} = \underline{\hspace{2cm}}$$ Make the denominator a perfect cube.

$$= \underline{\hspace{2cm}}$$ Simplify.

$$= \underline{\hspace{2cm}}$$ Quotient property

$$= \underline{\hspace{2cm}}$$ Simplify.

Example 7 *Adding and Subtracting Variable Expressions*

Perform the indicated operation. Assume all variables are positive.

a. $3\sqrt[3]{x} - \sqrt[3]{x} = \underline{\hspace{3cm}}$

b. $5x^2y^{1/2} + 7x^2y^{1/2} = \underline{\hspace{3cm}}$

✓ **Checkpoint** Simplify the expression. Assume all variables are positive.

5. $\dfrac{14xy^3z^5}{2x^{2/3}yz^2}$

6. $4\sqrt[3]{5y^4} - y\sqrt[3]{40y}$

Homework

7.3 Power Functions and Function Operations

Goals • Perform operations with functions.
• Use function operations to solve real-life problems.

Your Notes

VOCABULARY

Power function

Composition

OPERATIONS ON FUNCTIONS

Let f and g be any two functions. A new function h can be defined by performing any of the four basic operations (addition, subtraction, multiplication, and division) on f and g.

Operation Defined	Example: $f(x) = 2x$, $g(x) = x + 1$
Addition $h(x) = f(x) + g(x)$	$h(x) = 2x + (x + 1) = $ _____
Subtraction $h(x) = f(x) - g(x)$	$h(x) = 2x - (x + 1) = $ _____
Multiplication $h(x) = f(x) \cdot g(x)$	$h(x) = 2x(x + 1) = $ _____
Division $h(x) = \dfrac{f(x)}{g(x)}$	$h(x) = $ _____

The domain of h consists of the x-values that are in the domains of _____. Additionally, the domain of a quotient does not include x-values for which _____.

Example 1   *Adding and Subtracting Functions*

Let $f(x) = 3x^{1/2}$ and $g(x) = 2x^{1/2}$. Find (a) the sum of the functions, (b) the difference of the functions, and (c) the domains of the sum and difference.

a. $f(x) + g(x) = 3x^{1/2} + 2x^{1/2} =$ _____

b. $f(x) - g(x) = 3x^{1/2} - 2x^{1/2} =$ _____

c. The functions f and g each have the same domain— _____. So, the domains $f + g$ and $f - g$ also consist of _____.

Example 2   *Multiplying and Dividing Functions*

Let $f(x) = 2x$ and $g(x) = x^{1/2}$. Find (a) the product of the functions, (b) the quotient of the functions, and (c) the domains of the product and quotient.

a. $f(x) \cdot g(x) = (2x)(x^{1/2}) =$ _____

b. $\dfrac{f(x)}{g(x)} =$ _____

c. The domain of f consists of _____ and the domain of g consists of _____. So, the domain of $f \cdot g$ consists of _____. Because $g(0) =$ ___, the domain of $\dfrac{f}{g}$ is restricted to _____.

✔ *Checkpoint* Complete the following exercise.

1. Let $f(x) = 3x^{1/4}$ and $g(x) = -x^{1/4}$. Find (a) $f + g$, (b) $f - g$, (c) $f \cdot g$, (d) $\dfrac{f}{g}$, and (e) the domains.

Your Notes

COMPOSITION OF TWO FUNCTIONS

The **composition** of the function f with the function g is $h(x) =$ _____ . The domain of h is the set of all x-values such that x is in the domain of __ and $g(x)$ is in the domain of __.

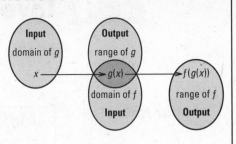

Input
domain of g

Output
range of g

x —— → $g(x)$ —— → $f(g(x))$

domain of f
Input

range of f
Output

Example 3 *Finding the Composition of Functions*

Let $f(x) = 2x^{-1}$ and $g(x) = x - 1$. Find the following.

a. $f(g(x))$ **b.** $g(f(x))$

c. $f(f(x))$ **d.** domain of each composition

Solution

a. $f(g(x)) = f(x - 1) =$ _____

b. $g(f(x)) = g(2x^{-1}) =$ _____

c. $f(f(x)) = f(2x^{-1}) =$ _____

d. The domain of $f(g(x))$ consists of _____

_____ . The domains of $g(f(x))$ and $f(f(x))$ consist of _____

_____ . Note that $f(f(x))$ simplifies to __ , but that result is not what determines the domain.

✓ *Checkpoint* Complete the following exercise.

2. Let $f(x) = 4x^{-1}$ and $g(x) = x - 3$. Find (a) $f(g(x))$, (b) $g(f(x))$, (c) $f(f(x))$, and (d) the domain of each composition.

Homework

7.4 Inverse Functions

• Find inverses of linear functions.
• Find inverses of nonlinear functions.

Your Notes

VOCABULARY

Inverse relation

Inverse functions

Example 1 *Finding an Inverse Relation*

Find an equation for the inverse of the relation $y = 3x - 1$.

Solution

$y = 3x - 1$ Write original equation.

_____   Switch x and y.

_____   Add ___ to each side.

_____   Divide each side by ___.

The inverse relation is $y =$ _____ .

INVERSE FUNCTIONS

Functions f and g are inverse functions of each other provided:

$f(g(x)) =$ ___   and $g(f(x)) =$ ___

The function g is denoted by f^{-1}, read as "f inverse."

Example 2   *Verifying Inverse Functions*

Verify that $f(x) = 3x - 1$ and $f^{-1}(x) = \dfrac{1}{3}x + \dfrac{1}{3}$ are inverses.

Solution

Show that $f(f^{-1}(x)) = $ ___ and $f^{-1}(f(x)) = $ ___.

$$f(f^{-1}(x)) = f\left(\dfrac{1}{3}x + \dfrac{1}{3}\right) \qquad\qquad f^{-1}(f(x)) = f^{-1}(3x - 1)$$

$$= \underline{\hspace{3cm}} \qquad\qquad\qquad = \underline{\hspace{3cm}}$$

$$= \underline{\hspace{3cm}} \qquad\qquad\qquad = \underline{\hspace{3cm}}$$

$$= \underline{\hspace{1cm}} \qquad\qquad\qquad\quad = \underline{\hspace{1cm}}$$

Example 3   *Finding an Inverse Power Function*

Find the inverse function of the function $f(x) = \dfrac{1}{4}x^2$, $x \le 0$.

Solution

$$f(x) = \dfrac{1}{4}x^2 \qquad \text{Write original function.}$$

$$y = \dfrac{1}{4}x^2 \qquad \text{Replace } f(x) \text{ with } y.$$

$$\qquad\qquad\qquad \text{Switch } x \text{ and } y.$$

$$\underline{\hspace{4cm}} \qquad \text{Multiply each side by ___.}$$

$$\underline{\hspace{4cm}} \qquad \text{Take square roots of each side.}$$

Because the domain of f is restricted to nonpositive values, the inverse function is $f^{-1}(x) = $ _____. (You would choose $f^{-1}(x) = $ _____ if the domain had been restricted to $x \ge 0$.)

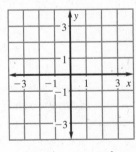

Check To check your work, graph f and f^{-1}. Note that the graph of $f^{-1}(x) = $ _____ is the reflection of the graph of $f(x) = \dfrac{1}{4}x^2$, $x \le 0$ in the line $y = x$.

Example 4   *Finding an Inverse Function*

Consider the function $f(x) = \frac{1}{3}x^3 + 2$. Determine whether the inverse function of f is a function. Then find the inverse function.

Begin by graphing the function and noticing that no _____ intersects the graph more than once. This tells you that the inverse function of f _____. To find an equation for f^{-1}, complete the following steps.

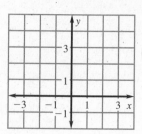

$$f(x) = \frac{1}{3}x^3 + 2 \qquad \text{Write original function.}$$

$$y = \frac{1}{3}x^3 + 2 \qquad \text{Replace } f(x) \text{ with } y.$$

_____   Switch x and y.

_____   Subtract ___ from each side.

_____   Multiply each side by ___.

_____   Take cube root of each side.

The inverse function is $f^{-1}(x) = $ _____.

✔ *Checkpoint* Find the inverse function.

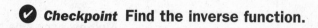

1. $y = \frac{1}{4}x - 2$ 2. $f(x) = x^3$ 3. $f(x) = \frac{1}{2}x^5 + 1$

Homework

7.5 Graphing Square Root and Cube Root Functions

Goals • Graph square root and cube root functions.
• Use radical functions to find real-life quantities.

Your Notes

VOCABULARY

Radical function

GRAPHS OF RADICAL FUNCTIONS

Follow these steps to graph $y = a\sqrt{x - h} + k$ or $y = a\sqrt[3]{x - h} + k$.

Step 1 Sketch the graph of $y = a\sqrt{x}$ or $y = a\sqrt[3]{x}$.

Step 2 Shift the graph h units horizontally and k units vertically.

Example 1 *Graphing a Square Root Function*

Graph $y = 2\sqrt{x + 1} + 1$.

Solution

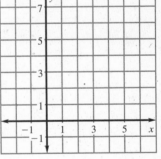

1. Sketch the graph of $y = 2\sqrt{x}$. Notice that it begins at the origin and passes through (__, __).

2. Note that for $y = 2\sqrt{x + 1} + 1$, 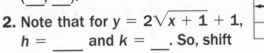 $h =$ ____ and $k =$ __. So, shift the graph _____. The result is a 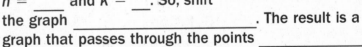 graph that passes through the points _____ _____.

Example 2   *Graphing a Cube Root Function*

Graph $y = -\sqrt[3]{x + 2} - 1$.

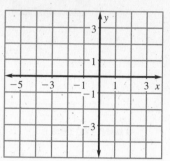

Solution

1. Sketch the graph of $y = -\sqrt[3]{x}$. Notice that it begins at the origin and passes through the points _____.

2. Note that for $y = -\sqrt[3]{x + 2} - 1$, $h =$ ____ and $k =$ ____. So, shift the graph _____ _____. The result is a graph that passes through the points _____.

✓ *Checkpoint* Graph the function.

1. $y = \sqrt{x - 2} + 2$

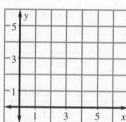

2. $y = 2\sqrt[3]{x - 1} - 2$

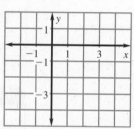

Example 3   *Finding Domain and Range*

State the domain and range of the function in (a) Example 1 and (b) Example 2.

Solution

a. From the graph of $y = 2\sqrt{x + 1} + 1$ in Example 1, you can see that the domain is _____ and the range is _____.

b. From the graph of $y = -\sqrt[3]{x + 2} - 1$ in Example 2, you can see that the domain and range are both _____ _____.

Your Notes

Example 4   *Modeling with a Square Root Function*

The equation of the radius *r* of a circle in terms of the area *A*

is $r = \sqrt{\dfrac{A}{\pi}}$. Use a graphing calculator to graph the model.

Then use the graph to estimate the area of a circle that has a radius of 2.76 units.

Solution

Graph _____ and _____.

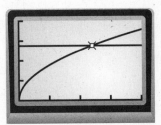

Choose a viewing window that shows the point where the graphs intersect. Then use the *Intersect* feature to find the *x*-coordinate of that point. You get *x* ≈ _____.

The area is about _____ square units.

✔ *Checkpoint* **Complete the following exercises.**

3. State the domain and range of the function in
   (a) Checkpoint 1 and (b) Checkpoint 2.

---

4. Graph the equation $y = -1.3\sqrt{x}$ on a graphing calculator. Then use the graph to estimate the value of *x* when *y* is −2.3.

Homework

7.6 Solving Radical Equations

Goals • Solve equations that contain radicals.
• Use radical equations to solve real-life problems.

VOCABULARY

Extraneous solution

Example 1 **Solving a Simple Radical Equation**

Solve $\sqrt[3]{x} - 4 = -3$.

$\sqrt[3]{x} - 4 = -3$ **Write original equation.**

_____   **Isolate radical.**

_____   **Cube each side.**

_____   **Simplify.**

The solution is ___. Check this in the original equation.

Example 2 **Solving an Equation with Rational Exponents**

Solve $-x^{2/3} = -49$.

$-x^{2/3} = -49$ **Write original equation.**

$x^{2/3} = $ ___   **Isolate radical.**

_____   **Raise each side to ___ power.**

_____   **Apply properties of roots.**

_____   **Simplify.**

The solution is ____. Check this in the original equation.

Example 3 *Solving an Equation with One Radical*

Solve $\sqrt{3x + 4} - 1 = 7$.

Solution

$\sqrt{3x + 4} - 1 = 7$ Write original equation.

    $\sqrt{3x + 4} = \underline{\ \ }$ Isolate radical.

_____   Square each side.

_____   Simplify.

_____   Subtract ___ from each side.

_____   Divide each side by ___.

Check $x = $ ____ in the original equation.

    $\sqrt{3(\underline{\ \ }) + 4} - 1 \overset{?}{=} 7$ Substitute for *x*.

            _____ $\overset{?}{=}$ __   Simplify.

            _____   Solution _____.

The solution is ___.

Example 4 *Solving an Equation with Two Radicals*

Solve $\sqrt{2x - 5} - \sqrt{x + 3} = 0$.

Solution

$\sqrt{2x - 5} - \sqrt{x + 3} = 0$ Write original equation.

_____   Add _____ to each side.

_____   Square each side.

_____   Simplify.

_____   Solve for *x*.

Check $x = $ __ in the original equation.

    $\sqrt{2(\underline{\ \ }) - 5} - \sqrt{\underline{\ \ } + 3} \overset{?}{=} 0$ Substitute for *x*.

        _____ − _____ $\overset{?}{=}$ __   Simplify.

            _____   Solution _____.

The solution is __.

Example 5 *An Equation with an Extraneous Solution*

Solve $x - 2 = \sqrt{x}$.

$x - 2 = \sqrt{x}$ Write original equation.

_____ $=$ _____   Square each side.

_____ $=$ __   Expand left side, simplify right.

_____ $= 0$ Write in standard form.

_____ $= 0$ Factor.

_____ $= 0$ or _____ $= 0$ Zero product property

$x = $ __ or $x = $ __   Simplify.

Check $x = $ __ and $x = $ __ in the original equation.

$x - 2 = \sqrt{x}$ Write original equation. $x - 2 = \sqrt{x}$

_____   Substitute for x.   _____

_____   Simplify.   _____

The only solution is __.

✔ **Checkpoint** Solve the equation.

1. $\sqrt[3]{x} + 7 = 5$ 2. $7x^{1/3} = 14$

3. $\sqrt{5x - 1} + 6 = 13$ 4. $\sqrt{x - 2} - \sqrt{5x + 2} = 0$

Homework

5. $x - 6 = \sqrt{3x}$

7.7 Statistics and Statistical Graphs

Goals • Use measures of central tendency and dispersion.
• Represent statistical data graphically.

Your Notes

VOCABULARY

Statistics

Mean ($\bar{x}$)

Median

Mode

Measures of dispersion

Range of data values

Standard deviation

Box-and-whisker plot

Lower quartile

Upper quartile

Histogram

Frequency of data values

Frequency distribution

Example 1 *Finding Measures of Central Tendency*

The scores for students on a test in two classes are shown.

Class A	Class B
44, 52, 53, 62, 70, 71, 71, 72, 74, 75, 75, 75, 76, 76, 78, 80, 81, 82, 82, 84, 85, 86, 90, 92, 93, 96, 97	48, 50, 56, 64, 68, 70, 71, 76, 76, 78, 78, 78, 80, 80, 80, 82, 82, 82, 83, 85, 85, 87, 88, 89, 91, 91, 94

Find the mean, median, and mode of the data listed above.

Solution

Class A: Mean: $\bar{x} = \dfrac{44 + 52 + \cdots + 97}{27} = $ _____ $\approx$ _____

Median: ___   Mode: ___

Class B: Mean: $\bar{x} = \dfrac{48 + 50 + \cdots + 94}{27} = $ _____ $\approx$ _____

Median: ___   Modes: _____

All three measures of central tendency are greater for _____ . So, _____ has better test scores overall.

Example 2 *Finding Ranges of Data Sets*

The ranges of the data sets in Example 1 are:

     Class A: **Class B:**

  Range = _____   Range = _____

Because _____ range of test scores is greater, its test scores are more spread out.

STANDARD DEVIATION OF A SET OF DATA

The standard deviation σ (read as "sigma") of $x_1, x_2, \ldots, x_n$ is:

$$\sigma = \sqrt{\dfrac{(\underline{\hspace{1cm}})^2 + (\underline{\hspace{1cm}})^2 + \cdots + (\underline{\hspace{1cm}})^2}{n}}$$

Your Notes

Example 3   *Finding Standard Deviations of Data Sets*

The standard deviations of the data sets in Example 1 are:

Class A: $\sigma \approx$

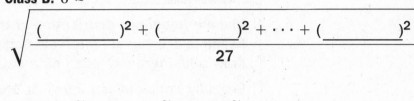

$$\sqrt{\dfrac{(\underline{\hspace{2cm}})^2 + (\underline{\hspace{2cm}})^2 + \cdots + (\underline{\hspace{2cm}})^2}{27}}$$

$$\approx \underline{\hspace{2cm}} \qquad \approx \underline{\hspace{1.5cm}} \approx \underline{\hspace{1cm}}$$

Class B: $\sigma \approx$

$$\sqrt{\dfrac{(\underline{\hspace{2cm}})^2 + (\underline{\hspace{2cm}})^2 + \cdots + (\underline{\hspace{2cm}})^2}{27}}$$

$$\approx \underline{\hspace{2cm}} \qquad \approx \underline{\hspace{1.5cm}} \approx \underline{\hspace{1cm}}$$

Because _____ standard deviation is greater, its test scores are more spread out about the mean.

Example 4   *Drawing Box-and-Whisker Plots*

Draw a box-and-whisker plot of each data set in Example 1.

Solution

Class A
The minimum is ___ and the maximum is ___. The median is ___. The lower quartile is ___ and the upper quartile is ___.

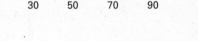

Class B
The minimum is ___ and the maximum is ___. The median is ___. The lower quartile is ___ and the upper quartile is ___.

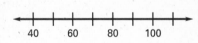

✅ **Checkpoint** Complete the following exercise.

1. The ages of management team members are 54, 62, 43, 56, 52, 61, 52, 46, 65, and 69. Find the mean, median, mode, range, and standard deviation of the ages.

Example 5 *Making Frequency Distributions and Histograms*

Make a frequency distribution of the data sets in Example 1 using six intervals beginning with 41–50. Then draw a histogram of each data set.

Begin by writing the six intervals. Then tally the data values by interval. Finally, count the tally marks to get the frequencies.

Class A			Class B		
Interval	Tally	Frequency	Interval	Tally	Frequency
41–50			41–50		
51–60			51–60		
61–70			61–70		
71–80			71–80		
81–90			81–90		
91–100			91–100		

Use the frequency distributions to draw the histograms. Draw and divide a horizontal axis into six equal sections, and label the sections with the intervals. Then draw a vertical axis for measuring the frequencies. Finally, draw bars of appropriate heights to represent the frequencies of the intervals.

Homework

8.1 Exponential Growth

Goals • Graph exponential growth functions.
• Use exponential growth models.

Your Notes

VOCABULARY

Exponential function

Asymptote

Exponential growth function

Growth factor

Example 1 *Graphing Functions of the Form $y = ab^x$*

Graph (a) $y = \dfrac{1}{4} \cdot 4^x$ and (b) $y = -\left(\dfrac{4}{3}\right)^x$.

Solution

a. Plot $\left(0, \underline{}\right)$ and $(1, \underline{})$. Then,

from left to right, draw a curve that
begins just _____ the x-axis,
passes through the two points, and
moves _____.

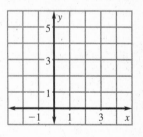

b. Plot $(0, \underline{})$ and $\left(1, \underline{}\right)$. Then,

from left to right, draw a curve that
begins just _____ the x-axis,
passes through the two points, and
moves _____.

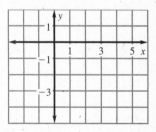

Example 2   *Graphing a General Exponential Function*

Graph $y = 2 \cdot 3^{x-1} - 3$. State the domain and range.

Begin by lightly sketching the graph of $y = 2 \cdot 3^x$, which passes through (0, __) and (1, __). Then translate the graph _____

_____. Notice that the graph passes through _____ and _____. The graph's asymptote is the line _____.
The domain is _____,
and the range is _____.

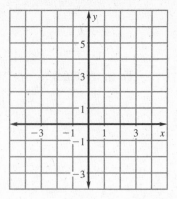

Example 3   *Modeling Exponential Growth*

In the last 10 years, an initial population of 44 deer in a state park grew by about 8% per year.

a. Write a model giving the number *d* of deer after *t* years. About how many deer were in the park after 5 years?

b. Graph the model and use the graph to estimate when there were 60 deer.

Solution

a. The initial amount is $a =$ ____ and the percent increase is $r =$ _____. So, the exponential growth model is:

$$d = a(1 + r)^t \qquad \text{Write exponential growth model.}$$

$$= \underline{\hspace{3cm}} \qquad \text{Substitute for } a \text{ and } r.$$

$$= \underline{\hspace{2.5cm}} \qquad \text{Simplify.}$$

Using this model, you can estimate the number of deer after 5 years ($t = 5$) to be $d =$ _____ $\approx$ ____ deer.

b. The graph passes through the points (0, ___) and (1, _____). To make an accurate graph, plot a few other points. Then draw a smooth curve through the points. Using the graph, you can estimate that the number of deer was 60 after about ___ years.

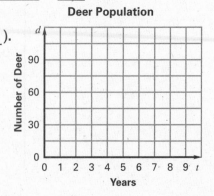

Deer Population

COMPOUND INTEREST

Consider an initial principal P deposited in an account that pays interest at an annual rate r (expressed as a decimal), compounded n times per year. The amount A in the account after t years can be modeled by the equation

$A = $ _____ .

_____

Example 4 *Finding the Balance in an Account*

You deposit $1400 in an account that pays 4% annual interest. Find the balance after 1 year if the interest is compounded with the given frequency.

a. annually   **b.** monthly   **c.** daily

Solution

a. $A = 1400$ Substitute for P, r, n, and t.

_____

$= 1400$ _____   Simplify.

$= $ _____   Use a calculator.

The balance at the end of 1 year is _____ .

b. $A = 1400$ Substitute for P, r, n, and t.

_____

$\approx$ _____   Simplify.

$\approx$ _____   Use a calculator.

The balance at the end of 1 year is _____ .

c. $A = 1400$ Substitute for P, r, n, and t.

_____

$\approx$ _____   Simplify.

$\approx$ _____   Use a calculator.

The balance at the end of 1 year is _____ .

✓ *Checkpoint* **Complete the following exercises.**

1. Graph $y = 2^x + 1$. State the domain and range.

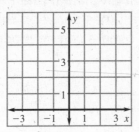

2. In 1998, the value of a cottage was $75,000. The value of the cottage rose 5% for each of the next 5 years. Write and graph a model giving the price *v* (in thousands of dollars) *t* years after 1998.

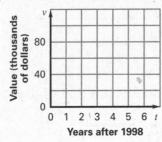

3. You deposit $800 in an account that pays 9% annual interest. Find the balance after one year if the interest is compounded (a) quarterly and (b) semiannually.

Homework

Exponential Decay

Goals • Graph exponential decay functions.
• Use exponential decay functions to model real-life situations.

Your Notes

VOCABULARY

Exponential decay function

Decay factor

Example 1 *Graphing Functions of the Form y = abˣ*

Graph the function (a) $y = 2\left(\dfrac{1}{3}\right)^x$ and (b) $y = -3\left(\dfrac{3}{4}\right)^x$.

Solution

a. Plot (0, ___) and $\left(1, \underline{\quad}\right)$. Then, from

right to left, draw a curve that begins

just _____ the x-axis, passes through

the two points, and moves _____

_____.

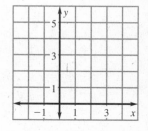

b. Plot (0, ____) and $\left(1, \underline{\quad}\right)$. Then,

from right to left, draw a curve that

begins just _____ the x-axis, passes

through the two points, and moves

_____.

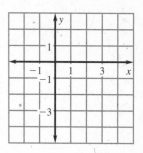

Example 2   *Graphing a General Exponential Function*

Graph $y = 3\left(\dfrac{1}{6}\right)^{x+3} - 2$. State the

domain and range.

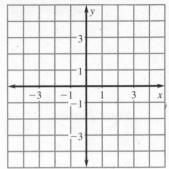

Solution

Begin by lightly sketching the graph

of $y = 3\left(\dfrac{1}{6}\right)^{x}$, which passes through

$(0, \underline{\hspace{0.4cm}})$ and $\left(1, \dfrac{}{}\right)$. Then translate the graph _____

_____. Notice that the graph passes

through _____ and _____. The graph's asymptote is

the line _____. The domain is _____, and the

range is _____.

✔ *Checkpoint* **Complete the following exercise.**

1. Graph $y = -\left(\dfrac{2}{5}\right)^{x-2} + 2$.

State whether the function is
an exponential growth or decay
function. State the domain and
the range of the function.

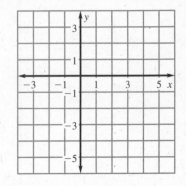

Example 3 *Modeling Exponential Decay*

A company buys a piece of machinery for $2500. The value y of the machine decreases by 10% each year.

a. Write an exponential decay model for the value of the machine. Use the model to estimate the value after 3 years.

b. Graph the model.

c. Use the graph to estimate when the value will be $2000.

Solution

a. Let t be the number of years since the machine was bought. The exponential decay model is:

$$y = a(1 - r)^t \qquad \text{Write exponential decay model.}$$

$$= \underline{\hspace{4cm}} \qquad \text{Substitute for } a \text{ and } r.$$

$$= \underline{\hspace{3cm}} \qquad \text{Simplify.}$$

When $t = 3$, the value is $y = \underline{\hspace{5cm}}$.

b. The graph passes through the points $(0, \underline{\hspace{1cm}})$ and $(1, \underline{\hspace{1cm}})$. The asymptote of the graph is the line $\underline{\hspace{1cm}}$.

c. Using the graph, you can estimate that the value of the machine will drop to $2000 after about $\underline{\hspace{0.5cm}}$ years.

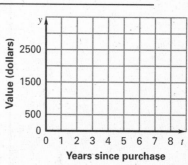

✔ *Checkpoint* **Complete the following exercise.**

2. A new riding lawnmower costs $3000. The value decreases by 8% each year. Write and graph an exponential decay model for the value of the lawnmower. Use the model to find the value after 4 years.

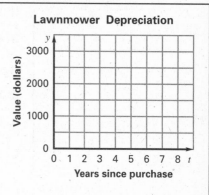

Lawnmower Depreciation

8.3 The Number e

Goals • Use *e* as the base of exponential functions.
• Use the natural base *e* in real-life situations.

Your Notes

> **THE NATURAL BASE e**
>
> The natural base *e* is irrational. It is defined as follows:
>
> As *n* approaches $+\infty$, $\left(1 + \dfrac{1}{n}\right)^n$ approaches
>
> $e \approx$ _____ .

Example 1   *Simplifying Natural Base Expressions*

Simplify the expression.

a. $e^2 \cdot e^6$ **b.** $\dfrac{6e^4}{2e^3}$ **c.** $(-4e^{3x})^2$

Solution

a. $e^2 \cdot e^6 = e$——   **b.** $\dfrac{6e^4}{2e^3} =$ _____

$\qquad\qquad = $ ___ $\qquad\qquad = $ ___

c. $(-4e^{3x})^2 =$ _____

$\qquad\qquad = $ _____

Example 2   *Evaluating Natural Base Expressions*

Use a calculator to evaluate the expression.

a. e^{-3} **b.** $e^{0.7}$

Solution

Expression	Keystrokes	Display
a. e^{-3}	[2nd] $[e^x]$ [(-)] ___ [ENTER]	
b. $e^{0.7}$	[2nd] $[e^x]$ ____ [ENTER]	

✔ **Checkpoint** **Simplify the expression.**

1. $e^{-7} \cdot e^8$

2. $\dfrac{(-3e^4)^3}{-9e^7}$

Use a calculator to evaluate the expression.

3. $e^{0.91}$

4. e^{-2}

Example 3 | *Graphing Natural Base Functions*

Graph the function. State the domain and range.

a. $y = 3e^{0.4x}$

b. $y = e^{-0.6(x + 3)} - 2$

Solution

a. Because _____
_____, the function
is an exponential _____
function. Plot the points (0, __)
and (1, _____) and draw the
curve.

The domain is _____,
and the range is _____
_____.

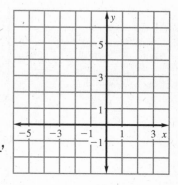

b. Because _____
_____, the
function is an exponential _____
function. Translate the graph of
$y = e^{-0.6x}$ to the _____
_____.

The domain is _____,
and the range is _____.

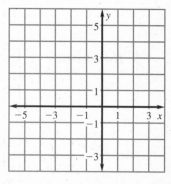

✅ **Checkpoint** Complete the following exercise.

5. Graph $y = e^{0.9x} + 1$. State the domain and the range.

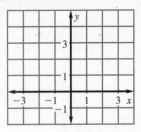

Example 4   *Finding the Balance in an Account*

You deposit $1400 in an account that pays 4% annual interest compounded continuously. What is the balance after 1 year?

Solution

Note that $P =$ _____, $r =$ _____, and $t =$ ___. So, the balance at the end of 1 year is:

$A = Pe^{rt} =$ _____

In Example 4 of Lesson 8.1, you found that the balance from daily compounding is _____ . So, continuous compounding earned only an additional _____ .

✅ **Checkpoint** Complete the following exercise.

6. You deposit $800 in an account that pays 9% annual interest compounded continuously. What is the balance after 1 year?

Homework

Logarithmic Functions

Goals • Evaluate logarithmic functions.
• Graph logarithmic functions.

Your Notes

VOCABULARY

Common logarithm

Natural logarithm

DEFINITION OF LOGARITHM WITH BASE *b*

Let *b* and *y* be positive numbers, $b \neq 1$. The **logarithm of *y* with base *b*** is denoted by $\log_b y$ and is defined as follows:

$\log_b y =$ ___ if and only if $b^x =$ ___

The expression $\log_b y$ is read as "log base *b* of *y*."

Example 1 *Rewriting Logarithmic Equations*

Logarithmic Form	Exponential Form
a. $\log_3 81 = 4$	_____
b. $\log_4 1 = 0$	_____
c. $\log_9 9 = 1$	_____
d. $\log_{10} 0.01 = -2$	_____
e. $\log_{1/4} 4 = -1$	_____

✔ *Checkpoint* **Write the equation in exponential form.**

1. $\log_3 3 = 1$ **2.** $\log_2 0.125 = -3$

SPECIAL LOGARITHMIC VALUES

Let b be a positive real number such that $b \neq 1$.

Logarithm of 1 $\log_b 1 = \underline{\ \ }$ because $b^{\underline{\ \ }} = 1$.

Logarithm of base b $\log_b b = \underline{\ \ }$ because $b^{\underline{\ \ }} = b$.

Example 2   *Evaluating Logarithmic Expressions*

Evaluate the expression.

a. $\log_2 64$ **b.** $\log_{1/2} 0.25$ **c.** $\log_{1/3} 27$ **d.** $\log_4 2$

Solution

To help you find the value of $\log_b y$, ask yourself what power of b gives you y.

a. 2 to what power gives 64?

    $2^{\underline{\ \ }} = 64$, so $\log_2 64 = \underline{\ \ }$

b. $\dfrac{1}{2}$ to what power gives 0.25?

    $\left(\dfrac{1}{2}\right)^{\underline{\ \ }} = 0.25$, so $\log_{1/2} 0.25 = \underline{\ \ }$

c. $\dfrac{1}{3}$ to what power gives 27?

    $\left(\dfrac{1}{3}\right)^{\underline{\ \ }} = 27$, so $\log_{1/3} 27 = \underline{\ \ \ \ }$

d. 4 to what power gives 2?

    $4^{\underline{\ \ }} = 2$, so $\log_4 2 = \underline{\ \ \ }$

✔ *Checkpoint* **Evaluate the expression.**

3. $\log_5 125$ **4.** $\log_8 2$

Example 3 *Using Inverse Properties*

Simplify the expression.

a. $10^{\log 2.3}$ **b.** $\log_2 8^x$

Solution

a. $10^{\log 2.3} =$ ___

b. $\log_2 8^x =$ _____

Example 4 *Finding Inverses*

Find the inverse of the function.

a. $y = \log_{1/2} x$ **b.** $y = \ln(x - 2)$

Solution

a. From the definition of logarithm, the inverse of

$y = \log_{1/2} x$ is _____ .
_____

b. $y = \ln(x - 2)$ Write original function.

_____ Switch x and y.

_____ Write in exponential form.

_____ $= y$ Solve for y.

The inverse of $y = \ln(x - 2)$ is $y =$ _____ .

✔ **Checkpoint** Simplify the expression.

5. $10^{\log x}$ **6.** $\log_3 81^x$

Find the inverse of the function.

7. $y = \log_2 x$ **8.** $y = \ln(x + 7)$

GRAPHS OF LOGARITHMIC FUNCTIONS

The graph of $y = \log_b (x - h) + k$ has these characteristics:

- The line $x =$ ___ is a vertical asymptote.

- The domain is _____, and the range is _____.

- If $b > 1$, the graph moves _____. If $0 < b < 1$, the graph moves _____.

Example 5 *Graphing Logarithmic Functions*

Graph the function. State the domain and range.

a. $y = \log_{1/2} (x - 2)$ **b.** $y = \log_2 (x + 1) + 2$

Solution

a. Plot several convenient points, such as $\left(\dfrac{5}{2}, \_\_\right)$ and $(4, \_\_)$.

The vertical line $x =$ ___ is an asymptote. From left to right, draw a curve that starts just to the right of the line $x =$ ___ and moves _____.

The domain is _____, and the range is _____.

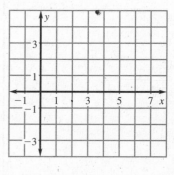

b. Plot several convenient points, such as $(0, \_\_)$ and $(1, \_\_)$. The vertical line $x =$ ____ is an asymptote. From left to right, draw a curve that starts just to the right of the line $x =$ ____ and moves _____.

The domain is _____, and the range is _____.

Homework

8.5 Properties of Logarithms

Goals • Use properties of logarithms.
• Use properties of logarithms to solve real-life problems.

Your Notes

PROPERTIES OF LOGARITHMS

Let b, u, and v be positive numbers such that $b \neq 1$.

Product Property $\quad \log_b uv = \log_b u \, \underline{\quad} \, \log_b v$

Quotient Property $\quad \log_b \dfrac{u}{v} = \log_b u \, \underline{\quad} \, \log_b \underline{\quad}$

Power Property $\quad \log_b u^n = \underline{\hspace{2cm}}$

Example 1 *Using Properties of Logarithms*

Use $\log_3 4 \approx 1.262$ and $\log_3 5 \approx 1.465$ to approximate the following.

a. $\log_3 \dfrac{4}{5}$ 　　　　**b.** $\log_3 20$ 　　　　**c.** $\log_3 16$

Solution

a. $\log_3 \dfrac{4}{5} = \log_3 4 \, \underline{\quad} \, \log_3 5 \approx \underline{\hspace{4cm}}$

b. $\log_3 20 = \log_3 (4 \cdot 5) = \log_3 4 \, \underline{\quad} \, \log_3 5 \approx$

$\underline{\hspace{4cm}}$

c. $\log_3 16 = \log_3 \underline{\quad} = \underline{\hspace{4cm}}$

✔ *Checkpoint* Use $\log_5 3 \approx 0.683$ and $\log_5 6 \approx 1.113$ to approximate the value of the expression.

1. $\log_5 2$ 　　　　　　　　**2.** $\log_5 18$

Example 2 *Expanding a Logarithmic Expression*

Expand $\log_4 \dfrac{x^2}{3y^3}$. Assume x and y are positive.

Solution

$\log_4 \dfrac{x^2}{3y^3} = $ _____ Quotient property

$= $ _____ Product property

$= $ _____ Power property

$= $ _____ Simplify.

Example 3 *Condensing a Logarithmic Expression*

Condense log 3 + 3 log 2 − log 6.

$\log 3 + 3 \log 2 - \log 6$

$= \log 3 + $ _____ $- \log 6$ Power property

$= \log$ _____ $- \log 6$ Product property

$= \log$ _____ Quotient property

$= $ _____ Simplify.

✔ *Checkpoint* **Complete the following exercises.**

3. Expand $\log_6 \dfrac{9x^3}{2y^2}$. 4. Condense $4 \log_3 x - 3 \log_3 y$.

CHANGE OF BASE FORMULA

Let u, b, and c be positive numbers with $b \neq 1$ and $c \neq 1$. Then:

$$\log_c u = \frac{\log_b u}{\log_b c}$$

In particular, $\log_c u = \underline{\hspace{1.5cm}}$ and $\log_c u = \underline{\hspace{1.5cm}}$.

Example 4   *Using the Change-of-Base Formula*

Evaluate $\log_5 6$ using common and natural logarithms.

Solution

Using common logarithms:

$$\log_5 6 = \underline{\hspace{1.5cm}} = \underline{\hspace{1.5cm}} \approx \underline{\hspace{1.5cm}} \approx \underline{\hspace{1.5cm}}$$

Using natural logarithms:

$$\log_5 6 = \underline{\hspace{1.5cm}} = \underline{\hspace{1.5cm}} \approx \underline{\hspace{1.5cm}} \approx \underline{\hspace{1.5cm}}$$

✔ *Checkpoint* **Complete the following exercise.**

5. Evaluate $\log_7 9$ using natural logarithms.

Homework

Solving Exponential and Logarithmic Equations

Goals • Solve exponential equations.
• Solve logarithmic equations.

Your Notes

Example 1 *Solving by Equating Exponents*

Solve $27^{2x} = 9^{x+2}$.

Solution

$27^{2x} = 9^{x+2}$	Write original equation.
$(\underline{\quad})^{2x} = (\underline{\quad})^{x+2}$	Rewrite each power with base __ .
$\underline{\quad\quad} = \underline{\quad\quad}$	Power of a power property
$\underline{\quad\quad} = \underline{\quad\quad}$	Equate exponents.
$x = \underline{\quad}$	Solve for x.

The solution is __ .

Check Substitute the solution into the original equation.

$27^{2 \cdot \underline{\quad}} \stackrel{?}{=} 9^{\underline{\quad}+2}$ Substitute for x.

$\underline{\quad\quad\quad}$ Solution checks.

Example 2 *Taking a Logarithm of Each Side*

Solve $4^x = 21$.

Solution

$4^x = 21$	Write original equation.
$\underline{\quad\quad} = \underline{\quad\quad}$	Take _____ of each side.
$x = \underline{\quad\quad}$	$\log_b b^x = x$
$x = \underline{\quad\quad}$	Use change-of-base formula with common logarithms.
$x \approx \underline{\quad\quad}$	Use a calculator.

The solution is about _____. Check this in the original equation.

Example 3   *Taking a Logarithm of Each Side*

Solve $3^{5x-2} + 2 = 6$.

Solution

$3^{5x-2} + 2 = 6$ Write original equation.

$\quad 3^{5x-2} = \underline{}$ Subtract ___ from each side.

_____   Take _____ of each side.

_____ $\log_b b^x = x$

_____   Add ___ to each side.

_____   Multiply each side by ___ .

$\qquad\qquad x \approx \underline{}$ Use a calculator.

The solution is about _____ .

Check Check the solution algebraically by substituting into the original equation. Or, check it graphically by graphing both sides of the equation and observing that the two graphs intersect at $x \approx$ _____ .

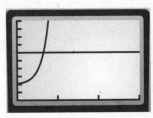

✓ **Checkpoint** Solve the equations.

1. $4^{3x-2} = 16^x$ **2.** $7^x = 46$

3. $10^{2x+1} - 4 = 3$

Example 4 *Solving a Logarithmic Equation*

Solve $\log_7 (3x - 1) = \log_7 (2x + 2)$.

Solution

$\log_7 (3x - 1) = \log_7 (2x + 2)$ Write original equation.

_____   Use same base property.

_____   Add __ to each side.

_____   Solve for x.

The solution is ___ .

Check Substitute the solution into the original equation.

$\log_7 (3x - 1) = \log_7 (2x + 2)$ Write original equation.

$\log_7 (\underline{\hspace{2cm}}) \overset{?}{=} \log_7 (\underline{\hspace{2cm}})$ Substitute for x.

_____   Solution checks.

Example 5 *Exponentiating Each Side*

Solve $\log_3 (2x + 3) = 3$.

Solution

$\log_3 (2x + 3) = 3$ Write original equation.

_____   Exponentiate each side using base __.

_____ $b^{\log_b x} = x$

_____   Solve for x.

The solution is ___ .

Check Substitute the solution into the original equation.

$\log_3 (2x + 3) = 3$ Write original equation.

$\log_3 (\underline{\hspace{2cm}}) \overset{?}{=} 3$ Substitute for x.

$\log_3 \underline{\hspace{1cm}} \overset{?}{=} 3$ Simplify.

_____   Solution checks.

Example 6   *Checking for Extraneous Solutions*

Solve log $2x$ + log $(5x + 15)$ = 2.

Solution

log $2x$ + log $(5x + 15)$ = 2	Write original equation.
log [_____] = 2	Product property of logarithms
_____	Exponentiate sides using base ____.
_____	$10^{\log x} = x$
_____	Write in standard form.
_____	Factor.
_____	Zero product property

The solutions appear to be _____. However, when you check these in the original equation or use a graphic check as shown at the right, you can see that _____ is the only solution. The solution is ___.

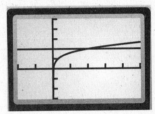

✓ **Checkpoint** Solve the equations.

4. $\log_5 (x + 6) = \log_5 (3x - 4)$ 5. $\log_6 (17x + 2) = 2$

6. $\log_2 4x + \log_2 (x + 3) = 4$

Homework

8.7 Modeling with Exponential and Power Functions

Goals • Model data with exponential functions.
• Model data with power functions.

Example 1   *Writing an Exponential Function*

Write an exponential function $y = ab^x$ whose graph passes through (1, 8) and (2, 32).

Solution

Substitute the coordinates of the two given points into $y = ab^x$ to obtain two equations in a and b.

$\underline{\quad} = ab^1$ Substitute for x and for y.

$\underline{\quad} = ab^2$ Substitute for x and for y.

To solve the system, solve for a in the first equation to get

$a = \underline{\quad}$, then substitute into the second equation.

$32 = \dfrac{\quad}{\quad} b^2$ Substitute for a.

$32 = \underline{\quad}$ Simplify.

$\underline{\quad\quad}$ Divide each side by $\underline{\quad}$.

Using $b = \underline{\quad}$, you then have $a = \dfrac{\quad}{\quad}$.

So, $y = \underline{\quad\quad}$.

✔ *Checkpoint* Complete the following exercise.

1. Write an exponential function $y = ab^x$ whose graph passes through (1, 4) and (3, 16).

Your Notes

Example 2 — Finding an Exponential Model

The table gives the amount *A* in a savings account *t* years after the account was opened.

t	0	1	2	3	4	5	6	7	8
A	145	190	250	330	440	600	780	990	1320

a. Draw a scatter plot of ln *A* versus *t*. Is an exponential model a good fit for the original data?

b. Find an exponential model for the original data.

Solution

a. Use a calculator to create a new table of values.

t	0	1	2	3	4	5	6	7	8
ln A									

Then plot the new points. The points lie close to a line, so an exponential model should be a good fit for the original data.

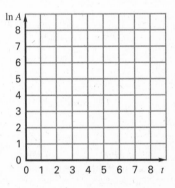

b. To find an exponential model $A = ab^t$, choose two points on the line, such as (1, _____) and (7, _____). Use these points to find an equation of the line. Then solve for *A*.

ln *A* = _____ **Equation of line**

A = _____ **Exponentiate each side using base *e*.**

A = _____ **Use properties of exponents.**

A = _____ **Exponential model**

✔ **Checkpoint** Complete the following exercise.

2. Find an exponential model to fit the data.
(0, 8.0), (1, 5.6), (2, 3.9), (3, 2.7), (4, 1.9), (5, 1.4), (6, 1.0), (7, 0.7), (8, 0.5)

Example 3 *Writing a Power Function*

Write a power function $y = ax^b$ whose graph passes through (3, 4) and (6, 7).

Solution

Substitute the coordinates of the two given points into $y = ax^b$ to obtain two equations in a and b.

$4 =$ _____   Substitute for x and for y.

$7 =$ _____   Substitute for x and for y.

To solve the system, solve for a in the first equation to get

$a =$ _____ , then substitute into the second equation.

_____   Substitute for a.

_____   Simplify.

_____   Divide each side by ___.

_____   Take _____ of each side.

                            Use the change-of-base formula with

_____   common logarithms.

_____   Use a calculator.

Using $b =$ _____ , you then have $a =$ _____.

So, $y =$ _____ .

✔ *Checkpoint* **Complete the following exercise.**

3. Write a power function $y = ax^b$ whose graph passes through (4, 11) and (8, 14).

| Example 4 | *Finding a Power Model* |

The table gives the approximate area *A* of circles with radius *r*.

r	1	2	3	4
A	3.142	12.566	28.274	50.265
r	5	6	7	8
A	78.540	113.097	153.938	201.062

a. Draw a scatter plot of ln *A* versus ln *r*. Is a power model a good fit for the original data?

b. Find a power model for the original data.

Solution

a. Use a calculator to create a new table of values.

ln *r*	0	0.693	1.099	1.386
ln *A*				
ln *r*	1.609	1.792	1.946	2.079
ln *A*				

Then plot the new points. The points lie close to a line, so an exponential model should be a good fit for the original data.

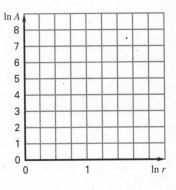

b. To find a power model $A = ar^b$, choose two points on the line, such as (1.386, _____) and (1.946, _____). Use these points to find an equation of the line. Then solve for *A*.

ln *A* = _____   **Equation of line**

ln *A* = _____   **Power property of logarithms**

A = _____   **Exponentiate each side.**

A = _____   **Use properties of exponents.**

A = _____   **Power model**

Homework

Logistic Growth Functions

Goals • Evaluate and graph logistic growth functions.
• Use logistic growth functions in real life.

Your Notes

VOCABULARY

Logistic growth function

Example 1 *Evaluating a Logistic Growth Function*

Evaluate $f(x) = \dfrac{24}{1 + 4e^{-3x}}$ for (a) $x = -1$ and (b) $x = 1$.

Solution

a. $f(-1) = $ _____ $\approx$ _____

b. $f(1) = $ _____ $\approx$ _____

✔ *Checkpoint* Complete the following exercise.

---

1. Evaluate $f(x) = \dfrac{11}{1 + e^{-2x}}$ for (a) $x = -2$, (b) $x = 0$, and (c) $x = 3$.

GRAPHS OF LOGISTIC GROWTH FUNCTIONS

The graph of $y = \dfrac{c}{1 + ae^{-rx}}$ has the following characteristics:

• The horizontal lines _____ and _____ are asymptotes.

• The y-intercept is _____ .

• The domain is _____ , and the range is _____ .

• The graph is _____ from left to right. To the left of its point of maximum growth, $\left(\dfrac{\ln a}{r}, \dfrac{c}{2}\right)$, the rate of increase is _____ . To the right, the rate of increase is _____ .

Example 2   *Graphing a Logistic Growth Function*

Graph $y = \dfrac{4}{1 + 3e^{-x}}$.

Solution

Begin by sketching the upper horizontal asymptote, $y = $ __ . Then plot the y-intercept at _____ and the point of maximum growth $\approx$ _____ . Finally, from _____ left to right, draw a curve that starts just above the x-axis, curves up to the _____ , and then levels off as it approaches the upper horizontal asymptote.

Example 3   *Solving a Logistic Growth Equation*

Solve $\dfrac{12}{1 + 6e^{-5x}} = 9$.

$\dfrac{12}{1 + 6e^{-5x}} = 9$ Write original equation.

_____   Multiply each side by _____.

_____   Use distributive property.

_____   Subtract ___ from each side.

_____   Divide each side by ___.

_____   Take _____ of each side.

_____   Divide each side by ___.

_____   Use a calculator.

The solution is about _____. Check this in the original equation.

✔ *Checkpoint* **Complete the following exercises.**

2. Graph $y = \dfrac{3}{1 + 0.5e^{-2x}}$.

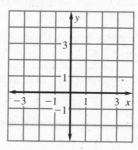

3. Solve $\dfrac{72}{1 + 11e^{-4.1x}} = 12$.

Example 4   *Using a Logistic Growth Model*

The average value V (in thousands) of a certain property can be modeled by $V = \dfrac{120}{1 + 14e^{-0.7x}}$ where x is the number of years since it was purchased. Graph and describe the function.

Solution

The initial value of the property

is $V =$

_____

$=$ _____ .

The value of the property increases more and more rapidly until

$x =$ _____ $\approx$ ____ years.

Then the rate of growth decreases. The value begins to level off to about _____ after about 10 years.

✔ *Checkpoint* **Complete the following exercise.**

4. Assume the model in Example 4 is $V = \dfrac{140}{1 + 4e^{-0.9x}}$.

What is the initial value of the property? The value of the property is increasing more and more rapidly until when? To what amount does the value of the property level off?

Homework

9.1 Inverse and Joint Variation

Goals • Write and use inverse variation models.
• Write and use joint variation models.

VOCABULARY

Inverse variation

Constant of variation

Joint variation

Example 1 *Classifying Direct and Inverse Variation*

Tell whether x and y show *direct variation*, *inverse variation*, or *neither*.

Given Equation	Rewritten Equation	Type of Variation
a. $y = x - 2$		_____
b. $2 = yx$	_____	_____
c. $x = \dfrac{y}{7}$	_____	_____

✔ *Checkpoint* Tell whether x and y show *direct variation*, *inverse variation*, or *neither*.

1. $yx = 1$ **2.** $\dfrac{y}{1.3} = x$ **3.** $y = x + 1$

Your Notes

Example 2   *Writing an Inverse Variation Equation*

The variables x and y vary inversely, and $y = 2$ when $x = 3$.

a. Write an equation that relates x and y.

b. Find y when $x = -2$.

Solution

a. $y = \dfrac{k}{x}$.   Write general equation for inverse variation.

$\underline{\quad} = \dfrac{k}{\square}$ Substitute for y and for x.

$\underline{\quad} = k$ Solve for k.

The inverse variation equation is $y = \underline{\quad}$.

b. When $x = -2$, the value of y is:

$y = \dfrac{\quad}{\underline{\quad}} = \underline{\quad}$

Example 3   *Checking Data for Inverse Variation*

Tell whether the following data show inverse variation. If they do, find a model for the relationship between a and b.

a	5	10	15	20	25
b	21	10.5	7	5.25	4.2

Solution

Each product ab is equal to _____. For instance, $(5)(21) =$ _____ and $(20)(5.25) =$ _____. So, the data _____ inverse variation. A model for the

relationship is $b = \dfrac{\quad}{\underline{\quad}}$.

Lesson 9.1 • **Algebra 2 Notetaking Guide**   205

Example 4 **Comparing Different Types of Variation**

Write an equation for the given relationship.

Relationship	Equation
a. v varies directly with u.	$v =$ ___
b. v varies inversely with u.	$v =$ ___
c. w varies jointly with t, u, and v.	$w =$ ___
d. v varies inversely with the cube of u.	$v =$ ___
e. w varies directly with u and inversely with v.	$w =$ ___

✓ **Checkpoint** Complete the following exercises.

4. The variables x and y vary inversely, and $y = 3.5$ when $x = 4$. Find an equation that relates x and y. Find y when $x = 6$.

5. Do the data below show inverse variation? If so, find a model for the relationship between x and y.

x	2	4	6	8	10
y	12	6	4	3	2.4

Homework

6. Write an equation for the given relationship: y varies jointly with x and z and varies inversely with the square of v.

9.2 Graphing Simple Rational Functions

Goals • Graph simple rational functions.
• Use the graph of a rational function to solve real-life problems.

Your Notes

VOCABULARY

Rational function

Hyperbola

Branches of a hyperbola

Example 1 *Graphing a Rational Function*

Graph $y = \dfrac{3}{x - 2} + 1$. State the domain and range.

Solution

Draw the asymptotes $x =$ ___ and $y =$ ___.

Plot two points to the left of the vertical asymptote, such as $(-1,$ ___$)$ and $(1,$ ___$)$, and two points to the right, such as $(3,$ ___$)$ and $(5,$ ___$)$.

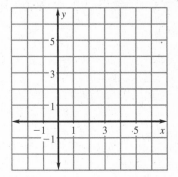

Use the asymptotes and plotted points to draw the branches of the hyperbola.

The domain is _____, and the range is _____.

Example 2   *Graphing a Rational Function*

Graph $y = \dfrac{4x - 2}{2x + 2}$. State the domain and range.

Solution

Draw the asymptotes. Solve $2x + 2 = 0$ for x to find the vertical asymptote _____. The horizontal asymptote is

$y = \dfrac{a}{c} = $ _____ .

Plot two points to the left of the vertical asymptote, such as $(-4, \_\_)$ and $(-2, \_\_)$, and two points to the right, such as $(0, \_\_)$ and $(2, \_\_)$.

Use the asymptotes and plotted points to draw the branches of the hyperbola.

The domain is _____ , and the range is _____ .

✔ *Checkpoint* **Complete the following exercise.**

1. Graph $y = \dfrac{-2}{x + 2} - 1$.

State the domain and range.

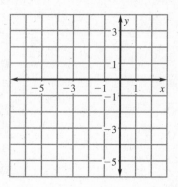

Example 3   *Writing a Rational Model*

You are arranging a dinner at a local restaurant. The cost to rent a dining room is $300. In addition to this one-time charge, the unit cost of each plate is $40.

a. Write a model that gives the average cost per person as a function of the number of people attending.

b. Graph the model and use it to estimate how many people must attend to drop the average cost to $45 per person.

c. Describe what happens to the average cost as the number of people attending increases.

Solution

a. The average cost is the total cost of the dinner divided by the number of people attending.

$$\text{Verbal Model} \quad \boxed{\text{Average cost}} = \frac{\boxed{\text{One-time charges}} + \boxed{\text{Unit cost}} \cdot \boxed{}}{\boxed{}}$$

Labels   Average cost = A   (dollars)

Average cost = A   (dollars)

One-time charges = ____   (dollars)

Unit cost = ____   (dollars)

Number attending = x   (people)

Algebraic Model $A =$ _____

b. The _____ is the vertical asymptote and the line _____ is the horizontal asymptote. The domain is _____ and the range·is _____. When $A = 45$, the value of x is ____. So, you need at least ____ people to attend for the average cost to drop to $45 per person.

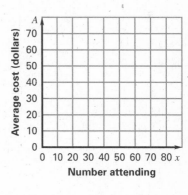

c. As the number of people attending increases, the average cost per person gets closer and closer to ____.

Homework

9.3 Graphing General Rational Functions

Goals • Graph general rational functions.
• Use the graph of a rational function to solve real-life problems

Your Notes

GRAPHS OF RATIONAL FUNCTIONS

Let $p(x)$ and $q(x)$ be polynomials with no common factors other than 1. The graph of the rational function

$$f(x) = \frac{p(x)}{q(x)} = \frac{a_m x^m + a_{m-1} x^{m-1} + \cdots + a_1 x + a_0}{b_n x^n + b_{n-1} x^{n-1} + \cdots + b_1 x + b_0}$$

has the following characteristics.

1. The x-intercepts of the graph of f are the real zeros of _____ .

2. The graph of f has a vertical asymptote at each real zero of _____ .

3. The graph of f has at most one horizontal asymptote.

• If $m < n$, the line _____ is a horizontal asymptote.

• If $m = n$, the line _____ is a horizontal asymptote.

• If $m > n$, the graph has _____ .
The graph's end behavior is the same as the graph of

$$y = \frac{a_m}{b_n} x^{m-n}.$$

Example 1   *Graphing a Rational Function (m < n)*

Graph $y = \dfrac{-12}{x^4 + 4}$. State the domain and range.

Solution

The numerator has no zeros, so there is _____.
The denominator has no real zeros, so there is _____
_____. The degree of the numerator (__) is less than
the degree of the denominator (__), so the line _____ is a
horizontal asymptote.

The graph passes through the
points $(-2,$ _____$),$ $(-1,$ _____$),$
$(0,$ ____$),$ $(1,$ _____$),$ and $(2,$ _____$).$
The domain is _____,
and the range is _____.

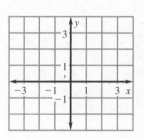

✔ *Checkpoint* **Complete the following exercise.**

1. Graph $y = \dfrac{10}{x^3 + 8}$.

State the domain and range.

Example 2   *Graphing a Rational Function (m = n)*

Graph $y = \dfrac{x^2 - 4}{x^2 - 1}$.

The numerator can be factored as _____ , so the x-intercepts of the graph are _____ . The denominator can be factored as _____ , so the denominator has zeros _____ . This implies that the lines _____ _____ are vertical asymptotes of the graph. The degree of the numerator (__) is equal to the degree of the denominator (__), so the horizontal asymptote is _____ . To draw _____ the graph, plot points between and beyond the vertical asymptotes.

	x	y
To the left of $x = -1$	−4	
	−2	
Between $x = -1$ and $x = 1$	−0.5	
	0	
	0.5	
To the right of $x = 1$	2	
	4	

✔ *Checkpoint* **Complete the following exercise.**

2. Graph $y = \dfrac{-x^3}{x^3 - 1}$.

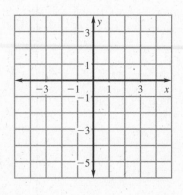

Example 3   **Graphing a Rational Function (m > n)**

Graph $y = \dfrac{x^2 - 5x + 4}{x - 5}$.

The numerator can be factored as _____ , so the x-intercepts of the graph are _____ . The only zero of the denominator is ___ , so the only vertical asymptote is _____ . The degree of the numerator (__) is greater than the degree of the denominator (__), so there is _____ _____ and the end behavior of the graph of f is the same as the end behavior of the graph of _____ .

To draw the graph, plot points to the left and right of the vertical asymptote.

x	y
0	
1	
3	
4	
6	
7	
9	

To the left of x = 5

To the right of x = 5

✔ **Checkpoint** **Complete the following exercise.**

3. Graph $y = \dfrac{x^2 - x - 5}{x - 2}$.

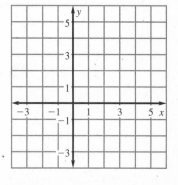

Multiplying and Dividing Rational Expressions

Goals • Multiply and divide rational expressions.
• Model real-life quantities using rational expressions.

Your Notes

VOCABULARY

Simplified form of a rational expression

SIMPLIFYING RATIONAL EXPRESSIONS

Let a, b, and c be nonzero real numbers or variable expressions. Then the following property applies:

$$\frac{a\cancel{c}}{b\cancel{c}} = \underline{\qquad}$$

Divide out common factor c.

Example 1   *Simplifying a Rational Expression*

Simplify: $\dfrac{x^2 - 2x - 3}{x^2 - 9}$

$\dfrac{x^2 - 2x - 3}{x^2 - 9} =$ _____

Factor numerator and denominator.

$=$ _____

Divide out common factor _____ and write simplified form.

✔ **Checkpoint** **Complete the following exercise.**

---

1. Simplify: $\dfrac{x^2 + 2x - 15}{x^2 + 6x + 5}$

Example 2 *Multiplying Rational Expressions*

Multiply: $\dfrac{3x^2 + 6x}{x^2 - 4x} \cdot \dfrac{x - 4}{x^2 + 9x + 14}$

Solution

$\dfrac{3x^2 + 6x}{x^2 - 4x} \cdot \dfrac{x - 4}{x^2 + 9x + 14}$

$=$ _____   **Factor numerators and denominators.**

$=$ _____   **Multiply numerators and denominators.**

$=$ _____   **Divide out common factors and write simplified form.**

Example 3 *Multiplying by a Polynomial*

Multiply: $\dfrac{2x}{x^3 - 1} \cdot (x^2 + x + 1)$

Solution

$\dfrac{2x}{x^3 - 1} \cdot (x^2 + x + 1)$

$= \dfrac{2x}{x^3 - 1} \cdot$ _____   **Write polynomial as rational expression.**

$=$ _____   **Factor and multiply.**

$=$ _____   **Divide out common factor and write simplified form.**

✔ **Checkpoint** Multiply the rational expressions.

2. $\dfrac{x-3}{xy^2} \cdot \dfrac{4x^2y^3}{x^2+x-12}$ 3. $\dfrac{-x}{x^3-8} \cdot (x^2+2x+4)$

Example 4   *Dividing Rational Expressions*

Divide: $\dfrac{x^2+4x+3}{4x^2+12x} \div \dfrac{x+1}{3}$

Solution

$\dfrac{x^2+4x+3}{4x^2+12x} \div \dfrac{x+1}{3}$

$= \dfrac{x^2+4x+3}{4x^2+12x} \cdot \underline{}$ **Multiply by reciprocal.**

$= \underline{}$ **Factor.**

$= \underline{}$ **Divide out common factors and write simplified form.**

✔ **Checkpoint** Divide the rational expressions.

4. $\dfrac{20x^2+x-1}{7x^3+x} \div \dfrac{4x+1}{x}$ 5. $\dfrac{x^3-4x}{2} \div (x^4-16)$

Homework

9.5 Addition, Subtraction, and Complex Fractions

Goals • Add and subtract rational expressions.
• Simplify complex fractions.

Your Notes

VOCABULARY

Complex fraction

Example 1 *Subtracting with Like Denominators*

$$\frac{11}{7x} - \frac{4}{7x} = \frac{\boxed{}}{7x} = \frac{\boxed{}}{7x} = \underline{}$$

Subtract numerators and simplify.

Example 2 *Adding with Unlike Denominators*

Add: $\dfrac{x + 2}{4x} + \dfrac{x}{3x^2 + 9x}$

First find the least common denominator.

Factor the denominators: $4x = \underline{}$

$3x^2 + 9x = \underline{}$

The LCD is $\underline{}$. Use this to rewrite each expression.

$$\frac{x + 2}{4x} + \frac{x}{3x^2 + 9x} = \frac{x + 2}{4x} + \frac{x}{\boxed{}}$$

$$= \frac{(x + 2)\boxed{}}{4x\boxed{}} + \frac{x\boxed{}}{\boxed{}}$$

$$= \underline{}$$

$$= \underline{}$$

Example 3   *Subtracting with Unlike Denominators*

Subtract: $\dfrac{2x}{x^2 - 1} - \dfrac{x + 2}{x^2 + 2x + 1}$

Solution

$\dfrac{2x}{x^2 - 1} - \dfrac{x + 2}{x^2 + 2x + 1}$

$= \dfrac{2x}{\boxed{}} - \dfrac{x + 2}{\boxed{}}$

$= \dfrac{}{}$

$= \dfrac{}{} \qquad = \dfrac{}{}$

✓ **Checkpoint** **Perform the indicated operation.**

1. $\dfrac{2}{3x} + \dfrac{4}{3x}$ 2. $\dfrac{1}{x + 5} - \dfrac{4}{x + 5}$

3. $\dfrac{3}{x^2 - 16} + \dfrac{x}{x^2 + 8x + 16}$ 4. $\dfrac{1}{4x^2} - \dfrac{5x}{2x^3 + 8x^2}$

Example 4 *Simplifying a Complex Fraction*

Simplify: $\dfrac{\dfrac{3}{x+1}}{\dfrac{3}{x+1}-\dfrac{1}{x}}$

Solution

$$\dfrac{\dfrac{3}{x+1}}{\dfrac{3}{x+1}-\dfrac{1}{x}} = \dfrac{\dfrac{3}{x+1}}{\boxed{}}$$

Add fractions in denominator.

$$= \dfrac{3}{x+1} \cdot \underline{}$$

Multiply by reciprocal.

$$= \underline{}$$

Divide out common factor and write in simplified form.

✔ *Checkpoint* **Complete the following exercise.**

5. Simplify: $\dfrac{\dfrac{x-2}{3x+1}}{\dfrac{1}{x}-\dfrac{2}{3x+1}}$

Homework

Solving Rational Equations

Goals • Solve rational equations.
• Use rational equations to solve real-life problems.

Your Notes

VOCABULARY

Cross multiplying

Example 1 *An Equation with One Solution*

Solve: $\dfrac{4}{3} - \dfrac{7}{x} = \dfrac{1}{6}$

$\dfrac{4}{3} - \dfrac{7}{x} = \dfrac{1}{6}$ Write original equation.

$\underline{\quad}\left(\dfrac{4}{3} - \dfrac{7}{x}\right) = \underline{\quad}\left(\dfrac{1}{6}\right)$ Multiply each side by LCD = ___.

_____   Simplify.

_____   Add ___ to each side.

_____   Subtract ___ from each side.

_____   Divide each side by ___.

The solution is ___. Check this in the original equation.

✔ *Checkpoint* **Complete the following exercise.**

---

1. Solve: $\dfrac{7}{2x} - \dfrac{5}{3} = \dfrac{1}{12}$

Example 2 *An Equation with an Extraneous Solution*

Solve: $\dfrac{x + 6}{x + 3} = 2 - \dfrac{5x + 12}{x + 3}$

The least common denominator is _____.

$$\dfrac{x + 6}{x + 3} = 2 - \dfrac{5x + 12}{x + 3}$$

$$\underline{} \cdot \dfrac{x + 6}{x + 3} = \underline{} \cdot 2 - \underline{} \cdot \dfrac{5x + 12}{x + 3}$$

$$\underline{}$$

$$\underline{}$$

$$\underline{}$$

$$\underline{}$$

The solution appears to be ____. After checking it in the original equation, however, you can conclude that ____ is an extraneous solution because it leads to _____.
So, the original equation has _____.

Example 3 *An Equation with Two Solutions*

Solve: $\dfrac{3x - 1}{x - 2} = 2 + \dfrac{12}{(x - 2)(x - 1)}$

The LCD is _____.

$$\dfrac{3x - 1}{x - 2} = 2 + \dfrac{12}{(x - 2)(x - 1)}$$

$$\underline{} = \underline{}$$

$$\underline{} = \underline{}$$

$$\underline{} = 0$$

$$\underline{} = 0$$

$$\underline{} = 0 \quad \text{or} \quad \underline{} = 0$$

$$x = \underline{} \quad \text{or} \quad x = \underline{}$$

The solutions are _____.

✔ *Checkpoint* **Solve the equation.**

2. $\dfrac{3x + 2}{x + 4} = 3 + \dfrac{x - 6}{x + 4}$ 3. $\dfrac{2(x + 3)}{x + 2} = 1 - \dfrac{5}{x^2 - 4}$

Example 4   *Solving an Equation by Cross Multiplying*

Solve: $\dfrac{3x - 2}{x^2 - 3x} = \dfrac{4}{x - 4}$

Solution

$$\dfrac{3x - 2}{x^2 - 3x} = \dfrac{4}{x - 4}$$ Write original equation.

$(3x - 2)\underline{\hspace{2cm}} = 4\underline{\hspace{2cm}}$ Cross multiply.

$\underline{\hspace{3cm}} = \underline{\hspace{2.5cm}}$ Simplify.

$0 = \underline{\hspace{2.5cm}}$ Write in standard form.

$0 = \underline{\hspace{2.5cm}}$ Factor.

$x = \underline{\hspace{1cm}}$ or $x = \underline{\hspace{0.7cm}}$ Zero product property

The solutions are $\underline{\hspace{2cm}}$. Check these in the original equation.

✔ *Checkpoint* **Complete the following exercise.**

Homework

4. Solve: $\dfrac{2x + 8}{x - 2} = \dfrac{x + 4}{x + 1}$

10.1 The Distance and Midpoint Formulas

Goals • Use the distance and midpoint formulas.
• Use the distance and midpoint formulas in real-life situations.

Your Notes

> **THE DISTANCE FORMULA**
>
> The distance d between the points (x_1, y_1) and (x_2, y_2) is as follows: $d = \sqrt{(x_2 - x_1)^2 + (y_2 - y_1)^2}$

Example 1 Finding the Distance Between Two Points

Find the distance between $(4, -5)$ and $(-2, 7)$.

Let $(x_1, y_1) = (4, -5)$ and $(x_2, y_2) = (-2, 7)$.

$d = \sqrt{(x_2 - x_1)^2 + (y_2 - y_1)^2}$ **Use distance formula.**

$= $ _____   **Substitute.**

$= $ _____   **Simplify.**

$= $ _____ $\approx$ _____   **Use a calculator.**

Example 2 Classifying a Triangle Using the Distance Formula

Classify $\triangle ABC$ as *scalene*, *isosceles*, or *equilateral*.

Solution

$AB = \sqrt{\rule{3cm}{0pt}} = \sqrt{\rule{0.6cm}{0pt}}$

$BC = \sqrt{\rule{3cm}{0pt}} = \sqrt{\rule{0.6cm}{0pt}}$

$AC = \sqrt{\rule{3cm}{0pt}} = \sqrt{\rule{0.6cm}{0pt}}$

Triangle ABC is _____.

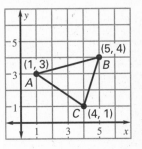

✓ *Checkpoint* **Complete the following exercises.**

1. Find the distance between the points (0, 2) and (−4, 5).

---

2. The vertices of a triangle are (1, 0), (1, 6), and (3, 3). Classify the triangle as *scalene*, *isosceles*, or *equilateral*.

THE MIDPOINT FORMULA

The midpoint of the line segment joining $A(x_1, y_1)$ and $B(x_2, y_2)$ is as follows:

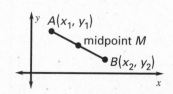

$$M\left(\frac{x_1 + x_2}{2}, \frac{y_1 + y_2}{2}\right)$$

Each coordinate of M is the _____ of the corresponding coordinates A and B.

Example 3   *Finding the Midpoint of a Segment*

Find the midpoint of the line segment joining (1, −4) and (−3, 5).

Solution

Let $(x_1, y_1) = (1, -4)$ and

$(x_2, y_2) = (-3, 5)$.

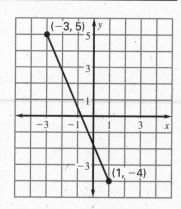

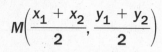

= _____ = _____

Example 4 *Finding a Perpendicular Bisector*

Write an equation for the perpendicular bisector of the line segment joining $A(-2, 3)$ and $B(2, 5)$.

Solution

First find the midpoint of the line segment:

$$\left(\frac{x_1 + x_2}{2}, \frac{y_1 + y_2}{2}\right) = \underline{\hspace{3cm}} = \underline{\hspace{1.5cm}}$$

Then find the slope of $\overline{AB}$:

$$m = \frac{y_2 - y_1}{x_2 - x_1} = \underline{\hspace{2cm}} \quad \underline{\hspace{1cm}} = \underline{\hspace{1cm}}$$

The slope of the perpendicular bisector is the $\underline{\hspace{3cm}}$

$\underline{\hspace{3cm}}$ of $\underline{\hspace{1cm}}$, or $m_\perp = \underline{\hspace{1cm}}$.

Because you know the slope of the perpendicular bisector and a point that the bisector passes through, you can use the $\underline{\hspace{3cm}}$ form to write its equation.

$$y - \underline{\hspace{0.5cm}} = \underline{\hspace{0.5cm}}(x - \underline{\hspace{0.5cm}})$$

$$y = \underline{\hspace{2cm}}$$

✔ **Checkpoint** **Complete the following exercises.**

3. Find the midpoint of the line segment joining $(-2, -1)$ and $(2, 3)$.

4. Write an equation for the perpendicular bisector of the line segment joining $A(-1, -3)$ and $B(3, 7)$.

10.2 Parabolas

Goals • Graph and write equations of parabolas.
• Use parabolas to solve real-life problems.

Your Notes

VOCABULARY

Focus

Directrix

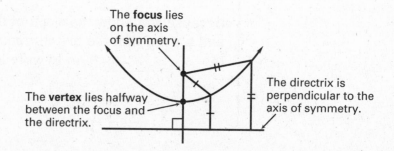

The **focus** lies on the axis of symmetry.

The **vertex** lies halfway between the focus and the directrix.

The directrix is perpendicular to the axis of symmetry.

STANDARD EQUATION OF A PARABOLA (VERTEX AT ORIGIN)

The **standard form of the equation of a parabola** with vertex at (0, 0) is as follows.

Equation	Focus	Directrix	Axis of Symmetry
$x^2 = 4py$	$(0, p)$	$y = -p$	Vertical ($x = 0$)
$y^2 = 4px$	$(p, 0)$	$x = -p$	Horizontal ($y = 0$)

Your Notes

Example 1 *Graphing an Equation of a Parabola*

Identify the focus and directrix of the parabola given by $x = 4y^2$. Draw the parabola.

$x = 4y^2$ Write original equation.

_____   Divide each side by ___ .

Because $4p =$ ___ , you know that $p =$ ___ . The focus is

$(p, 0) = \left(\underline{\quad}, 0 \right)$ and the directrix is $x = -p =$ ___ .

To draw the parabola, make a table of values and plot points. Because p ___ 0, the parabola opens to the _____ . So, only _____ x-values should be chosen.

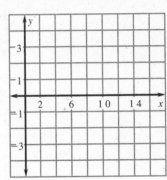

x	0	1	4	16
y				

✓ **Checkpoint** Complete the following exercise.

1. Identify the focus and directrix of the parabola given by $y = x^2$. Draw the parabola.

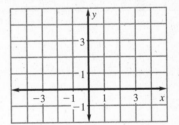

Example 2 *Writing an Equation of a Parabola*

Write an equation of the parabola.

Solution

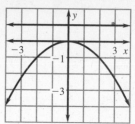

The graph shows that the vertex is _____ and the directrix is

__ = −p = __ . Substitute ____

for p in the standard equation for a parabola with a _____ axis of symmetry.

_____ **Standard form,** _____ **axis of symmetry**

_____ **Substitute for p.**

_____ **Simplify.**

✔ *Checkpoint* **Complete the following exercise.**

2. Write an equation of the parabola shown.

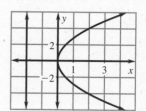

Homework

10.3 Circles

• Graph and write equations of circles.
• Use circles to solve real-life problems.

Your Notes

VOCABULARY

Circle

Center

Radius

**STANDARD EQUATION OF A CIRCLE
(CENTER AT ORIGIN)**

The **standard form of the equation of a circle** with center at
(0, 0) and radius *r* is as follows:

$$x^2 + y^2 = r^2$$

Example 1 *Graphing an Equation of a Circle*

Draw the circle given by $y^2 = 4 - x^2$.

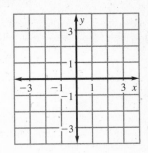

Solution

Write the equation in standard form.

$$y^2 = 4 - x^2 \quad \text{Original equation}$$

_____   Add ____ to
                 each side.

In this form you can see that the graph is a circle whose
center is the origin and whose radius is $r =$ ____ = __.
Plot several points that are __ units from the origin.
The points (__, 2), (2, __), (0, ____), and (____, 0) are
most convenient.

Draw a circle that passes through the four points.

Example 2 *Writing an Equation of a Circle*

The point $(3, -4)$ is on a circle whose center is the origin. Write the standard form of the equation of the circle.

Solution

Because the point $(3, -4)$ is on the circle, the radius of the circle must be the distance between the center and the point $(3, -4)$.

$r = \sqrt{\underline{}^2 + \underline{}^2}$ Use the distance formula.

$= \sqrt{\underline{}}$ Simplify.

$= \sqrt{\underline{}} = \underline{}$

Knowing that the radius is ___, you can use the standard form to find an equation of the circle.

$x^2 + y^2 = r^2$ **Standard form**

$x^2 + y^2 = \underline{}^2$ **Substitute for r.**

$x^2 + y^2 = \underline{}$ **Simplify.**

Example 3 *Finding a Tangent Line*

Write an equation of the line that is tangent to the circle $x^2 + y^2 = 5$ at $(-1, 2)$.

Solution

The slope of the radius through the point $(-1, 2)$ is:

$m = \dfrac{}{} = \dfrac{}{}$

Because the tangent line at $(-1, 2)$ is perpendicular to this radius, its slope must be the negative reciprocal of ____, or

$\dfrac{}{}$. So, an equation of the tangent line is as follows.

$y - \underline{} = \underline{}(x - \underline{})$ **Point-slope form**

$\dfrac{}{} = \dfrac{}{}$ **Distributive property**

$y = \dfrac{}{}$ **Add ___ to each side.**

Example 4 **Using a Circular Model**

The beam of a lighthouse can be seen for up to 20 miles. You are on a ship that is 19 miles west and 6 miles south of the lighthouse. Can you see the lighthouse beam?

$x^2 + y^2 < 20^2$ Inequality that describes the region lit

_____ $\overset{?}{<} 20^2$ Substitute for x and y.

_____ $\overset{?}{<}$ ____   Simplify.

_____   The inequality is ____.

You ____ see the lighthouse beam from the ship.

✔ **Checkpoint** Complete the following exercises.

1. Draw the circle given by $x^2 = 16 - y^2$.

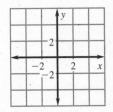

2. The point $(-2, 2)$ is on a circle whose center is the origin. Write the standard form of the equation of the circle.

3. Write an equation of the tangent line to the circle $x^2 + y^2 = 10$ at $(3, 1)$.

Homework

4. The beam of a lighthouse can be seen for up to 20 miles. You are on a ship that is 13 miles west and 16 miles north of the lighthouse. Can you see the lighthouse beam?

10.4 Ellipses

Goals • Graph and write equations of ellipses.
• Use ellipses in real-life situations.

Your Notes

VOCABULARY

Ellipse

Foci

Vertices

Major axis

Center

Co-vertices

Minor axis

CHARACTERISTICS OF AN ELLIPSE (CENTER AT THE ORIGIN)

The **standard form of the equation of an ellipse** with center at $(0, 0)$ and major and minor axes of lengths $2a$ and $2b$, where $a > b > 0$, is as follows.

Equation	Major Axis	Vertices	Co-vertices
$\dfrac{x^2}{a^2} + \dfrac{y^2}{b^2} = 1$	Horizontal	$(\pm a, 0)$	$(0, \pm b)$
$\dfrac{x^2}{b^2} + \dfrac{y^2}{a^2} = 1$	Vertical	$(0, \pm a)$	$(\pm b, 0)$

The foci of the ellipse lie on the major axis, c units from the center where $c^2 = a^2 - b^2$.

Example 1 *Graphing an Equation of an Ellipse*

Draw the ellipse given by $x^2 + 4y^2 = 36$. Identify the foci.

First rewrite the equation in standard form.

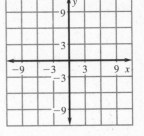

$$\underline{\hspace{2cm}} = 1 \quad \text{Standard form}$$

Because the denominator of the x^2-term is _____ than that of the y^2-term, the major axis is _____. So $a =$ __ and $b =$ __. Plot the vertices and co-vertices. Then draw the ellipse that passes through these four points.

The foci are $(c, 0)$ and $(-c, 0)$. To find the value of c, use the equation $c^2 = a^2 - b^2$.

$$c^2 = \underline{\hspace{0.5cm}}^2 - \underline{\hspace{0.5cm}}^2 = \underline{\hspace{1.5cm}} = \underline{\hspace{1cm}}$$

$$c = \underline{\hspace{1cm}} = \underline{\hspace{1cm}}$$

The foci are at _____ and _____.

Example 2 *Writing Equations of Ellipses*

Write an equation of the ellipse with the given characteristics and center at $(0, 0)$.

a. Vertex: $(-3, 0)$
   Co-vertex: $(0, 1)$

b. Vertex: $(0, 5)$
   Focus: $(0, -2)$

Solution

a. Because the vertex is on the __-axis and the co-vertex is on the __-axis, the major axis is _____ with $a =$ __ and $b =$ __.

An equation is _____.

b. Because the vertex and focus are points on a _____ line, the major axis is _____ with $a =$ __ and $c =$ __. To find b, use the equation $c^2 = a^2 - b^2$.

$$\underline{\hspace{0.5cm}}^2 = \underline{\hspace{0.5cm}}^2 - b^2 \implies b^2 = \underline{\hspace{1.5cm}} = \underline{\hspace{0.5cm}} \implies b = \underline{\hspace{1cm}}$$

An equation is _____.

✅ *Checkpoint* **Complete the following exercise.**

1. Draw the ellipse given by $25x^2 + 4y^2 = 100$. Identify the foci.

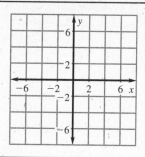

Write an equation of the ellipse with the given characteristics and center at (0, 0).

2. Vertex: $(-9, 0)$
Focus: $(5, 0)$

3. Vertex: $(0, 12)$
Co-vertex: $(4, 0)$

Example 3   *Writing an Equation of an Ellipse*

A putting surface at a golf course is the shape of an ellipse. It is 20 yards long and 14 yards wide. Write the equation of the putting surface.

Solution

The major axis is _____ with $a = \underline{\quad} = \underline{\quad}$ and

$b = \underline{\quad} = \underline{\quad}$. An equation is _____ .

✅ *Checkpoint* **Complete the following exercise.**

4. The area of an ellipse is given by $A = \pi ab$. Find the area of the putting surface in Example 3.

10.5 Hyperbolas

Goals • Graph and write equations of hyperbolas.
• Use hyperbolas to solve real-life problems.

Your Notes

VOCABULARY

Hyperbola

Foci

Vertices

Transverse axis

Center

CHARACTERISTICS OF A HYPERBOLA
(CENTER AT ORIGIN)

The **standard form of the equation of a hyperbola** with center at
(0, 0) is as follows.

Equation	Transverse Axis	Asymptotes	Vertices
$\dfrac{x^2}{a^2} - \dfrac{y^2}{b^2} = 1$	Horizontal	$y = \pm\dfrac{b}{a}x$	$(\pm a, 0)$
$\dfrac{y^2}{a^2} - \dfrac{x^2}{b^2} = 1$	Vertical	$y = \pm\dfrac{a}{b}x$	$(0, \pm a)$

The foci of the hyperbola lie on the transverse axis, c units
from the center where $c^2 = a^2 + b^2$.

Example 1   *Graphing an Equation of a Hyperbola*

Draw the hyperbola given by $9x^2 - 16y^2 = 144$.

First rewrite the equation in standard form.

$9x^2 - 16y^2 = 144$ **Write original equation.**

$$\underline{} = 1$$ **Standard form**

Note from the equation that $a^2 = \underline{}$ and $b^2 = \underline{}$, so $a = \underline{}$ and $b = \underline{}$. Because the x^2-term is $\underline{}$, the transverse axis is $\underline{}$ and the vertices are at $\underline{}$ and $\underline{}$.

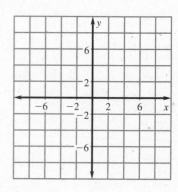

Example 2   *Writing an Equation of a Hyperbola*

Write an equation of the hyperbola with foci at $(-2, 0)$ and $(2, 0)$ and vertices at $(-1, 0)$ and $(1, 0)$.

Solution

The transverse axis is $\underline{}$ because the foci and vertices lie on the $\underline{}$-axis. Because the foci are each $\underline{}$ units from the center, $c = \underline{}$. Similarly, because the vertices are each $\underline{}$ unit from the center, $a = \underline{}$.

You can use these values of a and c to find b.

$b^2 = c^2 - a^2$

$b^2 = \underline{}^2 - \underline{}^2 = \underline{} = \underline{}$

$b = \underline{}$

Because the transverse axis is $\underline{}$, the standard form of the equation is as follows.

$$\underline{}$$ **Substitute for a and for b.**

$$\underline{}$$ **Simplify.**

✓ *Checkpoint* **Complete the following exercises.**

1. Draw the hyperbola given by
$9y^2 - 25x^2 = 225$.

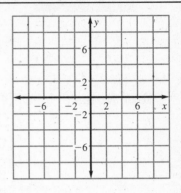

2. Write an equation of the hyperbola with foci at $(-8, 0)$ and $(8, 0)$ and vertices at $(-6, 0)$ and $(6, 0)$.

Example 3 *Using a Real-Life Hyperbola*

The diagram shows the hyperbolic cross section of a vase. Write an equation that models the curved sides of the vase.

Solution

From the diagram you can see that the transverse axis is _____ and $a =$ __. So the equation has this form:

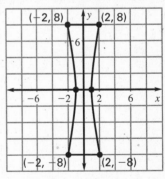

_____

Because the hyperbola passes through the point $(2, 8)$, you can substitute $x =$ __ and $y =$ __ into the equation and solve for b.

An equation of the hyperbola is _____ .

_____

Homework

Graphing and Classifying Conics

Goals • Write and graph equations of conics.
• Classify a conic using its equation.

Your Notes

VOCABULARY

Conic section

General second-degree equation

Discriminant

STANDARD FORM OF EQUATIONS OF TRANSLATED CONICS

In the following equations the point (h, k) is the vertex of the parabola and the center of the other conics.

Circle: $(x - h)^2 + (y - k)^2 = r^2$

Parabola: Horizontal axis

$(y - k)^2 = 4p(x - h)$

Vertical axis

$(x - h)^2 = 4p(y - k)$

Ellipse: Horizontal axis

$\dfrac{(x - h)^2}{a^2} + \dfrac{(y - k)^2}{b^2} = 1$

Vertical axis

$\dfrac{(x - h)^2}{b^2} + \dfrac{(y - k)^2}{a^2} = 1$

Hyperbola: Horizontal axis

$\dfrac{(x - h)^2}{a^2} - \dfrac{(y - k)^2}{b^2} = 1$

Vertical axis

$\dfrac{(y - k)^2}{a^2} - \dfrac{(x - h)^2}{b^2} = 1$

Example 1   *Writing an Equation of a Translated Parabola*

Write an equation of the parabola whose vertex is at $(1, -3)$ and whose focus is at $(1, -4)$.

Solution

Because the parabola opens _____, it has the form $(x - h)^2 = 4p(y - k)$, where p ___ 0.

The vertex is at $(1, -3)$, so $h =$ __ and $k =$ ____.

The distance between the vertex $(1, -3)$ and the focus $(1, -4)$ is $|p| = \sqrt{\underline{\hspace{4cm}}} =$ __

So $p =$ __ or $p =$ ____. Because p __ 0, $p =$ ____.

The standard form of the equation is _____.

Example 2   *Graphing the Equation of a Translated Circle*

Graph $(x + 1)^2 + (y + 2)^2 = 4$.

Solution

Compare the given equation to the standard form of the equation of a circle: $(x - h)^2 + (y - k)^2 = r^2$.

You can see that the graph is a circle with center at $(h, k) =$ _____ and radius $r =$ __.

Plot the center and several points that are each __ units from the center. Use points that are directly to the right and left of the center and directly above and below the center.

_____ = _____

_____ = _____

_____ = _____

_____ = _____

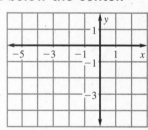

Draw a circle through the points.

✔ *Checkpoint* **Complete the following exercises.**

1. Write an equation of the parabola whose vertex is at (3, 5) and whose focus is at (5, 5).

_____

2. Graph $(x + 3)^2 + (y - 2)^2 = 9$.

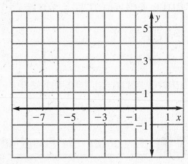

Example 3 *Writing an Equation of a Translated Ellipse*

Write an equation of the ellipse with foci at (−1, 0) and (3, 0) and vertices at (−3, 0) and (5, 0).

The ellipse has a _____ major axis, so its equation is of this form: $\dfrac{(x - h)^2}{a^2} + \dfrac{(y - k)^2}{b^2} = 1$.

The center is halfway between the vertices.

$(h, k) =$ _____ $=$ _____

The value of *a* is the distance between the vertex and the center. $a = \sqrt{\rule{3cm}{0.4pt}} = \sqrt{\rule{1.5cm}{0.4pt}} = \rule{0.8cm}{0.4pt}$

The value of *c* is the distance between the focus and the center. $c = \sqrt{\rule{3cm}{0.4pt}} = \sqrt{\rule{1.5cm}{0.4pt}} = \rule{0.8cm}{0.4pt}$

Substitute the values of *a* and *c* into the equation $b^2 = a^2 - c^2$.

$b^2 =$ _____ $=$ _____

The standard form of the equation is _____.

✓ *Checkpoint* **Complete the following exercise.**

3. Write an equation of the ellipse with foci at $(1, -1)$ and $(-5, -1)$ and vertices at $(4, -1)$ and $(-8, -1)$.

Example 4   *Graphing the Equation of a Translated Hyperbola*

Graph $\dfrac{(x-1)^2}{9} - (y-1)^2 = 1.$

The x^2-term is _____,
so the transverse axis is
_____. Because $a^2 =$ __
and $b^2 =$ __, you know that
$a =$ __ and $b =$ __.

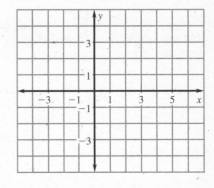

Plot the center at
$(h, k) =$ _____. Plot the
vertices __ units to the right
and left of the center at
_____ and _____.

Draw a rectangle that is centered at _____ and is $2a =$ __ units wide and $2b =$ __ units high.

Draw the asymptotes through the corners of the rectangle.

Draw the hyperbola so that it passes through the vertices and approaches the asymptotes.

CLASSIFYING CONICS

If the graph of $Ax^2 + Bxy + Cy^2 + Dx + Ey + F = 0$ is a conic, then the type of conic can be determined as follows.

Discriminant	Type of Conic
$B^2 - 4AC$ ___ 0, $B = 0$, and $A = C$	Circle
$B^2 - 4AC$ ___ 0 and either $B \neq 0$ or $A \neq 0$	Ellipse
$B^2 - 4AC$ ___ 0	Parabola
$B^2 - 4AC$ ___ 0	Hyperbola

If B ___ 0, each axis of the conic is horizontal or vertical.
If B ___ 0, the axes are neither horizontal nor vertical.

Example 5 *Classifying a Conic*

Classify the conic given by $x^2 + y^2 - 2x + 4y - 11 = 0$.

Because $A = C =$ ___ and $B =$ ___, the value of the discriminant is as follows: $B^2 - 4AC =$ _____ $=$ ___

Because $B^2 - 4AC$ ___ 0, the graph is a _____.

✓ *Checkpoint* **Complete the following exercises.**

4. Graph $\dfrac{(y - 2)^2}{4} - \dfrac{(x - 2)^2}{4} = 1$.

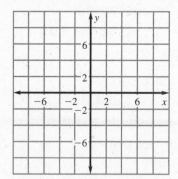

---

5. Classify the conic given by $y^2 - 18x + 84 = 0$.

10.7 Solving Quadratic Systems

Goals • Solve systems of quadratic equations.
       • Use quadratic systems to solve real-life problems.

Your Notes

Example 1	*Finding Points of Intersection*

Find the points of intersection of the graphs of $x^2 + y^2 = 5$ and $y = 2x$.

To find the points of intersection, substitute ____ for y in the equation of the circle.

$$x^2 + y^2 = 5 \qquad \text{Equation of circle}$$
$$x^2 + (\underline{\quad})^2 = 5 \qquad \text{Substitute for } y.$$
$$x^2 + \underline{\quad} = 5 \qquad \text{Expand the power.}$$
$$\underline{\quad} = 5 \qquad \text{Combine like terms.}$$
$$\underline{\quad} = \underline{\quad} \qquad \text{Divide by } \underline{\ }.$$
$$x = \underline{\quad} \qquad \text{Take square root of each side.}$$

To find the y-coordinates, substitute $x = \underline{\ }$ and $x = \underline{\quad}$ into the linear equation and solve for y.

The points of intersection are _____ and _____.

✔ **Checkpoint** Complete the following exercise.

1. Find the points of intersection of the graphs of $2x^2 + y^2 = 18$ and $y = -x + 3$.

Example 2 | *Solving a System by Substitution*

Find the points of intersection of the graphs in the system.

$$3x^2 - 3y^2 = 0 \quad \text{Equation 1}$$
$$3y^2 + x = 0 \quad \text{Equation 2}$$

Solution

Because Equation 2 has no x^2-term, solve that equation for x.

$$3y^2 + x = 0 \qquad\longrightarrow\qquad x = \underline{\hspace{1cm}}$$

Next, substitute _____ for x in Equation 1 and solve for y.

$$3(\underline{\hspace{1cm}})^2 - 3y^2 = 0 \qquad \text{Substitute for } x.$$
$$\underline{\hspace{1cm}} - 3y^2 = 0 \qquad \text{Expand the power.}$$
$$\underline{\hspace{2cm}} = 0 \qquad \text{Factor common monomial.}$$
$$\underline{\hspace{3cm}} = 0 \qquad \text{Difference of squares}$$
$$y = \underline{\hspace{0.5cm}}, y = \underline{\hspace{0.5cm}}, y = \underline{\hspace{0.5cm}} \qquad \text{Zero product property}$$

The graphs intersect at _____, _____, and _____.

Example 3 | *Solving a System by Linear Combination*

Find the points of intersection of the graphs in the system.

$$x^2 + y^2 - 20x + 64 = 0 \quad \text{Equation 1}$$
$$x^2 - y^2 - 16 = 0 \quad \text{Equation 2}$$

Solution

$$x^2 + y^2 - 20x + 64 = 0$$
$$\underline{x^2 - y^2 \qquad\qquad - 16 = 0}$$

$$\underline{\hspace{3cm}} \qquad \text{Add.}$$
$$\underline{\hspace{3cm}} \qquad \text{Factor.}$$
$$x = \underline{\hspace{0.5cm}} \text{ or } x = \underline{\hspace{0.5cm}} \qquad \text{Zero product property}$$

The graphs intersect at _____, _____, and _____.

✅ **Checkpoint** Complete the following exercise.

2. Find the points of intersection of the graphs.

$$2x^2 + 2y^2 - 26 = 0$$
$$-x^2 + y + 7 = 0$$

Example 4 *Solving a System of Quadratic Models*

A town is having a treasure hunt that begins at the courthouse. The contestants receive the following clues.

Clue 1: The treasure is 2 miles from the courthouse.

Clue 2: The treasure is 5 miles from the mall. (The mall is 1 mile west and 4 miles south of the courthouse.)

Clue 3: The treasure is 2 miles from the police station. (The police station is 4 miles east of the courthouse.)

Let each unit represent 1 mile. If the courthouse is at (0, 0) then the mall is at _____ and the police station is at _____. Write the equation of each circle.

Clue 1: _____

Clue 2: _____

Clue 3: _____

Subtract the equation for Clue 1 from the equation for Clue 2.

Subtract the equation for Clue 1 from the equation for Clue 3.

$x = \underline{}$

Homework

Use $x =$ ___ and Clue ___ to find y. The treasure is _____ _____ of the courthouse.

An Introduction to Sequences and Series

Goals • Use and write sequences.
• Use summation notation.

Your Notes

VOCABULARY

Terms

Sequence

Finite sequence

Infinite sequence

Series

Summation (or sigma) notation

Example 1 *Writing Terms of Sequences*

Write the first four terms of the sequence $g(n) = (-1)^{n+1}$.

$g(1) = $ _____ $= $ ___ $g(2) = $ _____ $= $ ___

$g(3) = $ _____ $= $ ___ $g(4) = $ _____ $= $ ___

✔ *Checkpoint* Complete the following exercise.

---

1. Write the first six terms of the sequence $f(n) = n(n + 3)$.

Example 2   *Writing Rules for Sequences*

For the sequence 1, 4, 9, 16,..., describe the pattern, write the next term, and write a rule for the nth term.

You can write the terms as $\underline{}^2$, $\underline{}^2$, $\underline{}^2$, $\underline{}^2$,....

The next term is $a_5 = \underline{} = \underline{}$. A rule for the nth term is $a_n = \underline{}$.

✔ **Checkpoint** Complete the following exercise.

2. For the sequence $-1, 2, -3, 4,\ldots$, describe the pattern, write the next term, and write a rule for the nth term.

Example 3   *Writing Series with Summation Notation*

Write each series with summation notation.

a. $1 + 3 + 5 + \cdots + 51$

b. $1 + \dfrac{1}{4} + \dfrac{1}{9} + \dfrac{1}{16} + \dfrac{1}{25} + \cdots$

Solution

a. Notice that the first term is _____, the second term is _____, the third is _____, and the last term is _____. So, the terms of the series can be written as:

$a_i = \underline{}$ where $i = 1, 2, 3, \ldots, \underline{}$.

The summation notation for the series is _____.

b. Notice that each denominator is a _____. So, the terms of the series can be written as:

$a_i = \dfrac{}{}$ where $i = 1, 2, 3, \ldots$.

The summation notation for the series is _____.

✓ *Checkpoint* Write each series with summation notation.

3. 9, 18, 27,..., 90   **4.** −3, −6, −9, −12,...

Example 4   *Using Summation Notation*

Find the sum of the series.

$$\sum_{k=1}^{3} 2k + 2 = (2(\_\_) + 2) + (2(\_\_) + 2) + (2(\_\_) + 2)$$

$$= \underline{\hspace{2cm}} = \underline{\hspace{1cm}}$$

✓ *Checkpoint* Complete the following exercise.

5. Find the sum of the series $\sum_{i=1}^{6} (i + 1)^2$.

FORMULAS FOR SPECIAL SERIES

1. $\sum_{i=1}^{n} 1 = n$ **2.** $\sum_{i=1}^{n} i = \dfrac{n(n + 1)}{2}$

3. $\sum_{i=1}^{n} i^2 = \dfrac{n(n + 1)(2n + 1)}{6}$

Homework

Example 5   *Using a Formula for a Sum*

Use the formulas for special series to find the sum of $\sum_{i=1}^{150} i$.

$$\sum_{i=1}^{150} i = \underline{\hspace{3cm}} = \underline{\hspace{3cm}} = \underline{\hspace{1.5cm}}$$

11.2 Arithmetic Sequences and Series

Goals • Use arithmetic sequences and series.
• Use arithmetic sequences and series in real life.

Your Notes

VOCABULARY

Arithmetic sequences

Common difference

Arithmetic series

Example 1 *Identifying Arithmetic Sequences*

Decide whether the sequence $-4, -1, 2, 5, \ldots$ is arithmetic.

Solution

$a_2 - a_1 = $ _____

$a_3 - a_2 = $ _____

$a_4 - a_3 = $ _____

The differences _____ constant, so the sequence _____ arithmetic.

RULE FOR AN ARITHMETIC SEQUENCE

The nth term of an arithmetic sequence with first term a_1 and common difference d is given by:

$$a_n = a_1 + (n - 1)d$$

Example 2   *Writing a Rule for the nth Term*

Write a rule for the *n*th term of the sequence 49, 38, 27, 16, 5, …. Then find a_{20}.

The sequence is arithmetic with first term $a_1 = $ ___ and common difference $d = $ _____ $= $ ____.

$$a_n = a_1 + (n - 1)d \qquad \text{Write general rule.}$$
$$= \underline{\quad} + (n - 1)\underline{\quad\quad} \qquad \text{Substitute for } a_1 \text{ and } d.$$
$$= \underline{\quad\quad\quad} \qquad \text{Simplify.}$$

The 20th term is $a_{20} = $ _____ $= $ _____.

✓ *Checkpoint* **Complete the following exercise.**

1. Write a rule for the *n*th term of the sequence −4, 3, 10, 17, 24,…. Then find a_{24}.

Example 3   *Finding the nth Term*

One term of an arithmetic sequence is $a_7 = 5$. The common difference is $d = -7$. Write a rule for the *n*th term.

Begin by finding the first term as follows.

$$a_n = a_1 + (n - 1)d \qquad \text{Write rule for } n\text{th term.}$$
$$a_7 = a_1 + (\underline{\;} - 1)d \qquad \text{Substitute } \underline{\;} \text{ for } n.$$
$$\underline{\;} = a_1 + (\underline{\;} - 1)(\underline{\quad}) \qquad \text{Substitute for } a_7 \text{ and } d.$$
$$\underline{\quad} = a_1 \qquad \text{Solve for } a_1.$$

So, a rule for the *n*th term is:

$$a_n = a_1 + (n - 1)d \qquad \text{Write a general rule.}$$
$$= \underline{\quad} + (n - 1)(\underline{\quad}) \qquad \text{Substitute for } a_1 \text{ and } d.$$
$$= \underline{\quad\quad\quad} \qquad \text{Simplify.}$$

Your Notes

Example 4 Finding the nth Term Given Two Terms

Two terms of an arithmetic sequence are $a_7 = 20$ and $a_{23} = 52$. Find (a) a rule for the nth term and (b) the value of n for which $a_n = 44$.

Solution

a. **Write** a system of equations using $a_n = a_1 + (n-1)d$ and substituting 23 for n and then 7 for n.

$$a_{23} = a_1 + (23-1)d \implies \underline{\quad} = a_1 + \underline{\quad}d$$
$$a_7 = a_1 + (7-1)d \implies \underline{\quad} = a_1 + \underline{\quad}d$$

Solve the system.

$\underline{\quad} = \underline{\quad}d$ Subtract equations.

$\underline{\quad} = d$ Solve for d.

$\underline{\quad} = a_1 + \underline{\quad}(\underline{\quad})$ Substitute for d.

$\underline{\quad} = a_1$ Solve for a_1.

Find a rule for a_n.

$a_n = a_1 + (n-1)d$ Write general rule.

$a_n = \underline{\quad} + (n-1)\underline{\quad}$ Substitute for a_1 and d.

$a_n = \underline{\quad}$ Simplify.

b. $a_n = \underline{\quad}$ Use the rule for a_n from part (a).

$\underline{\quad} = \underline{\quad}$ Substitute for a_n.

$\underline{\quad} = n$ Solve for n.

THE SUM OF A FINITE ARITHMETIC SERIES

The sum of the first n terms of an arithmetic series is:

$$S_n = n\left(\frac{a_1 + a_n}{2}\right)$$

In words, _____

_____ .

Example 5 **Finding a Sum**

Consider the arithmetic series $3 + 8 + 13 + 18 + 23 + \dots$. Find (a) the sum of the first 40 terms and (b) n such that $S_n = 570$.

a. To begin, notice that $a_1 = \underline{}$ and $d = \underline{}$. So, a formula for the nth term is:

$$a_n = \underline{} + (n - 1)\underline{} = \underline{}$$

The 40th term is $a_{40} = \underline{} = \underline{}$. So,

$$S_{40} = \underline{} = \underline{}$$

b.

$$\underline{} = \underline{} \qquad \text{Use rule for } S_n.$$

$$\underline{} = \underline{} \qquad \text{Multiply each side by 2.}$$

$$\underline{} = 0 \qquad \text{Write in standard form.}$$

$$\underline{} = 0 \qquad \text{Factor.}$$

$$n = \underline{} \qquad \text{Choose positive solution.}$$

✔ **Checkpoint** **Complete the following exercises.**

2. One term of an arithmetic sequence is $a_9 = 45$. The common difference is $d = -3$. Write the rule for the nth term.

3. Two terms of an arithmetic sequence are $a_5 = 0$ and $a_{13} = 32$. Find (a) a rule for the nth term and (b) the value of n for which $a_n = 12$.

Homework

4. Consider the arithmetic series $-16, -9, -2, 5, 12, \dots$. Find (a) the sum of the first 20 terms and (b) n such that $S_n = 338$.

11.3 Geometric Sequences and Series

Goals • Use geometric sequences and series.
• Use geometric sequences and series in real life.

Your Notes

VOCABULARY

Geometric sequence

Common ratio

Geometric series

Example 1 *Identifying Geometric Sequences*

Decide whether the sequence 625, 125, 25, 5, 1,... is geometric.

Solution

To decide whether a sequence is geometric, find the ratios of consecutive terms.

$$\frac{a_2}{a_1} = \underline{\hspace{1cm}} = \underline{\hspace{1cm}} \qquad \frac{a_3}{a_2} = \underline{\hspace{1cm}} = \underline{\hspace{1cm}}$$

$$\frac{a_4}{a_3} = \underline{\hspace{1cm}} = \underline{\hspace{1cm}} \qquad \frac{a_5}{a_4} = \underline{\hspace{1cm}}$$

The ratios are _____, so the sequence _____ geometric.

RULE FOR A GEOMETRIC SEQUENCE

The nth term of a geometric sequence with first term a_1 and common ratio r is given by:

$$a_n = a_1 r^{n-1}$$

Example 2   *Writing a Rule for the nth Term*

Write a rule for the *n*th term of the sequence 81, 108, 144, 192, 256,.... Then find a_{11}.

Solution

The sequence is geometric with first term $a_1 = $ ___ and

common ratio $r = $ _____ . So, a rule for the *n*th term is:

$$a_n = a_1 r^{n-1}$$ Write general rule.

$$= \underline{\hspace{2cm}}$$ Substitute for a_1 and r.

The 11th term is $a_{11} = \underline{\hspace{2cm}} = \underline{\hspace{2cm}}$.

✔ **Checkpoint** Complete the following exercise.

1. Write a rule for the *n*th term of the sequence 5, 10, 20, 40,.... Then find a_{25}.

Example 3   *Finding the nth Term*

One term of a geometric sequence is $a_2 = 6$. The common ratio is $r = 3$. Write a rule for the *n*th term.

Begin by finding the first term as follows.

$$a_n = a_1 r^{n-1}$$ Write general rule.

$$a_2 = a_1 r^{\underline{\hspace{0.5cm}} - 1}$$ Substitute for *n*.

$$\underline{\hspace{0.5cm}} = a_1 (\underline{\hspace{0.5cm}})^{\underline{\hspace{0.5cm}}}$$ Substitute for a_2 and *r*.

$$\underline{\hspace{0.5cm}} = a_1$$ Solve for a_1.

So, a rule for the *n*th term is $a_n = \underline{\hspace{2cm}}$.

Example 4 *Finding the nth Term Given Two Terms*

Two terms of a geometric sequence are $a_2 = -8$ and $a_7 = -256$. Find a rule for the nth term.

Solution

Write a system of equations using $a_n = a_1 r^{n-1}$ and substituting 2 for n and then 7 for n.

$a_2 = a_1 r^{2-1}$ ⟹ _____ **Equation 1**

$a_7 = a_1 r^{7-1}$ ⟹ _____ **Equation 2**

Solve the system.

$\underline{\quad\quad} = a_1$ Solve Equation 1 for a_1.

$-256 = \underline{\quad\quad}(r^6)$ Substitute for a_1 in Equation 2.

$-256 = \underline{\quad\quad}$ Simplify.

$\dfrac{\underline{\quad}}{\underline{\quad}} = \underline{\quad}$ Divide each side by -8.

$\underline{\quad} = r$ Solve for r.

$-8 = a_1 \underline{\quad}$ Substitute for r.

$\underline{\quad\quad} = a_1$ Solve for a_1.

A rule for the nth term is $a_n = $ _____.

✓ *Checkpoint* **Complete the following exercise.**

> **2.** Two terms of a geometric sequence are $a_4 = 250$ and $a_6 = 1562.5$. Find a rule for the nth term.

THE SUM OF A FINITE GEOMETRIC SERIES

The sum S_n of the first n terms of a geometric series with common ratio $r \neq 1$ is:

$$S_n = a_1 \left(\frac{1 - r^n}{1 - r} \right)$$

Example 5   *Finding a Sum*

Consider the geometric series $-1, -3, -9, -27, -81,...$
Find (a) the sum of the first 10 terms and (b) n such that
$S_n = -797,161$.

Solution

a. To begin, notice that $a_1 = \underline{\quad}$ and $r = \underline{\quad}$. So,

$$S_{10} = a_1\left(\frac{1 - r^{10}}{1 - r}\right) = \underline{\hspace{3cm}} = \underline{\hspace{2cm}}$$

b. $a_1\left(\dfrac{1 - r^n}{1 - r}\right) = S_n$ Write general rule.

$$\underline{\hspace{2cm}} = \underline{\hspace{3cm}}$$ Substitute for a_1, r, and S_n.

$$\underline{\hspace{2cm}} = \underline{\hspace{3cm}}$$ Simplify.

$$\underline{\hspace{2cm}} = \underline{\hspace{3cm}}$$ Multiply each side by ____.

$$\underline{\hspace{2cm}} = \underline{\hspace{3cm}}$$ Subtract __ from each side.

$$\underline{\hspace{2cm}} = \underline{\hspace{3cm}}$$ Divide each side by ____.

$$n = \underline{\hspace{3cm}} = \underline{\quad}$$ Solve for n.

 **Checkpoint** Complete the following exercise.

3. Consider the geometric series $7, -14, 28, -56, 112, ...$
Find (a) the sum of the first 11 terms and (b) n such that
$S_n = -2387$.

Homework

11.4 Infinite Geometric Series

Goals • Find sums of infinite geometric series.
• Use an infinite series as a model.

Your Notes

THE SUM OF AN INFINITE GEOMETRIC SERIES

The sum of an infinite geometric series with the first term a_1 and common ratio r is given by

$$S = \frac{a_1}{1-r}$$

provided $|r| < 1$. If $|r| \geq 1$, the series has _____.

Example 1 *Finding Sums of Infinite Geometric Series*

Find the sum of the infinite geometric series.

a. $\displaystyle\sum_{i=1}^{\infty} 4(0.5)^{i-1}$

b. $4 + 1 + \dfrac{1}{4} + \dfrac{1}{16} + \dfrac{1}{64} + \cdots$

Solution

a. For this series, $a_1 = $ __ and $r = $ ____.

$$S = \frac{a_1}{1-r} = \underline{\hspace{2cm}} = \underline{\hspace{0.7cm}}$$

b. For this series, $a_1 = $ __ and $r = $ ____.

$$S = \frac{a_1}{1-r} = \underline{\hspace{2cm}} = \underline{\hspace{0.7cm}}$$

✔ **Checkpoint** Find the sum of the infinite geometric series.

1. $\displaystyle\sum_{i=1}^{\infty} 9(0.1)^{i-1}$ 2. $80, 40, 20, 10, 5,\ldots$

Example 2 *Finding the Common Ratio*

An infinite geometric series with first term $a_1 = 6$ has a sum of 12. What is the common ratio of the series?

$$S = \frac{a_1}{1 - r}$$ Write rule for sum.

$$\underline{\quad} = \frac{\boxed{}}{1 - r}$$ Substitute for S and a_1.

$$\underline{\qquad\qquad}$$ Multiply each side by $(1 - r)$.

$$\underline{\qquad\quad}$$ Divide each side by ___.

$$r = \underline{\quad}$$ Solve for r.

The common ratio is $r = \dfrac{\quad}{\quad}$.

Example 3 *Writing a Repeating Decimal as a Fraction*

Write 0.323232... as a fraction.

$$0.323232\ldots = 32(\underline{\quad}) + 32(\underline{\quad})^2 + 32(\underline{\quad})^3 + \cdots$$

$$= \frac{a_1}{1 - r}$$ Write rule for sum.

$$= \underline{\qquad}$$ Substitute for a_1 and r.

$$= \underline{\qquad}$$ Write as a quotient of integers.

The repeating decimal 0.323232... is $\dfrac{\quad}{\quad}$ as a fraction.

✔ **Checkpoint** Complete the following exercise.

3. An infinite series with first term $a_1 = 228$ has a sum of 304. What is the common ratio of the series?

✓ *Checkpoint* **Complete the following exercise.**

4. Write 0.678678678… as a fraction.

Example 4 *Using an Infinite Series as a Model*

A pendulum swings 15 meters going left to right. On its swing back, it swings 85% as far as the first swing. Each successive swing is 85% of its previous swing. Find the total distance traveled by the pendulum when it finally stops.

Solution

The total distance traveled by the pendulum is:

$$d = 15 + 15(\underline{\quad}) + 15(\underline{\quad})^2 + 15(\underline{\quad})^3 + \cdots$$

$$= 15 + \frac{15(\boxed{})}{1 - \boxed{}} \quad \text{Excluding first term, find sum of series.}$$

$$= \underline{\qquad} \quad \text{Simplify fraction.}$$

$$= \underline{\quad} \quad \text{Simplify.}$$

The pendulum travels a total distance of _____.

✓ *Checkpoint* **Complete the following exercise.**

5. A pendulum swings 18 meters going left to right. On its swing back, it swings 75% as far as the first swing. Each successive swing is 75% of its previous swing. Find the total distance traveled.

11.5 Recursive Rules for Sequences

Goals • Evaluate and write recursive rules for sequences.
• Use recursive rules to solve real-life problems.

Your Notes

VOCABULARY

Explicit rule

Recursive rule

Factorial

Example 1 *Evaluating Recursive Rules*

Write the first five terms of the sequence.

a. $a_1 = 2, a_2 = 1, a_n = a_{n-2} - a_{n-1}$
b. $a_1 = -1, a_2 = 2, a_n = (a_{n-2})(a_{n-1})$

Solution

a. $a_1 = 2$ b. $a_1 = -1$

$a_2 = 1$ $a_2 = 2$

$a_3 = \underline{\hspace{2cm}} = \underline{\hspace{1cm}}$ $a_3 = \underline{\hspace{2cm}} = \underline{\hspace{1cm}}$

$a_4 = \underline{\hspace{2cm}} = \underline{\hspace{1cm}}$ $a_4 = \underline{\hspace{2cm}} = \underline{\hspace{1cm}}$

$a_5 = \underline{\hspace{2cm}} = \underline{\hspace{1cm}}$ $a_5 = \underline{\hspace{2cm}} = \underline{\hspace{1cm}}$

✔ **Checkpoint** Complete the following exercise.

1. Write the first five terms of the sequence.
$a_1 = 0, a_2 = 1, a_n = 2a_{n-2} + a_{n-1}$

Example 2 *Writing a Recursive Rule for an Arithmetic Sequence*

Write the indicated rule for the arithmetic sequence with $a_1 = 1$ and $d = 7$.

a. an explicit rule **b.** a recursive rule

Solution

a. From Lesson 11.2 you know that an explicit rule for the *n*th term of the arithmetic sequence is:

$$a_n = a_1 + (n - 1)d \qquad \text{General explicit rule for } a_n$$

$$= \underline{\hspace{2cm}} \qquad \text{Substitute for } a_1 \text{ and } d.$$

$$= \underline{\hspace{1.5cm}} \qquad \text{Simplify.}$$

b. To find the recursive equation, use the fact that you can obtain a_n by adding the common difference *d* to the previous term.

$$a_n = a_{n-1} + d \qquad \text{General recursive rule for } a_n$$

$$= \underline{\hspace{2cm}} \qquad \text{Substitute for } d.$$

A recursive rule for the sequence is $a_1 = \underline{\hspace{0.5cm}}$, $a_n = \underline{\hspace{2cm}}$.

Example 3 *Writing a Recursive Rule for a Geometric Sequence*

Write the indicated rule for the geometric sequence with $a_1 = 6$ and $r = 2$.

a. an explicit rule **b.** a recursive rule

Solution

a. From Lesson 11.3 you know that an explicit rule for the *n*th term of the geometric sequence is:

$$a_n = a_1 r^{n-1} \qquad \text{General explicit rule for } a_n$$

$$= \underline{\hspace{2cm}} \qquad \text{Substitute for } a_1 \text{ and } r.$$

b. To write a recursive rule, use the fact that you can obtain a_n by multiplying the previous term by *r*.

$$a_n = r \cdot a_{n-1} \qquad \text{General recursive rule for } a_n$$

$$= \underline{\hspace{2cm}} \qquad \text{Substitute for } r.$$

A recursive rule for the sequence is $a_1 = \underline{\hspace{0.5cm}}$, $a_n = \underline{\hspace{2cm}}$.

✔ *Checkpoint* Write the indicated rule for the arithmetic sequence with $a_1 = 9$ and $d = 5$.

2. an explicit rule   **3.** a recursive rule

Write the indicated rule for the geometric sequence with $a_1 = 8$ and $r = 0.5$.

4. an explicit rule   **5.** a recursive rule

Example 4   *Writing a Recursive Rule*

Write a recursive rule for the sequence 20, 15, 5, 10, −5,....

Solution

Beginning with the _____ term in the sequence, each term is the _____ of the two previous terms. So, a recursive rule is given by:

$a_1 = $ ____, $a_2 = $ ____, $a_n = $ _____ − _____

✔ *Checkpoint* Complete the following exercise.

6. Write a recursive rule for the sequence 3, 11, 19, 27, 35,....

Homework

12.1 The Fundamental Counting Principle and Permutations

Goals
- Use the fundamental counting principle.
- Use permutations.

Your Notes

VOCABULARY

Permutation

FUNDAMENTAL COUNTING PRINCIPLE

Two Events If one event can occur in m ways and another event can occur in n ways, then the number of ways that both events can occur is _____.

Three or More Events The fundamental counting principle can be extended to three or more events. For example, if three events can occur in m, n, and p ways, then the number of ways that all three events can occur is _____.

Example 1 *Using the Fundamental Counting Principle*

You are buying a sandwich. You have a choice of 5 meats, 4 cheeses, 3 dressings, and 8 other toppings. How many different sandwiches with one meat, one cheese, one dressing, and one other topping can you choose?

Solution

You can use the fundamental counting principle to find the total number of sandwiches.

Number of sandwiches = _____ = ____

Example 2 *Using the Fundamental Counting Principle*

A town has telephone numbers that begin with 432 or 437 followed by four digits. How many different telephone numbers are possible if the last four digits cannot be repeated?

Solution

If you cannot repeat digits, there are ____ choices for the first digit, but then only ___ remaining choices for the second digit, ___ remaining choices for the third digit, and ___ for the last digit.

Telephone numbers = _____ = _____

✔ *Checkpoint* **Complete the following exercises.**

1. If dressings were not a choice in Example 1, how many different sandwiches could be made?

_____

2. How many different telephone numbers in Example 2 are possible if digits can be repeated?

Example 3 *Finding the Number of Permutations*

Twenty-six golfers are competing in the final round of a local competition. How many different ways can 3 of the golfers finish first, second, and third?

Any of the ____ golfers can finish first, then any of the remaining ____ golfers can finish second, and finally any of the remaining ____ golfers can finish third. So, the number of ways that the golfers can place first, second, and third is _____ = _____ .

✔ *Checkpoint* **Complete the following exercise.**

3. Ten golfers are competing in a high school tournament. How many different ways can 3 of the golfers finish first, second, and third?

PERMUTATIONS OF n OBJECTS TAKEN r AT A TIME

The number of permutations of r objects taken from a group of n distinct objects is denoted by $_nP_r$ and is given by: $_nP_r = \dfrac{n!}{(n-r)!}$

Example 4   *Finding Permutations of n Objects Taken r at a Time*

You were left a list of 8 chores. In how many orders can you complete (a) 6 of the chores or (b) all 8 of the chores?

a. The number of permutations of 8 chores taken 6 at a time is:

$$_8P_6 = \underline{\hspace{2cm}} = \underline{\hspace{1.5cm}} = \underline{\hspace{2cm}} = \underline{\hspace{2cm}}$$

b. The number of permutations of 8 chores taken 8 at a time is:

$$_8P_8 = \underline{\hspace{2cm}} = \underline{\hspace{1.5cm}} = \underline{\hspace{1cm}} = \underline{\hspace{2cm}}$$

PERMUTATIONS WITH REPETITION

The number of distinguishable permutations of n objects where one object is repeated q_1 times, another is repeated q_2 times, and so on is: $\dfrac{n!}{q_1! \cdot q_2! \cdot ... \cdot q_k!}$

Example 5   *Finding Permutations with Repetition*

Find the number of distinguishable permutations of the letters in (a) **ALGEBRA** and (b) **MATHEMATICS**.

a. ALGEBRA has ___ letters of which ___ is repeated ___ times. So, the number of distinguishable permutations is

$$\frac{}{\underline{\qquad}\ \underline{\qquad\qquad}} = \underline{\qquad}\,.$$

b. MATHEMATICS has ___ letters of which _____ are each repeated ___ times. So, the number of distinguishable

permutations is $\dfrac{}{\underline{\qquad\qquad}\ \underline{\qquad\qquad}} = \underline{\qquad} =$

$\underline{\qquad\qquad}\,.$

✔ *Checkpoint* **Complete the following exercises.**

4. You were left a list of 5 chores to complete. In how many orders can you complete all 5 of the chores?

5. Find the number of distinguishable permutations of the letters in REPETITION.

Homework

12.2 Combinations and the Binomial Theorem

Goals • Use combinations.
• Use the binomial theorem.

Your Notes

VOCABULARY

Combination

Pascal's triangle

Binomial theorem

COMBINATIONS OF n OBJECTS TAKEN r AT A TIME

The number of combinations of r objects taken from a group of n distinct objects is denoted by $_nC_r$ and is given by:

$$_nC_r = \frac{n!}{(n-r)! \cdot r!}$$

| Example 1 | *Finding Combinations* |

Eighteen basketball players are competing for 5 starting positions. The players selected to start will make up the first team. If the order in which the players are selected is not important, how many different first teams are possible?

Solution

The number of ways to choose 5 players from 18 is:

$$_{18}C_5 = \underline{\hspace{3cm}} = \underline{\hspace{4cm}}$$

$$= \underline{\hspace{2cm}}$$

| Example 2 | *Deciding to Multiply or Add* |

A movie rental business is having a special on new releases. The new releases consist of 8 comedies, 3 family, 10 action, 7 dramas, and 2 mystery movies.

a. Suppose you want *exactly* 3 comedies and 2 dramas. How many different movie combinations can you rent?

b. Suppose you can afford *at most* 2 movies. How many movie combinations can you rent?

Solution

a. You can choose 3 of the 8 comedies and 2 of the 7 dramas. So, the number of possible movie combinations is:

$$_{8}C_3 \cdot {}_7C_2 = \underline{\hspace{3cm}} = \underline{\hspace{2cm}} = \underline{\hspace{1.5cm}}$$

b. You can rent 1 or 2 movies. Because there are ___ movies to choose from, the number of movie combinations is: $\underline{\hspace{0.5cm}}C_1 + \underline{\hspace{0.5cm}}C_2 = \underline{\hspace{2cm}} = \underline{\hspace{1cm}}$

✔ *Checkpoint* Complete the following exercise.

1. Use Example 2 to find the number of possible movie combinations if you choose 1 family and 2 action movies.

Example 3 **Subtracting Instead of Adding**

Your school soccer team has 9 scheduled games this season. You want to attend at least 2 games. How many different combinations of games can you attend?

For each of the 9 games, you can choose to attend or not attend the game, so there are ___ total combinations. If you attend at least 2 games, you do not attend only ___ or ___ game. So, the number of ways you can attend at least 2 games is:

$$\_\_\_ - (_9C\_\_ + {}_9C\_\_) = \rule{3cm}{0.4pt} = \_\_\_$$

THE BINOMIAL THEOREM

The binomial expansion of $(a + b)^n$ for any positive integer n is:

$$(a + b)^n = \sum_{r=0}^{n} {}_nC_r a^{n-r} b^r$$

Example 4 **Expanding a Power of a Simple Binomial Sum**

Expand $(x + 5)^3$.

$(x + 5)^3 = $ _____

$\quad\quad = $ _____

$\quad\quad = $ _____

Example 5 **Expanding a Power of a Binomial Difference**

Expand $(a - 2b)^4$.

$(a - 2b)^4 = $ _____

_____

$\quad\quad = $ _____

_____

$\quad\quad = $ _____

Example 6 **Finding a Coefficient in an Expansion**

Find the coefficient of y^6 in the expansion of $(8 - y)^8$.

$$(8 - y)^8 = \sum_{r=0}^{8} \underline{\hspace{3cm}}$$

The term that has y^6 is $\underline{\hspace{2cm}} = \underline{\hspace{2cm}} =$

$\underline{\hspace{2cm}}$.

The coefficient is $\underline{\hspace{1cm}}$.

✔ *Checkpoint* **Complete the following exercises.**

2. Your school band has a concert series of 10 performances. You want to attend at least one concert. How many different combinations of concerts can you attend?

3. Expand $(t + 2w)^3$.

4. Expand $(4 - b)^5$.

Homework

5. Find the coefficient of y^5 in the expansion of $(3y - 4)^7$.

12.3 An Introduction to Probability

Goals • Find theoretical and experimental probabilities.
• Find geometric probabilities.

Your Notes

VOCABULARY

Probability

Experimental probability

Geometric probability

THE THEORETICAL PROBABILITY OF AN EVENT

When all outcomes are equally likely, the **theoretical probability** that an event *A* will occur is:

$$P(A) = \frac{\text{number of outcomes in } A}{\text{total number of outcomes}}$$

The theoretical probability of an event is often simply called the probability of an event.

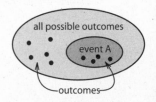

Example 1   *Finding Probabilities of Events*

A standard deck of 52 playing cards has 4 suits with 13 different cards in each suit. Find the probability of drawing a king.

Four outcomes correspond to drawing a king.

$$P(\text{drawing a king}) = \frac{\text{number of ways to draw king}}{\text{number of ways to draw card}}$$

$$= \underline{} = \underline{}$$

Example 2   *Probabilities with Permutations or Combinations*

There are 20 students in your gym class. Your teacher divides the class into two equal softball teams. Your team draws names one by one to determine the batting order. What is the probability that 1 of the 7 freshmen on the team will be chosen first, in any order?

P(1 of the 7 freshmen will be first) = _____ = _____

✔ **Checkpoint** Complete the following exercises.

1. Using a standard deck of playing cards, find the probability of (a) drawing a heart and (b) drawing a card less than or equal to 7.

---

2. Use Example 2 to find the probability that 3 of the 7 freshmen will be chosen last, in any order.

Example 3   *Finding Experimental Probabilities*

The first exam grades of students in a biology class are shown in the bar graph. Find the probability that a randomly chosen student in this biology class received a B or better.

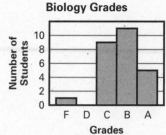

Biology Grades

Solution

The number of students in the biology class are ___ + ___ + ___ + ___ = ___ .

P(student received B or better) = _____ = _____ ≈ _____

Example 4   *Using Area to Find Probability*

You throw a dart at the board shown. Your dart is equally likely to hit any point inside the square board. Are you more likely to get 15 points or 10 points?

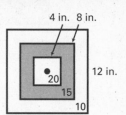

Solution

The two probabilities are as follows.

P(15 points)

$$= \frac{\text{area of middle square} - \text{area of inner square}}{\text{area of entire board}}$$

$$= \underline{\hspace{2cm}} \approx \underline{\hspace{1.5cm}}$$

P(10 points)

$$= \frac{\text{area of entire board} - \text{area of middle square}}{\text{area of entire board}}$$

$$= \underline{\hspace{2cm}} \approx \underline{\hspace{1.5cm}}$$

You are more likely to get ___ points.

✔ **Checkpoint** Complete the following exercises.

3. Use Example 3 to find the probability that a randomly chosen student in the biology class received a C or lower.

4. Use Example 4 to find the probability of getting 20 points.

Homework

12.4 Probability of Compound Events

Goals • Find probabilities of unions and intersections.
• Use complements to find probabilities.

Your Notes

VOCABULARY

Compound event

Mutually exclusive events

Complement

PROBABILITY OF COMPOUND EVENTS

If A and B are two events, then the probability of A or B is:
$P(A \text{ or } B) =$ _____

If A and B are mutually exclusive, then the probability of A or B is: $P(A \text{ or } B) =$ _____

Example 1 *Probability of Mutually Exclusive Events*

You roll a number cube. What is the probability of rolling a 3 or 4?

Let event A be rolling a 3, and let event B be rolling a 4. Event A has __ outcome and event B has __ outcome.

$P(A \text{ or } B) =$ _____ $=$ _____ $\approx$ _____

✔ *Checkpoint* **Complete the following exercise.**

1. You roll a number cube. What is the probability of rolling a 2 or an odd number?

Example 2 *Probability of a Compound Event*

You roll a number cube. What is the probability of rolling a number less than 4 or an even number?

Solution

Let event *A* be rolling a number less than 4, and let event *B* be rolling an even number. Event *A* has __ outcomes and event *B* has __ outcomes. Of these, _____ outcome is common to *A* and *B*. So, the probability of rolling a number less than 4 or an even number is:

$P(A \text{ or } B) = $ _____

$= $ _____ $\approx$ _____

Example 3 *Using Intersection to Find Probability*

In a poll of 50 students, 19 were student council members and 33 played a winter sport. Forty-eight out of 50 were student council members or played a winter sport. What is the probability that a student is a student council member and played a winter sport?

Solution

Let event *A* represent being a student council member, and let event *B* represent playing a winter sport. From the given information you know that:

$P(A) = \underline{\quad}$, $P(B) = \underline{\quad}$, and $P(A \text{ or } B) = \underline{\quad}$

The probability that a student who was polled was a student council member and played a winter sport is $P(A \text{ and } B)$.

$P(A \text{ or } B) = $ _____   Write general formula.

$= \dfrac{\quad}{\quad}$ _____   Substitute.

$P(A \text{ and } B) = $ _____   Solve for $P(A \text{ and } B)$.

$P(A \text{ and } B) = \dfrac{\quad}{\quad} = \dfrac{\quad}{\quad} = $ _____   Simplify.

Your Notes

✔ *Checkpoint* **Complete the following exercises.**

2. You roll a number cube. What is the probability of rolling a number greater than 4 or an odd number?

3. In a poll of 100 college students, 48 are members of a fraternity or sorority, and 63 play intramural sports. Thirty-nine out of 100 are members of a fraternity or sorority or play intramural sports. What is the probability that a student is a member of a fraternity or sorority and plays intramural sports?

PROBABILITY OF THE COMPLEMENT OF AN EVENT

The probability of the complement of A is
$P(A') =$ _____.

Example 4 *Probabilities of Complements*

When two number cubes are tossed, there are 36 possible outcomes. Find the probability that the sum is not 5.

Solution

$P(\text{sum is not 5}) =$ _____

$=$ _____

$=$ _____

$=$ ____ $\approx$ _____

Homework

Probability of Independent and Dependent Events

Goals • Find the probability of independent events.
• Find the probability of dependent events.

Your Notes

VOCABULARY

Independent

Dependent events

Conditional probability

PROBABILITY OF INDEPENDENT EVENTS

If A and B are independent events, then the probability that both A and B will occur is $P(A \text{ and } B) = $ _____ .

Example 1 *Probability of Two Independent Events*

A cereal company claims that 3 in every 25 people win a prize. What is the probability that you do not win a prize twice in a row?

Solution

Let event A be not winning the prize on your first try, and event B be not winning the prize on your second try. The two events are independent. So, the probability is:

$P(A \text{ and } B) = $ _____

$= $ _____ $= $ _____ $= $ _____

✔ Checkpoint Complete the following exercise.

1. A company claims that 3 in every 13 people win a prize. What is the probability that you could win twice in a row?

Example 2 *Solving a Probability Equation*

A manufacturer has found that 3 out of every 1100 light bulbs are defective. How many light bulbs can you order before the probability that at least one bulb is defective reaches 75%?

Solution

Let n be the number of light bulbs you order. From the given information you know that

P(bulb is not defective) = _____ ≈ _____.

Use the probability and the fact that each bulb ordered represents an independent event to find the value of n.

P(at least one bulb is defective) = _____

$1 - P$(no bulbs are defective) = _____   Complement

_____ = ____   Substitute.

_____ = ____   Subtract 1.

_____ = ____   Divide each side by −1.

$n = $ _____   Solve for n.

$n ≈ $ ____   Calculator

✔ Checkpoint Complete the following exercise.

2. How many light bulbs can you order before the probability that at least one bulb is defective reaches 10%?

Your Notes

PROBABILITY OF DEPENDENT EVENTS

If *A* and *B* are dependent events, then the probability that both *A* and *B* occur is *P*(*A* and *B*) = _____ .

Example 3 *Finding Conditional Probabilities*

The table shows the number of males and females with certain hair colors. Find (a) the probability that a listed person has red hair and (b) the probability that a female has red hair.

	Brown hair	Blonde hair	Red hair	Black hair	Other hair
Male	42	11	3	17	27
Female	47	16	13	9	15

Solution

a. *P*(red hair) = $\dfrac{\text{number people with red hair}}{\text{total number of people}}$

   = $\dfrac{\quad}{\quad}$ = _____

b. *P*(red hair | female) = $\dfrac{\text{number of red hair females}}{\text{total number of females}}$

   = $\dfrac{\quad}{\quad}$ = _____

✔ *Checkpoint* Complete the following exercise.

3. Use the table in Example 3 to find the probability that a male has black hair.

Example 4 *Comparing Dependent and Independent Events*

You randomly select two marbles from a bag that contains 14 green, 7 blue, and 9 red marbles. What is the probability that the first marble is blue and the second marble is not blue if (a) you replace the first marble before selecting the second and (b) you do not replace the first marble?

a. If you replace the first marble before selecting the second marble, then A and B are _____ events. So, the probability is:

$P(A \text{ and } B) = $ _____ $= \dfrac{}{} \cdot \dfrac{}{}$

$\approx$ _____

b. If you do not replace the first marble before selecting the second marble, then A and B are _____ events. So, the probability is:

$P(A \text{ and } B) = $ _____ $= \dfrac{}{} \cdot \dfrac{}{}$

$\approx$ _____

Example 5 *Probability of Three Dependent Events*

Your teacher passes around a basket with 6 red erasers, 9 blue erasers, and 7 green erasers. If you and your two neighbors are the first to randomly select an eraser, what is the probability that all three of you select green erasers?

$P(A \text{ and } B \text{ and } C) = $ _____

$= \dfrac{}{} \cdot \dfrac{}{} \approx$ _____

✔ **Checkpoint** Complete the following exercise.

Homework

4. Use Example 5 to find the probability that you and your two neighbors all select a blue eraser.

12.6 Binomial Distributions

Goals • Find binomial probabilities.
• Test a hypothesis.

Your Notes

VOCABULARY

Binomial experiment

Binomial distribution

Symmetric distribution

Skewed distribution

Hypothesis testing

FINDING A BINOMIAL PROBABILITY

For a binomial experiment consisting of n trials, the probability of exactly k successes is

$P(k \text{ successes}) = $ _____

where the probability of success on each trial is p.

Example 1   *Finding a Binomial Probability*

A survey taken in your math class found that 88% of the students are not afraid of heights. Suppose that you randomly survey 5 students. What is the probability that exactly 4 of them will not be afraid of heights?

Let $p = 0.88$ be the probability that a randomly selected student is not afraid of heights. By surveying 5 students, you are conducting $n = 5$ independent trials. The probability of getting exactly $k = 4$ successes is:

$P(k = 4) =$ _____

$=$ _____

$\approx$ _____

Example 2   *Drawing and Interpreting a Binomial Distribution*

Draw and interpret a histogram of the binomial distribution for the survey in Example 1. Then find the probability that at most 4 students surveyed are not afraid of heights.

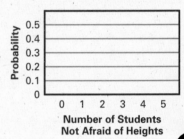

Solution

$P(k = 0) =$ _____ $\approx$ _____

$P(k = 1) =$ _____ $\approx$ _____

$P(k = 2) =$ _____ $\approx$ _____

$P(k = 3) =$ _____ $\approx$ _____

$P(k = 4) =$ _____ $\approx$ _____

$P(k = 5) =$ _____ $\approx$ _____

The distribution is _____. The probability is greatest for $k =$ ___. So the most likely number of people not afraid of heights is ___.

The probability of getting at most $k = 4$ successes is:

$P(k \leq 4) = 1 - P(k \geq \_\_)$

$= 1 - P(\_\_)$

$=$ _____ $=$ _____

✓ Checkpoint Complete the following exercises.

1. A survey taken in your math class found that 68% of the students are afraid of snakes. Suppose that you randomly survey 5 students. What is the probability that exactly 3 of them will be afraid of snakes?

2. Draw and interpret a histogram of the binomial distribution for the survey in Checkpoint 1. Then find the probability that at most 3 students surveyed are afraid of snakes.

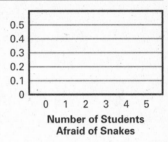

Number of Students
Afraid of Snakes

HYPOTHESIS TESTING

Step 1 State the hypothesis you are testing. The hypothesis should make a statement about some _____ _____ (mean, standard deviation, or proportion) of a population.

Step 2 Collect data from a _____ of the population and compute the _____ of the sample.

Step 3 Assume that the hypothesis is _____ and calculate the resulting probability of obtaining the sample statistical measure or a more extreme sample statistical measure. If this probability is _____, you should _____ the hypothesis.

Example 3 *Testing a Hypothesis*

To test the claim that 88% of students are not afraid of heights, you conduct a survey of 10 randomly selected students. In your survey only 7 students were not afraid of heights. Should you reject the claim? Explain.

Solution

1. Assume the claim *88% of students are not afraid of heights* is true.

2. Form the binomial distribution for the probability of selecting exactly k students out of 10 who are not afraid of heights.

3. Calculate the probability that you could randomly select 7 or fewer students out of 10 who are not afraid of heights.

$$P(k \leq 7) = 1 - P(\underline{\hspace{1.5cm}})$$

$$= \underline{\hspace{4cm}}$$

$$\approx \underline{\hspace{4cm}}$$

$$\approx \underline{\hspace{2cm}}$$

y-axis values: 0.5, 0.4, 0.3, 0.2, 0.1, 0

x-axis values: 0 1 2 3 4 5 6 7 8 9 10

**Number of Students
Not Afraid of Heights**

If it is true that *88% of students are not afraid of heights*, then there is an ____ % probability of finding only 7 or fewer students in a random sample of 10. With a probability this _____, you _____ reject the claim.

Homework

12.7 Normal Distributions

Goals • Calculate probabilities using normal distributions.
• Approximate binomial distributions.

Your Notes

VOCABULARY

Normal curve

AREAS UNDER A NORMAL CURVE

The mean $\bar{x}$ and the standard deviation σ of a normal distribution determine the following areas.

• The total area under the curve is ___ .

• _____ of the area lies within ___ standard deviation of the mean.

• _____ of the area lies within ___ standard deviations of the mean.

• _____ of the area lies within ___ standard deviations of the mean.

Example 1 *Using a Normal Distribution*

The verbal section of the 2003 SAT exam is normally distributed with a mean of 507 and a standard deviation of 111. What is the probability that a randomly chosen test taker will score between 507–618?

Solution

The score of 507 is the _____ and the score of 618 is _____ standard deviation to the _____ of the mean. So, the probability that a randomly chosen test taker will score between 507 and 618 is _____ .

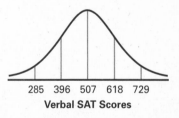
285 396 507 618 729
Verbal SAT Scores

Example 2   *Using a Normal Distribution (Compound Event)*

Use the information in Example 1. If you randomly choose 5 test takers, what is the probability that all five score at least 507?

Solution

A score of 507 is the _____. The probability of randomly selecting a test taker that scored 507 or better is:

$$P(x \geq 507) = \underline{\quad\quad} + \underline{\quad\quad} + \underline{\quad\quad} + \underline{\quad\quad}$$
$$= \underline{\quad\quad}$$

Randomly choosing test takers are independent events, so the probability that all five randomly chosen test takers score 507 or better is:

$$P(\text{all score 507 or better}) = (\underline{\quad})^5 = \underline{\quad\quad\quad}$$

✓ *Checkpoint* **Complete the following exercises.**

1. Use Example 1 to find the percent of SAT test takers that will score between 396 and 729.

2. Use the information in Example 1. If you randomly choose 2 test takers, what is the probability that both score less than 396?

NORMAL APPROXIMATION OF A BINOMIAL DISTRIBUTION

Consider the binomial distribution consisting of n trials with probability p of success on each trial. If $np \geq 5$ and $n(1 - p) \geq 5$, then the binomial distribution can be approximated by a normal distribution with a mean of $\bar{x} =$ ____ and a standard deviation of $\sigma = \sqrt{np(1 - p)}$.

Example 3 *Finding a Binomial Probability*

Suppose that a local high school conducted a poll and found that 41% of juniors and seniors had a part-time job. You are conducting a random survey of 149 juniors and seniors. What is the probability that at least 79 juniors or seniors have a part-time job?

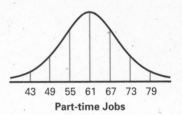

43 49 55 61 67 73 79
Part-time Jobs

Solution

Approximate the answer with a normal distribution having a mean of $\bar{x} =$ _____ $\approx$ ____ and a standard deviation of

$\sigma =$ _____ $\approx$ ___. For this distribution, 79 is

_____ standard deviations to the right of the mean. So, the probability that you will find at least 79 juniors or seniors at your high school that have part-time jobs is:

$P(x \geq 79) =$ _____

✔ *Checkpoint* **Complete the following exercise.**

3. Use the information in Example 3 to find the probability that at most 49 juniors or seniors have a part-time job.

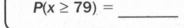

Homework

Right Triangle Trigonometry

Goals • Use trigonometric relationships to evaluate trigonometric functions of acute angles.
• Use trigonometric functions to solve real-life problems.

Your Notes

VOCABULARY

Solving a right triangle

Angle of elevation

Angle of depression

RIGHT TRIANGLE DEFINITION OF TRIGONOMETRIC FUNCTIONS

Let θ be an acute angle of a right triangle. The six trigonometric functions of θ are defined as follows.

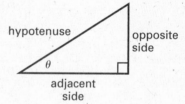

$\sin \theta = \dfrac{\text{opp}}{\boxed{}}$　　$\cos \theta = \dfrac{\boxed{}}{\text{hyp}}$　　$\tan \theta = \dfrac{\text{opp}}{\boxed{}}$

$\csc \theta = \dfrac{\boxed{}}{\text{opp}}$　　$\sec \theta = \dfrac{\text{hyp}}{\boxed{}}$　　$\cot \theta = \dfrac{\boxed{}}{\text{opp}}$

The abbreviations *opp*, *adj*, and *hyp* represent the lengths of the three sides of the right triangle. Note that the ratios in the second row are the reciprocals of the ratios in the first row. That is:

$\csc \theta = \dfrac{1}{\boxed{}}$　　$\sec \theta = \dfrac{1}{\boxed{}}$　　$\cot \theta = \dfrac{1}{\boxed{}}$

Example 1 *Evaluating Trigonometric Functions*

Evaluate the six trigonometric
functions of the angle θ shown in
the right triangle.

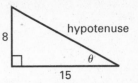

Solution

The length of the hypotenuse is:

$$\sqrt{8^2 + 15^2} = \sqrt{} = \underline{}$$ **Use Pythagorean theorem.**

$$\sin \theta = \frac{\text{opp}}{\boxed{}} = \frac{\boxed{}}{\boxed{}} \qquad \cos \theta = \frac{\boxed{}}{\text{hyp}} = \frac{\boxed{}}{\boxed{}}$$

$$\tan \theta = \frac{\text{opp}}{\boxed{}} = \frac{\boxed{}}{\boxed{}} \qquad \csc \theta = \frac{\boxed{}}{\text{opp}} = \frac{\boxed{}}{\boxed{}}$$

$$\sec \theta = \frac{\text{hyp}}{\boxed{}} = \frac{\boxed{}}{\boxed{}} \qquad \cot \theta = \frac{\boxed{}}{\text{opp}} = \frac{\boxed{}}{\boxed{}}$$

✔ *Checkpoint* **Complete the following exercise.**

1. Evaluate the six
trigonometric functions
of the angles shown in
the right triangles.

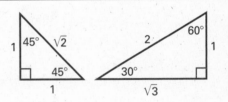

Your Notes

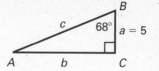

Example 2   *Solving a Right Triangle*

Solve △*ABC*.

Angles *A* and *B* are complementary angles, so $A = 90° - \_\_\_° = \_\_\_°$.

$$\frac{b}{5} = \tan 68°$$

$$\frac{c}{5} = \sec 68° = \frac{1}{\boxed{}} \approx \_\_\_\_$$

$$b \approx \_\_\_\_$$

$$c \approx \_\_\_\_$$

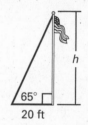

Example 3   *Finding the Height of a Flag Pole*

You are measuring the height of a flag pole. You stand 20 feet from the base of the pole. You measure the angle of elevation from a point on the ground to the top of the pole to be 65°. Estimate the height of the pole to the nearest foot.

Solution

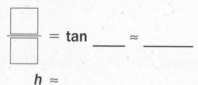

$$\frac{\boxed{}}{\boxed{}} = \tan \_\_\_ \approx \_\_\_\_$$

$$h \approx \_\_\_$$

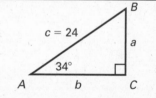

Answer The height of the flag pole is about ____ feet.

✔ **Checkpoint** Complete the following exercises.

2. Solve △*ABC*.

$c = 24$, $34°$, a, b, A, B, C

3. A cable to a radio tower makes an angle of 54° with the ground. If the cable is 240 feet, how far above the ground does it meet the tower? Round to the nearest foot.

Homework

290   **Algebra 2 Notetaking Guide** • Chapter 13

13.2 General Angles and Radian Measure

Goals • Measure angles in standard position using degree measure and radian measure.
• Calculate arc lengths and areas of sectors.

Your Notes

VOCABULARY

Initial side and terminal side

Standard position

Coterminal

Radian

Sector

Central angle

Example 1 *Drawing an Angle in Standard Position*

Draw an angle with a measure of −80° in standard position. Then tell in which quadrant the terminal side lies.

The terminal side is 80° _____ from the positive *x*-axis and is located in Quadrant ___.

Example 2   *Finding Coterminal Angles*

Find one positive angle and one negative angle that are coterminal with (a) 145° and (b) −395°.

a. Positive coterminal angle: 145° + 360° = _____°

Negative coterminal angle: 145° − 360° = _____°

b. Positive coterminal angle: −395° + 2(360°) = _____°

Negative coterminal angle: −395° − 360° = _____°

✓ *Checkpoint* Draw an angle with the given measure in standard position. Then find one positive and one negative coterminal angle.

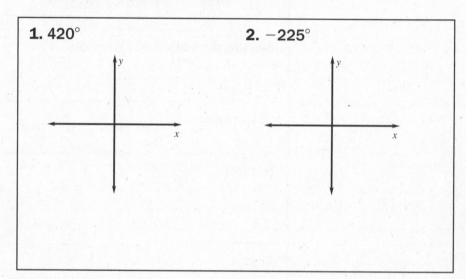

1. 420°   **2.** −225°

CONVERSIONS BETWEEN DEGREES AND RADIANS

To convert from degrees to radians, multiply by $\dfrac{\pi \text{ radians}}{180°}$.

To convert from radians to degrees, multiply by $\dfrac{180°}{\pi \text{ radians}}$.

Example 3   *Converting Between Degrees and Radians*

Convert $\dfrac{\pi}{8}$ radians to degrees.

$$\dfrac{\pi}{8} = \dfrac{\pi}{8}\left(\underline{}\right) = \underline{}°$$

✅ **Checkpoint** Convert the degree measure to radians and the radian measure to degrees.

3. $270°$

4. $-\dfrac{5\pi}{3}$

ARC LENGTH AND AREA OF A SECTOR

The arc length s and area A of a sector with radius r and central angle θ (measured in radians) are as follows.

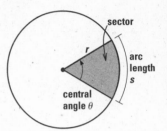

Arc length: $s = r\theta$ Area: $A = \dfrac{1}{2}r^2\theta$

Example 4   *Finding Arc Length and Area*

Find the arc length and area of a sector with a radius of 3 meters and a central angle of 40°.

First convert the angle measure to radians.

$$\theta = 40°\left(\underline{\hspace{3cm}}\right) = \underline{\hspace{1cm}} \text{ radians}$$

Arc length: $s = r\theta = \underline{\hspace{1.5cm}} = \underline{\hspace{1cm}}$ meters

Area: $A = \dfrac{1}{2}r^2\theta = \underline{\hspace{2.5cm}} = \underline{\hspace{0.5cm}}$ square meters

---

✅ **Checkpoint** Complete the following exercise.

Homework

5. Find the arc length and area of a sector with a radius of 8 inches and a central angle of 18°.

13.3 Trigonometric Functions of Any Angle

Goals • Evaluate trigonometric functions of any angle.
• Use trigonometric functions to solve real-life problems.

Your Notes

VOCABULARY

Quadrantal angle

Reference angle

GENERAL DEFINITION OF TRIGONOMETRIC FUNCTIONS

Let θ be an angle in standard position
and (x, y) be any point (except the origin)
on the terminal side of θ. The
six trigonometric functions of θ are
defined as follows.

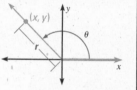

$$\sin \theta = \frac{\Box}{r} \qquad \csc \theta = \frac{\Box}{y}, y \neq 0$$

Pythagorean theorem gives
$r = \sqrt{x^2 + y^2}.$

$$\cos \theta = \frac{x}{\Box} \qquad \sec \theta = \frac{\Box}{x}, x \neq 0$$

$$\tan \theta = \frac{\Box}{x}, x \neq 0 \quad \cot \theta = \frac{\Box}{y}, y \neq 0$$

For _____ angles, these definitions give the same values
as those given by the definitions in Lesson 13.1.

Example 1 — *Evaluating Trigonometric Functions Given a Point*

Let $(-5, 12)$ be a point on the terminal side of an angle θ in standard position. Evaluate the six trigonometric functions of θ.

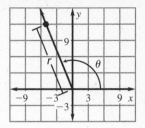

Solution

Use the Pythagorean theorem to find the value of r.

$$r = \sqrt{x^2 + y^2} = \sqrt{\underline{\quad}^2 + \underline{\quad}^2} = \sqrt{\underline{\quad}} = \underline{\quad}$$

Using $x = -5$, $y = 12$, and $r = \underline{\quad}$, you can write the following.

$\sin \theta = \dfrac{\Box}{r} = \underline{\quad}$ 　　　　 $\cos \theta = \dfrac{x}{\Box} = \underline{\quad}$

$\tan \theta = \dfrac{\Box}{x} = \underline{\quad}$ 　　　　 $\csc \theta = \dfrac{\Box}{y} = \underline{\quad}$

$\sec \theta = \dfrac{\Box}{x} = \underline{\quad}$ 　　　　 $\cot \theta = \dfrac{\Box}{y} = \underline{\quad}$

Example 2 — *Finding Reference Angles*

Find the reference angle θ' for (a) $\theta = -125°$ and (b) $\theta = \dfrac{11\pi}{6}$.

Solution

a. Because θ is coterminal with $\underline{\quad}°$ and

$\underline{\quad}° < \theta < \underline{\quad}°$, $\theta' = \underline{\quad}° - \underline{\quad}° = \underline{\quad}°$.

b. Because $\underline{\quad} < \theta < \underline{\quad}$, $\theta' = \underline{\quad} - \underline{\quad} = \underline{\quad}$.

✔ *Checkpoint* **Complete the following exercises.**

1. Let (40, −9) be a point on the terminal side of an angle θ in standard position. Evaluate the six trigonometric functions of θ.

___

2. Find the reference angle θ' for (a) $\theta = 145°$ and (b) $\theta = \dfrac{8\pi}{7}$.

EVALUATING TRIGONOMETRIC FUNCTIONS

Use these steps to evaluate a trigonometric function of any angle θ.

1. Find the reference angle ___.

2. Evaluate the trigonometric function for the angle ___.

3. Use the quadrant in which ___ lies to determine the sign of the trigonometric function value of ___. (See diagram at the right.)

Quadrant II	y	Quadrant I
$\sin \theta$, $\csc \theta$: +		$\sin \theta$, $\csc \theta$: +
$\cos \theta$, $\sec \theta$: −		$\cos \theta$, $\sec \theta$: +
$\tan \theta$, $\cot \theta$: −		$\tan \theta$, $\cot \theta$: +
Quadrant III		Quadrant IV x
$\sin \theta$, $\csc \theta$: −		$\sin \theta$, $\csc \theta$: −
$\cos \theta$, $\sec \theta$: −		$\cos \theta$, $\sec \theta$: +
$\tan \theta$, $\cot \theta$: +		$\tan \theta$, $\cot \theta$: −

Example 3 *Using Reference Angles*

Evaluate (a) sin 480° and (b) cot $\left(-\dfrac{5\pi}{6}\right)$.

Solution

a. The angle 480° is coterminal with _____. The reference

angle is $\theta' =$ _____ − _____ = _____ . The sine function is

_____ in Quadrant II, so sin 480° = sin _____ = _____ .

b. The angle $-\dfrac{5\pi}{6}$ is coterminal with _____ . The reference

angle is $\theta' =$ _____ − __ = _____ . The cotangent function is

_____ in Quadrant III, so $\cot\left(-\dfrac{5\pi}{6}\right) = \cot$ _____ = _____ .

✔ *Checkpoint* **Evaluate the function without using
a calculator.**

3. cos (−150°)   4. sec $\dfrac{7\pi}{4}$

Homework

13.4 Inverse Trigonometric Functions

Goals
- Evaluate inverse trigonometric functions.
- Use inverse trigonometric functions to solve real-life problems.

Your Notes

INVERSE TRIGONOMETRIC FUNCTIONS

- If $-1 \le a \le 1$, then the inverse sine of a is $\sin^{-1} a = \theta$ where $\sin \theta = a$ and $-\dfrac{\pi}{2} \le \theta \le \dfrac{\pi}{2}$ (or $-90° \le \theta \le 90°$).

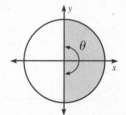

- If $-1 \le a \le 1$, then the inverse cosine of a is $\cos^{-1} a = \theta$ where $\cos \theta = a$ and $0 \le \theta \le \pi$ (or $0° \le \theta \le 180°$).

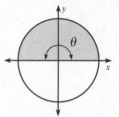

- If a is any real number, then the inverse tangent of a is $\tan^{-1} a = \theta$ where $\tan \theta = a$ and $-\dfrac{\pi}{2} < \theta < \dfrac{\pi}{2}$ (or $-90° < \theta < 90°$).

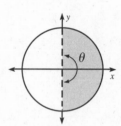

Example 1   *Evaluating Inverse Trigonometric Functions*

Evaluate the expression in both radians and degrees.

a. $\sin^{-1}\left(\dfrac{3}{2}\right)$　　　　　　　b. $\tan^{-1}\sqrt{3}$

Solution

a. There is _____ whose sine is $\dfrac{3}{2}$. So, $\sin^{-1}\left(\dfrac{3}{2}\right)$ is _____.

b. The angle whose tangent is $\sqrt{3}$ is:

$\theta = \tan^{-1}\sqrt{3} = \underline{\quad}$　　or　　$\theta = \tan^{-1}\sqrt{3} = \underline{\quad}°$

✔ *Checkpoint* **Evaluate the expression in both radians and degrees.**

1. $\sin^{-1}(-0.5)$

_____

2. $\cos^{-1}\left(\dfrac{\sqrt{2}}{2}\right)$

_____

3. $\tan^{-1}\dfrac{\sqrt{3}}{3}$

Example 2   *Finding an Angle Measure*

Find the measure of the angle θ.

In the right triangle, you are given the opposite side and the hypotenuse. You can write:

$$\sin\theta = \frac{\text{opp}}{\text{hyp}} = \underline{}$$

Use a calculator to find the measure of θ.

$$\theta = \sin^{-1}\underline{} \approx \underline{} \text{ radians} \quad \text{or} \quad \theta = \sin^{-1}\underline{} \approx \underline{}^{\circ}$$

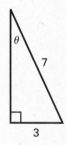

✓ *Checkpoint* Find the measure of the angle θ. Round to three significant digits.

4.

5.

Example 3   *Solving a Trigonometric Equation*

Solve the equation $\cos \theta = \dfrac{1}{3}$ where $270° < \theta < 360°$.

In the interval $0° < \theta < 180°$, the angle whose cosine is $\dfrac{1}{3}$ is $\cos^{-1} \dfrac{1}{3} \approx$ _____°. This angle is in Quadrant I. In Quadrant IV (where $270° < \theta < 360°$), the angle that has the same cosine value is:

$\theta \approx$ _____° $-$ _____° $=$ _____°

✓ *Checkpoint* Solve the equation for θ. Round to three significant digits.

6. $\sin \theta = -0.75$; $180° < \theta < 270°$

Homework

7. $\tan \theta = -2.7$; $90° < \theta < 180°$

13.5 The Law of Sines

Goals • Use the law of sines to find the sides and angles of a triangle.
• Find the area of any triangle.

Your Notes

LAW OF SINES

If $\triangle ABC$ has sides of length a, b, and c as shown, then:

$$\frac{\boxed{}}{a} = \frac{\sin B}{\boxed{}} = \frac{\boxed{}}{c}$$

An equivalent form is $\dfrac{a}{\boxed{}} = \dfrac{\boxed{}}{\sin B} = \dfrac{c}{\boxed{}}$.

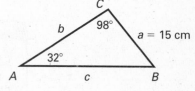

Example 1   *The AAS or ASA Case*

Solve $\triangle ABC$.

Solution

The third angle of $\triangle ABC$ is:

$B = 180° - 32° - 98° = \underline{}°$

By the law of sines you can write:

$$\frac{15}{\boxed{}} = \frac{b}{\sin \boxed{}} = \frac{c}{\boxed{}}$$

You can then solve for b and c as follows.

$$\frac{b}{\sin \boxed{}} = \frac{15}{\boxed{}} \qquad\qquad \frac{c}{\boxed{}} = \frac{15}{\boxed{}}$$

$$b = \frac{\boxed{}}{\boxed{}} \qquad\qquad c = \frac{\boxed{}}{\boxed{}}$$

$$b \approx \underline{} \text{ cm} \qquad\qquad c \approx \underline{} \text{ cm}$$

Your Notes

POSSIBLE TRIANGLES IN THE SSA CASE

Consider a triangle in which you are given a, b, and A.

A IS OBTUSE.   **A IS ACUTE.**

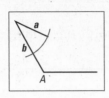

$a \leq b$

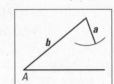

$b \sin A > a$

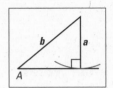

$b \sin A = a$

_____

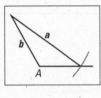

$a > b$

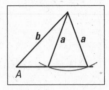

$b \sin A < a < b$

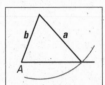

$a > b$

_____   _____   _____

Example 2   *The SSA Case—One Triangle*

Solve $\triangle ABC$.

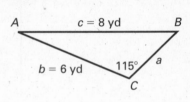

Because C is _____ and the side opposite C is _____ than the given adjacent side, you know that _____ can be formed.

$$\frac{\sin B}{\boxed{}} = \frac{\boxed{}}{8} \implies \sin B =$$

$$\underline{\hspace{3cm}}$$

$$\sin B \approx \underline{\hspace{2cm}} \implies B \approx \underline{\hspace{1cm}}^\circ$$

So, $A \approx 180^\circ - 115^\circ - \underline{\hspace{1cm}}^\circ = \underline{\hspace{1cm}}^\circ$

$$\frac{a}{\sin \boxed{}} = \frac{8}{\boxed{}} \implies a = $$

$$\underline{\hspace{3cm}}$$

$$\implies a \approx \underline{\hspace{1cm}} \text{ yd}$$

AREA OF A TRIANGLE

The area of any triangle is given by one half the product of the lengths of two sides times the sine of their included angle. For △ABC shown, there are three ways to calculate the area:

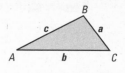

Area = _____   Area = _____   Area = _____

Example 3 *Finding a Triangle's Area*

Find the area of △ABC.

$$\frac{1}{2}ab \sin C = \frac{1}{2}\,\underline{\hspace{3cm}}$$

$$\approx \underline{\hspace{1.5cm}} \text{ in.}^2$$

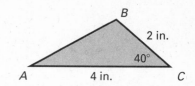

✓ *Checkpoint* Decide whether the given measurements can form exactly *one triangle*, exactly *two triangles*, or *no triangle.*

1. $C = 121°, c = 11, b = 7$ 2. $A = 15°, a = 13, b = 5$

---

3. $B = 91°, b = 18, c = 21$ 4. $C = 51°, c = 8, b = 10$

Solve △ABC and then find its area.

5.

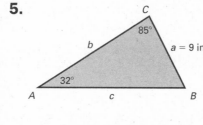

Homework

13.6 The Law of Cosines

Goals • Use the law of cosines to find the sides and angles of a triangle.
• Use Heron's formula to find the area of a triangle.

Your Notes

LAW OF COSINES

If $\triangle ABC$ has sides of length a, b, and c as shown, then:

$a^2 = b^2 + c^2 - 2bc \cos A$

$b^2 = $ _____

$c^2 = $ _____

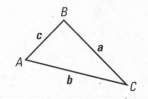

Example 1 **The SAS Case**

Solve $\triangle ABC$ with $b = 20$, $c = 10$, and $A = 41°$.

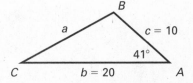

Solution

$a^2 = b^2 + c^2 - 2bc \cos A$ **Law of cosines**

$a^2 = $ _____   **Substitute.**

$a^2 \approx$ _____   **Simplify.**

$a \approx \sqrt{\rule{2em}{0.4pt}} \approx$ _____   **Take square root.**

You can use either the law of cosines or the law of sines to find a second angle.

$\dfrac{\sin \boxed{}}{\boxed{}} = \dfrac{\sin C}{\boxed{}}$ **Use law of sines and substitute for A, a, and C.**

$\sin C = \dfrac{\rule{4em}{0.4pt}}{}$

$\sin C \approx$ _____   **Simplify.**

$C \approx \sin^{-1}$ _____ $\approx$ _____ °   **Use inverse sine.**

The third angle is: $B \approx 180° - 41° -$ _____ ° $\approx$ _____ °.

Example 2 **The SSS Case**

Solve △ABC.

Find the angle opposite the longest side, $\overline{AB}$.

$$\cos C = \frac{a^2 + b^2 - c^2}{2ab}$$

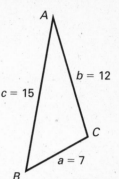

$$= \frac{\boxed{}}{\boxed{}} \approx \underline{}$$

Use the inverse cosine function to find C.

$$C = \cos^{-1} \underline{} \approx \underline{}^\circ$$

Use the law of sines to find A.

$$\frac{\sin A}{a} = \frac{\sin C}{c}$$ **Write law of sines.**

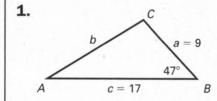 = 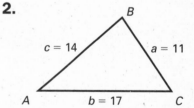   **Substitute.**

$$\sin A = \underline{}$$ **Multiply each side by __.**

$$\sin A \approx \underline{}$$ **Simplify.**

$$A \approx \sin^{-1} \underline{} \approx \underline{}^\circ$$ **Use inverse sine.**

The third angle is: $B \approx 180° - \underline{}^\circ - \underline{}^\circ \approx \underline{}^\circ.$

✔ **Checkpoint** Solve △ABC.

1.

2.

HERON'S AREA FORMULA

The area of the triangle with sides of length a, b, and c is

Area = _____

where s = _____ . The variable s is called the

_____

semiperimeter, or half-perimeter, of the triangle.

Example 3   *Finding the Area of a Triangle*

Find the area of $\triangle ABC$.

Begin by finding the semiperimeter.

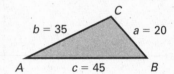

$s = $

_____

$= $ _____ $= $ _____

_____

Now use Heron's formula to find the area of $\triangle ABC$.

Area = _____

$= $ _____

$= $ _____

$\approx$ _____ square units

✔ **Checkpoint** Find the area of $\triangle ABC$ having the given side lengths.

3. $a = 15$, $b = 18$, $c = 21$ **4.** $a = 24$, $b = 36$, $c = 42$

Homework

13.7 Parametric Equations and Projectile Motion

Goals • Use parametric equations to represent motion in a plane.
• Use parametric equations to represent projectile motion.

Your Notes

VOCABULARY

Parametric equations

Parameter

Example 1 *Graphing a Set of Parametric Equations*

Graph $x = -t + 8$ and $y = 2t - 3$ for $0 \le t \le 4$.

Solution

Begin by making a table of values.

t	0	1	2	3	4
x					
y					

Plot the points (x, y) in the table and then connect the points with a line segment.

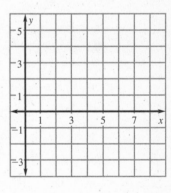

Example 2 *Eliminating the Parameter*

Write an *xy*-equation for the parametric equations in Example 1: $x = -t + 8$ and $y = 2t - 3$ for $0 \leq t \leq 4$. State the domain for the equation.

Solution

First solve one of the parametric equations for *t*.

$$x = -t + 8 \qquad \text{Write original equation.}$$

$$\underline{\hspace{2cm}} = -t \qquad \text{Subtract } \underline{\hspace{0.5cm}} \text{ from each side.}$$

$$\underline{\hspace{2.5cm}} = t \qquad \text{Multiply each side by } \underline{\hspace{0.7cm}}.$$

Then substitute for *t* in the other parametric equation.

$$y = 2t - 3 \qquad \text{Write original equation.}$$

$$y = 2(\underline{\hspace{2cm}}) - 3 \qquad \text{Substitute for } t.$$

$$y = \underline{\hspace{2.5cm}} \qquad \text{Simplify.}$$

This process is called $\underline{\hspace{6cm}}$ because the parameter *t* is not in the final equation. When $t = 0$, $x = \underline{\hspace{0.7cm}}$ and when $t = 4$, $x = \underline{\hspace{0.7cm}}$. So, the domain of the *xy*-equation is $\underline{\hspace{0.7cm}} \leq x \leq \underline{\hspace{0.7cm}}$.

✅ *Checkpoint* Write an *xy*-equation for the parametric equations. State the domain.

1. $x = 3t$ and $y = -6t$ for $0 \leq t \leq 4$

2. $x = 2t + 5$ and $y = 3t - 2$ for $0 \leq t \leq 6$

Your Notes

Example 3 *Modeling Projectile Motion*

Archery An archer releases an arrow from a bow 5 feet above the ground. The arrow leaves the bow at an angle of 12° and at an initial velocity of 230 feet per second.

a. Write a set of parametric equations for the motion.

b. Assuming the ground is level, find how far the arrow traveled before it hit the ground.

Solution

a. Use $v =$ _____ ft/sec, $\theta =$ ____°, $(x_0, y_0) =$ _____, and $g =$ ____ ft/sec^2.

$$x = (v \cos \theta)t + x_0 \quad \text{and} \quad y = -\frac{1}{2}gt^2 + (v \sin \theta)t + y_0$$

$\approx$ _____ $\qquad\qquad\qquad \approx$ _____

b. The arrow hits the ground when $y = 0$.

_____ $= 0$ **Substitute for y.**

$t =$ **Quadratic formula**

_____

$t \approx$ ____ seconds   **Simplify and choose positive *t*-value.**

When $t =$ ____ seconds, the arrow's location will have an x-value of $x =$ _____ $\approx$ ____ feet. So, the arrow traveled about ____ feet.

✔ *Checkpoint* **Complete the following exercise.**

3. Repeat Example 3 for an arrow released $5\frac{1}{2}$ feet above the ground at an angle of 13° with an initial velocity of 220 ft/sec.

Homework

Graphing Sine, Cosine, and Tangent Functions

Goals • Graph sine and cosine functions.
• Graph tangent functions.

Your Notes

VOCABULARY

Periodic

Cycle

Period

Amplitude

Frequency

CHARACTERISTICS OF $y = a \sin bx$ **AND** $y = a \cos bx$

The amplitude and period of the graphs of $y = a \sin bx$ and $y = a \cos bx$, where a and b are nonzero real numbers, are as follows:

$$\text{amplitude} = |a| \quad \text{and} \quad \text{period} = \frac{2\pi}{|b|}$$

Examples The graph of $y = 2 \sin 4x$ has amplitude ___ and

period _____ . The graph of $y = \frac{1}{3} \cos 2\pi x$ has

amplitude ___ and period _____ .

Example 1 *Graphing a Sine Function*

Graph the function $y = \sin 4x$.

The amplitude is $a =$ ___ and the period is ___ = ___ .

Intercepts: (___ , 0); (___ , 0); (___ , 0)

Maximum: (___ , 1)

Minimum: $\left(\dfrac{3\pi}{8}, \underline{\hspace{1cm}} \right)$

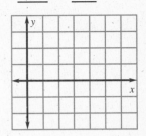

Example 2 *Graphing a Cosine Function*

Graph $y = 2 \cos 2\pi x$.

Solution

The amplitude is $a =$ ___ and the period is ___ = ___ .

Intercepts: (___ , ___); (___ , ___)

Maximums: (___ , ___); (___ , ___)

Minimum: (___ , ___)

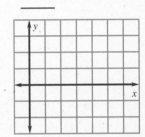

✓ *Checkpoint* Graph the function.

1. $y = 0.25 \sin x$

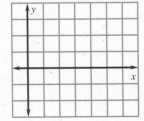

2. $y = 4 \cos 2x$

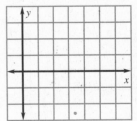

CHARACTERISTICS OF y = a tan bx

If a and b are nonzero real numbers, the graph of
$y = a \tan bx$ has these characteristics:

- The period is $\dfrac{\pi}{|b|}$.

- There are vertical asymptotes at odd multiples of $\dfrac{\pi}{2|b|}$.

Example The graph of $y = 5 \tan 3x$ has period $\dfrac{\pi}{3}$ and

asymptote at $x = (2n + 1)\dfrac{\pi}{2(3)} = \dfrac{\pi}{6} + \dfrac{n\pi}{3}$ where n is any integer.

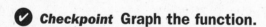

Example 3   *Graphing a Tangent Function*

Graph y = 3 tan 2x.

The period is $\dfrac{\pi}{b} = \underline{\quad}$.

Intercept: $(\underline{\quad}, \underline{\quad})$

Asymptotes: $x = \underline{\quad} \cdot \underline{\quad} = \underline{\quad}$;

$x = \underline{\quad} \cdot \underline{\quad} = \underline{\quad}$

Halfway points: $\left(\underline{\quad} \cdot \underline{\quad}, \underline{\quad}\right) = \left(\underline{\quad}, \underline{\quad}\right)$;

$\left(\underline{\quad} \cdot \underline{\quad}, \underline{\quad}\right) = \left(\underline{\quad}, \underline{\quad}\right)$

✔ *Checkpoint* **Graph the function.**

3. $y = 6 \tan x$

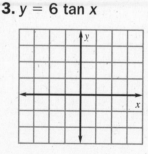

14.2 Translations and Reflections of Trigonometric Graphs

Goals • Graph translations and reflections of sine and cosine graphs.
• Graph translations and reflections of tangent graphs.

Your Notes

TRANSFORMATIONS OF SINE AND COSINE GRAPHS

To obtain the graph of

$$y = a \sin b(x - h) + k \quad \text{or} \quad y = a \cos b(x - h) + k,$$

transform the graph of $y = |a| \sin bx$ or $y = |a| \cos bx$ as follows.

Vertical shift Shift the graph ___ units vertically.

Horizontal shift Shift the graph ___ units horizontally.

Reflection If $a < 0$, reflect the graph in the line $y =$ ___ after any vertical and horizontal shifts have been performed.

Example 1 *Graphing a Vertical Translation*

Graph $y = 4 + 4 \sin x$.

Because the graph is a transformation of the graph of
$y = 4 \sin x$, the amplitude is ___ and the period is ___.
By comparing the given equation to the general equation
$y = a \sin b(x - h) + k$, you can see that $h =$ ___, $k =$ ___,
and a ___ 0. Therefore, translate the graph of $y = 4 \sin x$
___ units. The graph oscillates ___ units up and down
from the center line $y =$ ___. So, the maximum value of the
function is ___ and the minimum value of the function is ___.

The five key points are:

On $y = k$: _____

Maximum: _____

Minimum: _____

Example 2   *Graphing a Horizontal Translation*

Graph $y = 4 \cos 2\left(x - \dfrac{\pi}{2}\right)$.

Solution

Because the graph is a transformation of the graph of $y = 4 \cos 2x$, the amplitude is ___ and the period is

$\dfrac{}{\underline{}}$ = ___ . By comparing the given

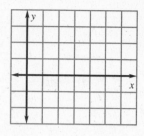

equation to the general equation $y = a \cos b(x - h) + k$, you can see

that $h = \underline{}$, $k = $ ___ , and a ___ 0. Therefore, translate the

graph of $y = 4 \cos 2x$ $\underline{}$ units. The five key points are:

On $y = k$: $\underline{}$ = $\underline{}$;

$\underline{}$ = $\underline{}$

Maximums: $\underline{}$ = $\underline{}$;

$\underline{}$ = $\underline{}$

Minimum: $\underline{}$ = $\underline{}$

Example 3 *Graphing a Reflection*

Graph $y = -2 \cos x$.

Because the graph is a reflection of the graph of $y = 2 \cos x$, the amplitude is ___ and the period is ___. When you plot the five key points on the graph, note that the intercepts are the same as they are for the graph of $y = 2 \cos x$. However, when the graph is reflected in the *x*-axis, the _____ become _____ and the _____ becomes a _____.

The five key points are:

On $y = k$: _____ ; _____

Minimums: _____ ; _____

Maximum: _____ = _____

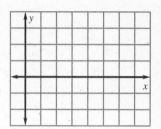

✔ *Checkpoint* **Graph the function.**

1. $y = -2 + \cos x$

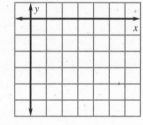

2. $y = 4 \sin 4\left(x - \dfrac{\pi}{4}\right)$

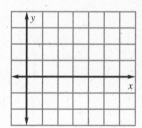

3. $y = -2 \sin x$

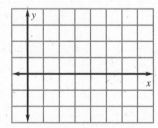

Example 4   *Combining a Translation and a Reflection*

Graph $y = -\dfrac{1}{2}\sin(2x - 4\pi) + 2$.

Begin by rewriting the function in the form $y = a\sin b(x - h) + k$:

$$y = -\frac{1}{2}\sin(2x - 4\pi) + 2$$

$$= \underline{\hspace{3cm}}$$

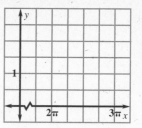

The amplitude is $\underline{\hspace{1cm}}$ and the period is $\underline{\hspace{1.5cm}}$. Since

$h = \underline{\hspace{0.8cm}}$, $k = \underline{\hspace{0.5cm}}$, and $a \underline{\hspace{0.4cm}} 0$, the graph of $y = \dfrac{1}{2}\sin 2x$ is

shifted $\underline{\hspace{1.5cm}}$ units, $\underline{\hspace{1.5cm}}$ units, then reflected in the

line $y = \underline{\hspace{0.5cm}}$. The five key points are:

On $y = k$: $\underline{\hspace{3cm}} = \underline{\hspace{2cm}}$;

$\underline{\hspace{3cm}} \underline{\hspace{2cm}} = \underline{\hspace{2cm}}$;

$\underline{\hspace{3cm}} \underline{\hspace{2cm}} = \underline{\hspace{2cm}}$

Minimum: $\underline{\hspace{3cm}} = \underline{\hspace{2cm}}$

$\underline{\hspace{4cm}} \underline{\hspace{2cm}}$

Maximum: $\underline{\hspace{3cm}} = \underline{\hspace{2cm}}$

$\underline{\hspace{4cm}} \underline{\hspace{2cm}}$

TRANSFORMATIONS OF TANGENT GRAPHS

To obtain the graph of $y = a\tan b(x - h) + k$, transform the graph of $y = |a|\tan bx$ as follows.

- Shift the graph $\underline{\hspace{0.5cm}}$ units vertically and $\underline{\hspace{0.5cm}}$ units horizontally.

- Then, if $a < 0$, reflect the graph in the line $y = \underline{\hspace{0.5cm}}$.

Example 5 **Combining a Translation and a Reflection**

Graph $y = -\tan\left(x - \dfrac{\pi}{2}\right) + 1$.

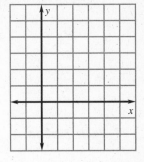

The graph is a transformation of the graph of $y = \tan x$, so the period is ___. By comparing the given equation to $y = a \tan b(x - h) + k$, you can see that $h = $ ___ , $k = $ ___ , and a ___ 0.

Therefore, translate the graph of

$y = \tan x$ _____ units and then reflect it in the _____.

Asymptotes: _____ ;

_____

/ _____

On $y = k$: $(h, k) = $

_____

Halfway Points: = ___ ;

_____ _____

= ___

_____ _____

✔ *Checkpoint* **Graph the function.**

4. $y = -\dfrac{1}{4}\cos\left(\dfrac{1}{2}x + \dfrac{1}{4}\pi\right) - 1$

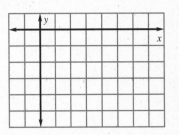

Homework

14.3 Verifying Trigonometric Identities

Goals • Use trigonometric identities to simplify trigonometric expressions and to verify other identities.
• Use trigonometric identities to solve real-life problems.

Your Notes

VOCABULARY
Trigonometric identity

FUNDAMENTAL TRIGONOMETRIC IDENTITIES

Reciprocal Identities

$$\csc \theta = \frac{1}{\boxed{}} \qquad \sec \theta = \frac{1}{\boxed{}} \qquad \cot \theta = \frac{1}{\boxed{}}$$

Tangent and Cotangent Identities

$$\tan \theta = \frac{\sin \theta}{\boxed{}} \qquad \cot \theta = \frac{\cos \theta}{\boxed{}}$$

Pythagorean Identities

$$\sin^2 \theta + \underline{} = 1 \qquad 1 + \tan^2 \theta = \underline{}$$

$$1 + \cot^2 \theta = \underline{}$$

Cofunction Identities

$$\sin \left(\frac{\pi}{2} - \theta \right) = \underline{} \qquad \cos \left(\frac{\pi}{2} - \theta \right) = \underline{}$$

$$\tan \left(\frac{\pi}{2} - \theta \right) = \underline{}$$

Negative Angle Identities

$$\sin (-\theta) = \underline{} \qquad \cos (-\theta) = \underline{}$$

$$\tan (-\theta) = \underline{}$$

Example 1 *Finding Trigonometric Values*

Given that $\cos \theta = \dfrac{8}{17}$ and $\dfrac{3\pi}{2} < \theta < 2\pi$, find the values of the other five trigonometric functions of θ.

$\sin^2 \theta + \underline{\hspace{1.5cm}} = 1$ Write Pythagorean identity.

$\sin^2 \theta + \underline{\hspace{1cm}} = 1$ Substitute.

$\sin^2 \theta = \underline{\hspace{1cm}}$ Simplify.

$\sin \theta = \underline{\hspace{1cm}}$ Take square roots of each side.

$\sin \theta = \underline{\hspace{1cm}}$ Because θ is in Quadrant IV, $\sin \theta$ is $\underline{\hspace{1.5cm}}$.

Now you can find the other four trigonometric functions.

$\tan \theta = \underline{\hspace{1cm}} = \underline{\hspace{1.5cm}}$ $\cot \theta = \underline{\hspace{1cm}} = \underline{\hspace{1.5cm}}$

$\csc \theta = \underline{\hspace{1cm}} = \underline{\hspace{1.5cm}}$ $\sec \theta = \underline{\hspace{1cm}} = \underline{\hspace{1.5cm}}$

✔ *Checkpoint* **Complete the following exercise.**

1. Given that $\sin \theta = -\dfrac{20}{29}$ and $\pi < \theta < \dfrac{3\pi}{2}$, find the values of the other five trigonometric functions of θ.

Example 2   *Simplifying a Trigonometric Expression*

Simplify the expression $\tan\left(\dfrac{\pi}{2} - x\right)\cot x$.

$\tan\left(\dfrac{\pi}{2} - x\right)\cot x = $ _____ $\cot x$ Cofunction identity

$= $ _____   Simplify.

Example 3   *Verifying a Trigonometric Identity*

Verify the identity $\sin\left(\dfrac{\pi}{2} - x\right)\sec x = 1$.

$\sin\left(\dfrac{\pi}{2} - x\right)\sec x = $ _____ $\sec x$ Cofunction identity

$= $ _____   Reciprocal identity

$= $ _   Simplify.

✔ *Checkpoint* Simplify the expression.

2. $\csc x \tan x$	**3.** $\sin x \cos^2 x - \sin x$

Verify the identity.

4. $\cos(-x)\sec x = 1$	**5.** $\sin x \tan x + \cos x = \sec x$

14.4 Solving Trigonometric Equations

Goals • Solve a trigonometric equation.
• Solve real-life trigonometric equations.

| **Example 1** | *Solving a Trigonometric Equation* |

Solve $2 \cos x - \sqrt{3} = 0$.

First isolate cos x on one side of the equation.

$2 \cos x - \sqrt{3} = 0$ Write original equation.

$2 \cos x = \underline{\hspace{1cm}}$ Add _____ to each side.

$\cos x = \dfrac{}{\underline{\hspace{1cm}}}$ Divide each side by __.

Two solutions of $\cos x = \dfrac{}{\underline{\hspace{1cm}}}$ in the interval $0 \le x < 2\pi$ are

$x = \cos^{-1} \dfrac{}{\underline{\hspace{1cm}}} \; \underline{\hspace{0.5cm}} = \underline{\hspace{0.8cm}}$ and $x = 2\pi - \underline{\hspace{0.8cm}} = \underline{\hspace{0.8cm}}$.

Because $y = \cos x$ is a _____ function, there are _____ other solutions. The general solution can be written as:

$x = \underline{\hspace{0.8cm}} + 2n\pi$ or $x = \underline{\hspace{0.8cm}} + 2n\pi$ n is any integer.

✓ *Checkpoint* **Find the general solution of the equation.**

| **1.** $4 \sin x - 2\sqrt{3} = 0$ | **2.** $7 - 6 \cos x = 1$ |

Example 2 **Solving a Trigonometric Equation in an Interval**

Solve cos x + 1 = sin x in the interval $0 \leq x < 2\pi$.

cos x + 1 = sin x		Write original equation.
_____ = _____		Square both sides.
_____ = _____		Multiply.
_____ = _____		Pythagorean identity
_____ = 0		Combine like terms.
_____ = 0		Divide each side by ___.
_____ = 0		Factor.
_____ = 0 or _____ = 0		Zero product property
cos x = ____		Solve for cos x.
x = ___ , x = ___ .		Solve for x.

The apparent solution _____ does not check in the original equation. The only solutions in the interval $0 \leq x < 2\pi$ are x = ___ and x = ___.

✅ **Checkpoint** Solve the equation in the interval $0 < x < 2\pi$.

3. $4\cos^2 x - 1 = 0$ 4. $\sec x \csc x = 2 \csc x$

Example 3 *Using the Quadratic Formula*

Solve $\sin^2 x - 4 \sin x + 2 = 0$ in the interval $0 \le x \le \pi$.

Solution

Because the equation is in the form $au^2 + bu + c = 0$, use the quadratic formula to solve for $u = \sin x$.

$\sin^2 x - 4 \sin x + 2 = 0$ **Original equation**

$\sin x = $ _____   **Quadratic formula**

$\dfrac{}{}$

$= \dfrac{}{}$ $= $ _____   **Simplify.**

$\approx$ _____   or   _____   **Use a calculator.**

$x \approx \sin^{-1}$ _____   or $x \approx \sin^{-1}$ _____   **Use inverse sine.**

_____ $\approx$ _____   **Use a calculator.**

In the interval $0 \le x \le \pi$, the solution is $x \approx$ _____ .

✓ *Checkpoint* **Solve the equation in the interval $0 < x < \pi$.**

5. $\cos^2 x = 2 + 2 \cos x$ **6.** $2 \sin^2 x - 4 \sin x = -1$

Homework

14.5 Modeling with Trigonometric Functions

Goals • Model data with a sine or cosine function.
• Use technology to write a trigonometric model.

Your Notes

Example 1 *Writing Trigonometric Functions*

Write a function for the sinusoid.

Solution

The maximum and minimum values of the function do not occur at points equidistant from the x-axis, so the curve has a vertical shift. The value of k is:

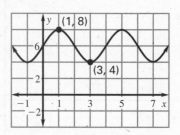

$$k = \frac{M + m}{2} = \frac{\boxed{}}{2} = \underline{}$$

The graph crosses the y-axis at $y = k$, so the graph is a _____ curve with no horizontal shift. The function has the

form $y = $ _____. The period is $\frac{2\pi}{b} = $ __, so $b = $ ____ .

The amplitude is $|a| = \frac{M - m}{2} = \frac{\boxed{}}{2} = $ __. The graph

is not a reflection, so $a = $ _____. The function is

$y = $ _____ .

✔ *Checkpoint* Write a function for the sinusoid.

1.

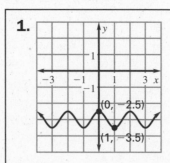

Example 2 *Modeling a Sinusoid*

Ocean Tides The height in a bay varies sinusoidally over time. On a certain day, a high tide of 11 feet occurred at midnight and a low tide of 2 feet occurred at 6:00 A.M. Write a model for the height (in feet) of the water as a function of time t (in hours since midnight).

Solution

The vertical shift for the model is

$$k = \frac{M + m}{2} = \frac{\boxed{}}{2} = \frac{\boxed{}}{2} = \underline{}.$$

When $t = 0$, the height is at its _____, so the model is a _____ function with a __ 0 and no _____.

The amplitude is $|a| = \frac{M - m}{2} = \frac{\boxed{}}{2} = \frac{\boxed{}}{2} = \underline{}.$

Because __ > __, a = ____. The period is

$p = 2[(\text{low time}) - (\text{high time})] = 2(\underline{} - \underline{}) = \underline{}.$

So, $\frac{2\pi}{b} = $ ___, which means $b = \underline{}$.

A model for the height of the water as a function of time is

$h = $ _____.

✔ **Checkpoint** Complete the following exercise.

2. The height in a bay varies sinusoidally over time. On a certain day, a low tide of 3 feet occurred at midnight and a high tide of 9 feet occurred at 7:00 A.M. Write a model for the height (in feet) of the water as a function of time t (in hours since midnight).

Example 3 **Using Sinusoidal Regression**

Cooling Degree-Days For any given day, the number of degrees that the average temperature is above 65°F is called the cooling degree-days for that day. This figure is used to calculate how much is spent to maintain comfortable indoor temperatures. The table below gives the total number C of cooling degree-days for each month t in Lihue, Hawaii, with $t = 1$ representing January. Find a model for the data.
(Source: National Climatic Data Center)

t	1	2	3	4	5	6
C	207	188	239	266	323	382
t	7	8	9	10	11	12
C	433	455	435	408	327	257

Solution

Begin by entering the data in a graphing calculator. Use the graphing calculator's sinusoidal regression feature to get a model.

$C \approx$ _____

✔ *Checkpoint* **Complete the following exercise.**

3. The average daily low temperature T (in degrees Fahrenheit) in Nome, Alaska, is given in the table. Time t is measured in months, with $t = 0$ representing January 1. Find a model for the data.
(Source: National Climatic Data Center)

t	0.5	1.5	2.5	3.5	4.5	5.5
T	−1.8	−2.3	1	12.4	31.1	40.6
t	6.5	7.5	8.5	9.5	10.5	11.5
T	46.6	45.2	37.2	22.9	10.8	0.9

Homework

14.6 Using Sum and Difference Formulas

Goals • Evaluate trigonometric functions of the sum or difference of two angles.
• Use sum and difference formulas to solve real-life problems.

Your Notes

SUM AND DIFFERENCE FORMULAS

Sum Formulas

$\sin (u + v) =$ _____

$\cos (u + v) =$ _____

$\tan (u + v) =$
_____

Difference Formulas

$\sin (u - v) =$ _____

$\cos (u - v) =$ _____

$\tan (u - v) =$
_____

Example 1 *Evaluating a Trigonometric Expression*

Find the exact value of $\sin 105°$.

Solution

$\sin 105° = \sin (60° + 45°)$ **Substitute for 105°.**

$=$ _____   **Sum formula**

$=$ _____   **Evaluate.**

$=$ _____   **Simplify.**

Example 2 *Using a Difference Formula*

Find cos $(u - v)$ given that sin $u = \dfrac{5}{13}$ with $\dfrac{\pi}{2} < u < \pi$ and

cos $v = -\dfrac{3}{5}$ with $\dfrac{\pi}{2} < v < \pi$.

Using a Pythagorean identity and quadrant signs gives

cos $u =$ _____ and sin $v =$ ___.

cos $(u - v) =$ _____   Difference
formula for cosine

$=$ _____   Substitute.

$=$ ___   Simplify.

✔ *Checkpoint* **Complete the following exercises.**

1. Find the exact value of cos $\dfrac{11\pi}{12}$.

_____

2. Find sin $(u + v)$ given that sin $u = -\dfrac{7}{25}$ with $\pi < u < \dfrac{3\pi}{2}$

and cos $v = -\dfrac{4}{5}$ with $\pi < v < \dfrac{3\pi}{2}$.

Example 3 *Simplifying an Expression*

Simplify the expression tan $(x + 3\pi)$.

tan $(x + 3\pi) =$ _____   Difference formula
for tangent

$=$ _____   Evaluate.

$=$ _____   Simplify.

Example 4 *Solving a Trigonometric Equation*

Solve $\sin\left(x + \dfrac{\pi}{3}\right) + \sin\left(x - \dfrac{\pi}{3}\right) = 1$ for $0 \le x < 2\pi$.

$$\sin\left(x + \dfrac{\pi}{3}\right) + \sin\left(x - \dfrac{\pi}{3}\right) = 1$$

$$+$$

_____

$$= 1$$

_____

$$= 1$$

_____

$$= 1$$

_____

$$\underline{} = 1$$

In the interval $0 \le x < 2\pi$, the solution is $x = \underline{}$.

✔ *Checkpoint* **Complete the following exercises.**

3. Simplify the expression $\cos(\pi + x)$.

_____

4. Solve $\tan(x + \pi) + 2\sin(x + \pi) = 0$ for $0 \le x < 2\pi$.

Homework

14.7 Using Double- and Half-Angle Formulas

Goals • Evaluate expressions using double- and half-angle formulas.
• Use double- and half-angle formulas to solve real-life problems.

Your Notes

DOUBLE-ANGLE AND HALF-ANGLE FORMULAS

Double-Angle Formulas

$\cos 2u =$ _____ $\sin 2u =$ _____

$\cos 2u =$ _____ $\tan 2u =$ _____

$\cos 2u =$ _____   _____

Half-Angle Formulas

$\sin \dfrac{u}{2} =$ _____ $\tan \dfrac{u}{2} =$ _____

$\cos \dfrac{u}{2} =$ _____ $\tan \dfrac{u}{2} =$ _____

Example 1 *Evaluating Trigonometric Expressions*

Find the exact value of $\tan \dfrac{\pi}{12}$.

Solution

Use the fact that $\dfrac{\pi}{12}$ is half of ____ .

$\tan \dfrac{\pi}{12} = \tan \dfrac{1}{2}\left(\underline{} \right) = \dfrac{}{}$ _____ = _____

$= $ _____

Example 2 **Evaluating Trigonometric Expressions**

For $\cos u = \dfrac{5}{13}$ with $0 < u < \dfrac{\pi}{2}$, find (a) $\sin \dfrac{u}{2}$ and (b) $\sin 2u$.

a. Because $\dfrac{u}{2}$ is in Quadrant ___, $\sin \dfrac{u}{2}$ is _____.

$$\sin \dfrac{u}{2} = \underline{\hspace{2.5cm}} \quad = \underline{\hspace{2.5cm}} \quad = \underline{\hspace{2cm}}$$

$$= \underline{\hspace{2cm}}$$

b. Use a Pythagorean identity to conclude that $\sin u = \underline{\hspace{1cm}}$.

$$\sin 2u = \underline{\hspace{3cm}} \quad = \underline{\hspace{2.5cm}} \quad = \underline{\hspace{1cm}}$$

✔ **Checkpoint** **Complete the following exercises.**

1. Find the exact value of $\tan \dfrac{7\pi}{8}$.

2. Given $\cos u = -\dfrac{20}{29}$ with $\dfrac{\pi}{2} < u < \pi$, find $\sin 2u$.

Example 3 **Verifying a Trigonometric Identity**

Verify the identity $\cos 3x = \cos^3 x - 3\sin^2 x \cos x$.

$$\cos 3x = \cos(2x + x)$$

$$= \underline{\hspace{4cm}}$$

$$= \underline{\hspace{5cm}}$$

$$= \underline{\hspace{5cm}}$$

$$= \underline{\hspace{4cm}}$$

Example 4   *Solving a Trigonometric Equation*

Solve $\tan \dfrac{x}{2} = \sin x$ for $0 \le x < 2\pi$.

$$\tan \dfrac{x}{2} = \sin x \qquad\qquad \text{Write original equation.}$$

$$\dfrac{\rule{2cm}{0.4pt}}{\rule{2cm}{0.4pt}} = \sin x \qquad\qquad \text{Use a half-angle formula.}$$

$$\dfrac{\rule{2cm}{0.4pt}}{\rule{2cm}{0.4pt}} = \sin^2 x \qquad\qquad \text{Multiply each side by } \sin x.$$

$$\rule{2cm}{0.4pt} = \rule{2cm}{0.4pt} \qquad\qquad \text{Use a Pythagorean identity.}$$

$$\rule{2cm}{0.4pt} = 0 \qquad\qquad \text{Subtract } \underline{\hspace{2cm}} \text{ from each side.}$$

$$\rule{2cm}{0.4pt} = 0 \qquad\qquad \text{Factor.}$$

$$\rule{1.5cm}{0.4pt} = 0 \quad \text{or} \quad \rule{2cm}{0.4pt} = 0 \qquad \text{Zero product property}$$

$$x = \underline{\hspace{0.6cm}} , \quad \dfrac{\rule{1cm}{0.4pt}}{\rule{1cm}{0.4pt}} \qquad \dfrac{\rule{1cm}{0.4pt}}{\rule{1cm}{0.4pt}} = \underline{\hspace{0.4cm}}$$

$$x = \underline{\hspace{0.4cm}}$$

✔ *Checkpoint* **Complete the following exercises.**

3. Verify the identity $\sin 4x = 4 \sin x \cos x(1 - 2 \sin^2 x)$.

4. Solve $\cos 2x + \sin x = 0$ for $0 \le x < 2\pi$.

Homework